What readers are saying about
The Rails View

This is a must-read for Rails developers looking to juice up their skills for a world of web apps that increasingly includes mobile browsers and a lot more JavaScript.

➤ **Yehuda Katz**
  Driving force behind Rails 3.0 and Co-founder, Tilde

In the past several years, I've been privileged to work with some of the world's leading Rails developers. If asked to name the best view-layer Rails developer I've met, I'd have a hard time picking between two names: Bruce Williams and John Athayde. This book is a rare opportunity to look into the minds of two of the leading experts on an area that receives far too little attention. Read, apply, and reread.

➤ **Chad Fowler**
  VP Engineering, LivingSocial

Finally! An authoritative and up-to-date guide to everything view-related in Rails 3. If you're stabbing in the dark when putting together your Rails apps' views, *The Rails View* provides a big confidence boost and shows how to get things done the right way.

➤ **Peter Cooper**
  Editor, Ruby Inside and Ruby Weekly

The Rails view layer has always been a morass, but this book reins it in with details of how to build views as software, not just as markup. This book represents the wisdom gained from years' worth of building maintainable interfaces by two of the best and brightest minds in our business. I have been writing Ruby code for over a decade and Rails code since its inception, and out of all the Ruby books I've read, I value this one the most.

➤ **Rich Kilmer**
    Director, RubyCentral

The Rails View

Creating a Beautiful and Maintainable User Experience

John Athayde
Bruce Williams

The Pragmatic Bookshelf

Dallas, Texas • Raleigh, North Carolina

Many of the designations used by manufacturers and sellers to distinguish their products are claimed as trademarks. Where those designations appear in this book, and The Pragmatic Programmers, LLC was aware of a trademark claim, the designations have been printed in initial capital letters or in all capitals. The Pragmatic Starter Kit, The Pragmatic Programmer, Pragmatic Programming, Pragmatic Bookshelf, PragProg and the linking *g* device are trademarks of The Pragmatic Programmers, LLC.

Every precaution was taken in the preparation of this book. However, the publisher assumes no responsibility for errors or omissions, or for damages that may result from the use of information (including program listings) contained herein.

Our Pragmatic courses, workshops, and other products can help you and your team create better software and have more fun. For more information, as well as the latest Pragmatic titles, please visit us at *http://pragprog.com.*

The team that produced this book includes:

Brian Hogan (editor)
Potomac Indexing, LLC (indexer)
Molly McBeath (copyeditor)
David J Kelly (typesetter)
Janet Furlow (producer)
Juliet Benda (rights)
Ellie Callahan (support)

Printed in the United States of America.
ISBN-13: 978-1-93435-687-6
Printed on acid-free paper.
Book version: P1.0—March 2012

Contents

Part I — Appendices

Acknowledgments

We have many people to thank for making this very ambitious book possible.

First of all, as this is a book about Rails, a lot of credit must go to the creator of the framework, David Heinemeier Hansson, the members of rails-core (past and present), and other contributors. The ideas in this book are distilled from years of discussion and collaboration with the Rails and Ruby communities.

Throughout our careers we've drawn inspiration and motivation from a number of web luminaries, and we would be remiss in failing to mention at least a few of them: Dan Cederholm, Molly Holzschlag, Paul Irish, Jeremy Keith, Steve Krug, Eric Meyer, Jakob Nielsen, Mark Pilgrim, and Jeffrey Zeldman.

We were surprised to learn that a number of people actually volunteered to read the book before it was complete, thereby putting their own sanity at risk. We'd like to thank these brave souls for their help in identifying issues, suggesting topics, and otherwise vastly improving the text: Derek Bailey, Kevin Beam, David A. Black, David Bock, Daniel Bretoi, Jeff Casimir, BJ Clark, Jeff Cohen, Justin Dell, Joel Friedman, Jeremy Hinegardner, Mark Margolis, Dan Reedy, Sam Rose, Loren Sands-Ramshaw, Diego Scataglini, Tibor Simac, Charley Stran, Mark Tabler, and Lynn M. Wallenstein.

This book simply would not have been completed if not for our amazing editor, Brian Hogan. He continuously challenged our preconceptions and helped to clarify our intent, all with seemingly unbounded patience and class. And we promise, Brian, we'll never again utilize *utilize* in our writing (except for that time right there).

Many thanks to Rich Kilmer, Chad Fowler, Aaron Batalion, and our colleagues in the engineering, design, and product teams at LivingSocial. You keep us hungry to win every day, constantly building pressure to innovate, which makes us better designers and developers.

John would like to thank his supportive wife, Whitney, for her patience and encouragement throughout the process; his parents, grandparents, and extended family for their love and support and for purchasing that Mac SE back in the day with Hypercard installed; all the members of #caboose for their patience and discussion over the years; Justin Hankins and Sara Flemming for all the years of experimenting in HTML, CSS, and Rails with Meticulous; and Amy Hoy for an intense year of business, design, and development boot camp while running Hyphenated People with him. He also thanks Bruce for agreeing to be a coauthor so that this book could rise to its potential.

Bruce credits the care and support of his wife, Melissa, and his two sons, Braedyn and Jamis, for the uncharacteristic level of determination and attention he's managed to focus on this single project, which broke any number of personal records. Also, Bruce's life would have turned out very differently were it not for the love of his mother, Monique, and father, Bruce (the elder), and a varied and distributed family he's proud to call his own, even if they do occasionally call him for tech support. To his coauthor, Bruce offers an equal share of sincere thanks and rampant design skill jealousy. Some things do not change. Finally, Bruce would like to dedicate his work on this book to the memory of his brother, Tristan Eppler.

John Athayde & Bruce Williams

March 2012

john@therailsview.com | bruce@therailsview.com

Preface

In 2004, Rails was born and the web discovered the MVC (model-view-controller) pattern in earnest, which brought a whole new level of productivity and *fun* to a world of developers and designers.

You'll find no end of books that provide a firm foundation for writing controllers and models (which benefit greatly from being written top-to-bottom in plain Ruby), but when it comes to views—that meeting place of Ruby, HTML, JavaScript, and CSS (not to mention developers and designers)—what's a disciplined craftsman to do?

This book aims to widen the discussion of Rails best practices to include solid, objective principles we can follow when building and refactoring views. By the time you're finished reading, you'll understand how you can structure your front end to be less brittle and more effective and boost your team's productivity.

Taming the Wild West

For all the advantages that Rails has over traditional, everything-in-the-view approaches like vanilla PHP or ASP, it's also fostered a culture of complacency around how views are structured and maintained.

After all, with all the controller and model logic extracted and the addition of helpers, what could go wrong?

While many of the elements that comprise the view are seen as easy (HTML, for example), the view layer in its entirety is an incredibly complex thing. This complexity can be so daunting that developers and designers just give up and use tables, hackery, and any tweak they can just to make it look somewhat right on the front end.

There are a lot of reasons for this. Many developers are uneasy around the view layer, being in such a hurry to get out of it and back to "real code" that they slap things together and leave a mess. Technical debt in the view layer often goes unpaid, and knowledge of good markup practices can be years behind or even considered irrelevant. After all, it works all right!

Designers can be uneasy around generated code and, without training, see ERB blocks as a sort of magical wonderland they can't hope to understand. Helpers are just black boxes, and the underlying model relationships and controller context that drive our views are just as opaque. Many designers are so visually focused that they, too, disregard the importance and usefulness of correct, modern markup. After all, it looks all right!

It's easy for the view layer to become a no-man's-land that no one owns or adequately polices or a junkyard that no one feels safe to walk through.

In this book we'll work hard to convince you not to abdicate responsibility for the view layer. We'll work together to learn how we can build application views sustainably from the ground up, discover useful refactoring patterns and helpful tools, and tackle integrating disparate technologies like Ruby, HTML, and JavaScript into a cohesive unit that's more than just a stumbling block between you and the new features you need to implement.

Who Should Read This Book?

If you're a designer working with Rails or a Rails developer working in the view layer, this book is for you. We'll cover the technical issues present in the view layer, and we'll also highlight some unique challenges that mixed teams of developers and designers face when working together.

Ruby and Rails Versions

The Rails View was built on top of Rails 3.2.1 and Ruby 1.9.3 and should be compatible with future stable releases for quite some time. In the event that we have small compatibility issues with future versions, we will post updates in the online forum on the book's website.[1]

Much of the content and code would need to be modified to work with some earlier versions due to our coverage of the Rails 3.1+ asset pipeline and use of the new Ruby 1.9 Hash literal syntax.

You can check your Rails version with the following command:

```
% rails -v
```

---

1. http://www.pragprog.com/titles/warv/

You can use gem install with the -v option to manually get the appropriate version.

```
% gem install rails -v 3.2.1
```

To manage your Ruby versions, we recommend RVM (Ruby Version Manager).[2]

What Is in the Book?

We'll learn how to build solid, maintainable views in Rails over the next nine chapters.

In Chapter 1, *Creating an Application Layout*, on page 1, we look at how to build the view structure for a new application from the ground up and get our layout files in order to provide a firm foundation for the rest of our application.

In Chapter 2, *Improving Readability*, on page 49, we look at how we can make our templates easier to read and more naturally convey their intent.

In Chapter 3, *Adding Cascading Style Sheets*, on page 73, we'll introduce you to the asset pipeline, explain the new SCSS format, customize the Sprockets configuration, and talk about how we can package assets into reusable units.

In Chapter 4, *Adding JavaScript*, on page 101, we'll continue our discussion of the asset pipeline, highlighting CoffeeScript, the Rails UJS drivers, and some organizational techniques for including JavaScript plugins in our applications.

In Chapter 5, *Building Maintainable Forms*, on page 119, we tackle forms, investigate creating our own form builders, and use some existing libraries to make complex forms easier to build and maintain.

In Chapter 6, *Using Presenters*, on page 143, we learn some techniques to make displaying complex information as easy and maintainable as possible from the view, building abstractions with our own custom Ruby classes.

In Chapter 7, *Handling Mobile Views*, on page 163, we discuss the challenges we face with supporting different screen resolutions and geometries, including mobile devices, and what solutions exist to aid in reusing templates and styling or whether to separate them altogether.

---

2. http://rvm.beginrescueend.com

In Chapter 8, *Working with Email*, on page 189, we discover some tips and tricks to make sending rich email less frustrating and designing emails less dependent on trial-and-error.

Finally, in Chapter 9, *Optimizing Performance*, on page 207, we'll learn the basics of measuring and solving application and business performance problems.

How to Read This Book

Each chapter in this book builds upon the content in the previous chapter. While examples will center around the ArtFlow application that we'll begin to build in Chapter 1, *Creating an Application Layout*, on page 1, chapters can be read sequentially or by jumping around to focus on a specific problem. You should be able to pull the code from our repository for any given chapter and work with it.

Chapter 1, *Creating an Application Layout*, on page 1, covers a lot of HTML and CSS that may seem out of place for a Rails book, but we feel these topics are critical to writing good views. Spend some time refreshing yourself on this subject matter even if you are already familiar with it. You may find some surprises in there!

Online Resources

The book's website has links to an interactive discussion forum as well as to errata for the book.[3] You'll also find the source code for all the projects we built. Readers of the ebook can click the gray box above the code excerpts to download that snippet directly.

If you find a mistake, please create an entry on the errata page so we can address it. If you have an electronic copy of this book, use the links in the footer of each page to easily submit errata to us.

Let's get started by looking at how views work and by digging into how we deliver those to our application's visitors.

Creating an Application Layout

The foundation of every Rails application's view layer is the layout. The layout provides a consistent, common structure for application pages, it sets the stage for the content our controllers render, and it pulls in the client-size scripts and style sheets that our interface needs to look and behave correctly.

In this chapter we're going to approach building an application layout from scratch, converting a design mockup into a real layout file while discovering some new markup and Rails view best practices along the way.

This layout is the first piece of a new application we're building for a design studio. The application is called ArtFlow, and it will be used to track designer progress, take client feedback, and act as a digital asset manager for assets after the project is complete.

Often projects live in project management applications (such as Basecamp) or through a string of emails with changes broken up into multiple emails. The logical flow of taking a concept to production will be one part of the application. After the project is complete and the team has moved on, there's a desire by clients to see previous campaigns they've run and look at their creative assets. Often clients will look at how certain pieces performed and base a new job on an existing creative asset. We want to be able to provide an easy way for clients to find those assets and for our design shop clients to see and track them as well (instead of keeping the assets in a folder hidden on a file server and identified only by the client's name).

The modeling at this stage of the application will be fairly straightforward and will consist of creations, designers, projects, campaigns, and clients. Creations (the designs themselves) originate from a designer and belong to a project. The project belongs to a client through a campaign. It will be structured something like Figure 1, *ArtFlow models*, on page 2.

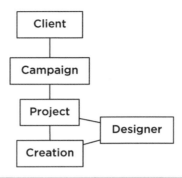

Figure 1—ArtFlow models

All of the view work we'll be doing to manage these records will sit on top of our layout, so it's important we build a good foundation from the beginning. Let's dive in, starting with the helpful mockup our user interface designer put together for the application.

1.1 Creating a Basic Layout

It's Monday morning, and we've been tasked to get the basic layout for ArtFlow put together. Our designer mocked up a nice-looking screen (as seen in Figure 2, *The ArtFlow mockup*, on page 3) that we will break up into our global layout and styles. The main layout for our application lives in app/views/layouts/application.html.erb and the style sheet is located at app/assets/style sheets/application.css.

These follow a paradigm for each controller as well. A controller named projects_controller.rb will look for a file in the layouts directory named projects.html.erb. We can also override this either on the controller or by the action of telling the controller to render a specific layout. At the controller level we would add layout "{layoutname}", and in an action we would use render :layout =>"{layoutname}".

In the past versions of Ruby on Rails, we have used HTML4 and XHTML, but Rails 3 generates an HTML5 layout when a new project is created. HTML5 provides some additional, enhanced functionality on browsers that support it while gracefully degrading on browsers that don't. We'll learn more about this as we build out our application, and the first step is getting familiar with some new tags.

We aren't going to cover HTML5 in its entirety here. Our editor, Brian Hogan, already wrote an awesome book on *HTML5 and CSS3* [Hog10], and you should

Figure 2—The ArtFlow mockup

pick that up. You can also look at Mark Pilgrim's excellent site,[1] and check out his accompanying book, *HTML5: Up and Running* [Pil10]. You can also drink from the fire hose with the HTML5 Specification.[2] In addition, there's the great resource dedicated to HTML5 called HTML5 Doctor.[3] HTML5 is a specification unto itself, but be careful. People frequently use the acronym *HTML5* to refer to a number of technologies described in different W3C specifications, including HTML5 itself (including canvas, video, web storage, and more), CSS3, Web Sockets, Web Workers, Geolocation, and more.

We're going to focus on the new tags that we can start using today, and we'll touch on some other pieces as we move through the various problems we encounter as we build ArtFlow.

HTML5 and Semantic Markup

Hierarchy and context—these two things are what we're really creating when we mark up a document. We build relationships between pieces of content

---

1. http://www.diveintohtml5.info
2. http://www.w3.org/TR/html5/ and the more user-friendly http://developers.whatwg.org/.
3. http://www.html5doctor.com/

that describe the structure of the document and provide hooks for us to style those pieces of content in separate style sheets. Maintaining this separation of concerns is one of our rules, on page 233.

In the past we've been dependent on the <div> element, which has very little semantic meaning on its own. While there were many semantic HTML elements in earlier versions of HTML, most were very specific and limited in scope (e.g., definition lists).

HTML5 has changed that. Now that we have several new, more semantic HTML elements available for overall page structure, we can provide a greater level of meaning in our documents, make the relationships between pieces of data more apparent, and make the whole document more readable.

There are also many more tags from earlier versions of HTML that we should also employ in our markup, such as definition lists (<dl>), which in the new version of the spec are to be used for any key-value pair. When writing HTML, we should try to add as much semantic meaning as possible, (again) as stated in our rules, on page 233.

Let's look at our new HTML5 tags and briefly see what each is used for:

- abbr: An abbreviation or acronym where the title attribute has the full, spelled-out version or meaning.

- article: A unique item, sometimes in a list. Common examples would be an article in a magazine or blog or an item on an e-commerce site.

- aside: Akin to a true sidebar within an article in print magazines, this is not to be used for our sidebar column. Pull quotes, breakout content, and similar objects would fit in this element.

- audio: An audio or sound stream. Various browsers support various codecs, including .wav, .ogg, and .mp3, depending.

- canvas: A canvas element is used for rendering graphics on the fly within a page. It is raster/bitmap-based and should not be used for things that have a better option (e.g., don't render a heading with canvas).

- datalist: A set of options inside an input when it is a list.

- details: A disclosure widget, where the user can find additional information or controls; for example, a file transfer window that has a series of key/value pairs about the transfer would be a definition list wrapped in a details element.

- figcaption: The caption for a figure.

- figure: Some kind of content that interrupts the main flow of content, such as a photo, illustration, chart, etc. that is referenced from the content. The rule of thumb is that you should be able to be remove it from the flow of the content (that is, to another page) without affecting the flow.

- footer: The footer of a given section of a document or of the document itself. This often contains copyright information, links, contact information, and more.

- header: A heading of a given section of a document or of the document itself. This will contain various h1 through h6 elements but can also contain other information.

- hgroup: A wrapper around multiple <header> elements when used adjacent to each other in a section—a heading and subheading that are related.

- mark: A tag to be used to mark or highlight content for reference purposes to bring the reader's attention to something or due to relevance in a search.

- meter: An element that reports a scalar value within a known range, or anything that could be from 0 to 100 percent (or where there is a known maximum value).

- nav: Navigation for a document or to other documents. Not every group of links is a <nav> item, however, and it should not be used in places such as footers, etc.

- output: The result from a calculation.

- progress: The completion progress of a task, either in relationship from 0 to 100 percent or in an unknown state.

- section: A generic document or web app section. It is a themed group and sometimes has a header and a footer within it.

- summary: A caption or summary of the parent <details> element and its contents.

- time: A time element, such as a created_at or updated_at column, in our models.

- video: Similar to audio but for a video or movie.

There are also quite a few new HTML5 form elements, which we will discuss in Chapter 5, *Building Maintainable Forms*, on page 119.

These are all things we would have probably used <div> tags for in the past, but now we can call them what they are! Let's look at our mockups and figure out where to use these new, more descriptive tags. We won't be using all of these in our build-out, but we should be aware of them so we can identify the proper tag to use for any content piece we encounter as we build our application.

Beyond Tags: Microformats and ARIA Roles

While the breadth of HTML tags gives us a lot of options to use, we should consider combining these meaningful tags with other techniques such as microformats and ARIA roles to provide as much meaning as possible.

Microformats arose from XHTML as a way to provide more meaning to content in a web page.[4] While there are some well-established microformats, such as hCard and hAddress, the concepts of a microformat are open-source and community-based design principles for formatting data.

ARIA roles are part of the WAI (Web Accessibility Initiative), and ARIA stands for *accessible rich Internet applications*.[5] These are attributes added to tags to let the browser better understand the role of an element or group of elements on a page. Whenever you see role="{value}" or aria-value{something}={value} as we build out our code, it means we're using ARIA roles to provide more meaning.

Analyzing the Design

Since the core user interaction with our application is managing creations, we'll start with our creation index. This page has many of the elements that are used site-wide, and since our designer was nice enough to standardize screens across the app, we'll be able to build out a good chunk of the design concept in one place.

Looking at Figure 3, *The creation index as we plan to break it up*, on page 7, we see a header, notifications, navigation, a sidebar, and a footer (in addition to our main creation listing). Now that we know how to decompose our mockup, let's start converting it into markup—once we have some standard boilerplate in place.

1.2 Setting Up a Boilerplate

A boilerplate refers to the standard view code that we use in every application we build. It's a great way to standardize toolsets and quickly get things moving early in the development cycle. There are as many different boilerplates as

---

4. http://www.microformats.org
5. http://www.w3.org/TR/wai-aria/

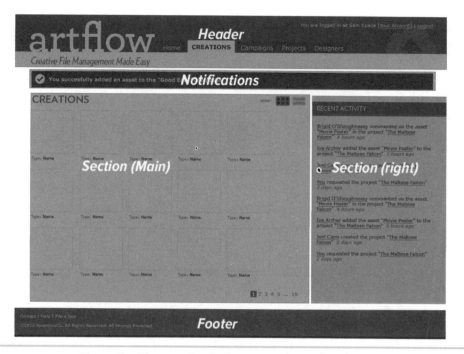

Figure 3—The creation index as we plan to break it up

there are stars in the sky, but let's look at the most common example, the one that Rails generates for us. The standard site-wide layout is located in app/views/layouts/application.html.erb.

```
<!DOCTYPE html>
<html>
<head>
  <title>Artflow</title>
  <%= stylesheet_link_tag    "application" %>
  <%= javascript_include_tag "application" %>
  <%= csrf_meta_tags %>
</head>
<body>

<%= yield %>

</body>
</html>
```

Here is the initial Rails application.html.erb. It says we're using HTML5 with the DOCTYPE (which appears simply as <!DOCTYPE html>), loads all the style sheets and JavaScript files from their respective directories, and puts the content rendered by the controller action where yield is placed.

> **Joe asks:**
> # Are Boilerplates Mandatory?
>
> Not at all. They are simply a codified way of doing things, similar to how Rails codifies certain things about how we build web applications. Boilerplates are also something that each team will develop over time and standardize for its particular needs. We have separate boilerplates for our public and internal-facing applications, and we often update them as best practices change and experience shows us a better way.

This file is intentionally sparse, as the core team put in only the HTML that is absolutely needed to make Rails deliver a view to a browser. The team could have put in a full boilerplate of various code pieces, but they left it to us to extend the basics.

Now let's add in some additional elements that we'll need, starting with our charset. Browsers need to map characters to unicode, and giving them a charset lets each browser do that correctly—otherwise we have nasty little things showing up in our text. We use UTF-8 because it provides the best features across the most devices and works for XML and HTML. We need to specify a character encoding or we can have various issues arise in our page.[6]

```
<head>
➤   <meta charset="utf-8">
    <title>ArtFlow</title>
    <!-- The rest of our head -->
</head>
```

We sometimes run across documents that use other encodings, such as ASCII or the ISO-8859-1 and its variations. These encodings are fine in English and for specific languages, but the new standards of UTF-8, -16, or -24 support almost every language in the world. HTML5 spec states that "authors are encouraged to use UTF-8," so we'll use that. UTF-8 makes internationalization much easier to deal with, and it lets us mix character sets in the same page. More information is available online.[7]

This is the same as the much longer (and older style) seen here:

```
<head>
➤   <meta http-equiv="Content-Type" content="text/html;charset=utf-8">
    <title>ArtFlow</title>
    <!-- The rest of our head -->
</head>
```

---

6. http://blog.whatwg.org/the-road-to-html-5-character-encoding
7. http://htmlpurifier.org/docs/enduser-utf8.html#whyutf8

Both work just fine with all the major browsers, and the shorter declaration is cleaner. Now that we have the charset in place, let's start to set up our code base for all the browsers we will support.

Turning on HTML5 for Internet Explorer and Older Browsers

We need to support MSIE 7 and 8 for this application. While large parts of it are being used internally and we can limit the browser support from an IT perspective, our customers' clients may be using all sorts of browsers to access the site. How do we balance providing better semantic markup and code with keeping our sanity while debugging browsers (which we cover in more depth in Section 1.8, *Testing Internet Explorer*, on page 41) with backwards compatibility?

Modernizr to the Rescue!

Modernizr is a library that uses JavaScript to detect the availability of native support for next-generation web technologies ranging from HTML5 to CSS3 and more.[8] It classes the <html> element with this information and allows for the loading of polyfills to include functionality in browsers without native support.[9] It also contains an HTML5 shiv to enable many of the new tags we looked at above. This shiv allows them to be styled, but we will need to add them to our reset/normalize style sheet (which we do in *Getting Browsers on the Same Page*, on page 10) in order to get them working the same across all browsers.

Modernizr's HTML shiv does a few things for us. First, the shiv tells the DOM (document object model) that there are some new elements that the DOM can address. Some browsers assume that if an element is a tag and the browser doesn't know about it, the tag was intended to be something new and the browser will treat the tag as a generic element. Internet Explorer does not. We could have typed the following for each new element:

```
<script>document.createElement("blah");</script>
```

Instead of typing the above for every new HTML element we want to use, this script takes care of creating those elements as well as some other things. It creates an array of the new tags we want to use and then applies .createElement(); to each. It also applied the IE HTML5 Print Protector so that these elements will print properly.[10]

---

8.   http://www.modernizr.com
9.   https://github.com/Modernizr/Modernizr/wiki/HTML5-Cross-browser-Polyfills
10.   http://www.iecss.com/print-protector/

We will roll our own custom version at http://modernizr.com/download/ to only include the functionality that we need and place it in our assets/javascripts folder. Next we'll add this to our manifest file in app/assets/javascripts/application.js (a directory we talk about in more depth in Chapter 4, *Adding JavaScript*, on page 101):

artflow/layout/app/assets/javascripts/application.js
```
//= require modernizr-1.7.custom
//= require jquery
//= require jquery_ujs
//= require_tree .
```

For concerns about what we can support today, we can take a look at http://html5readiness.com/ or http://www.caniuse.com/ and see which browsers support which elements (and at what point that support was introduced). While the spec is not yet final, most browsers have some implementation for many of the elements of the HTML5 family of tools.

Once we have this in place, the new HTML5 elements are now addressable in the DOM for both JavaScript and CSS styling. Now we need to make sure all the browsers are starting from a blank slate, stylistically speaking.

Getting Browsers on the Same Page

Now that all our browsers will recognize the HTML tags we're tossing at them, we'll look at another browser problem we have to solve.

Browsers have their own built-in style sheets that they use as basic presentation defaults. They also contribute and become the foundation for the styles we add, and as you might expect, these browser presentation defaults are nowhere near consistent. Each browser family will render things differently. List tags are rendered with left margins in one browser and left padding in another. There are extensive subtle presentation changes with elements having different top and bottom margins, line height, indentation, font presentation, and more.

The problem results in a lot of hacks to target specific browsers through JavaScript. Instead of this, we're going to get browsers on the same page by using a technique called *reset*.

Eric Meyer, who came up with the first reset.css, explains the semantic rationale as follows:[11]

> There's another reason we want to reset a whole lot of styles on a whole lot of elements. Not only do we want to strip off the padding and margins, but we also want all elements to have a consistent font size, weight, style, and family. Yes,

---

11. http://meyerweb.com/eric/thoughts/2007/04/18/reset-reasoning/

> **Joe asks:**
> ## What About Google's Chrome Frame?
>
> The Chrome Frame by Google is a plugin that effectively turns Internet Explorer into Google Chrome if the website it is browsing calls for it.[a] While this is a great tool, we can't be sure that our users will have it, nor do we want to force them to download it in order to use our app. We can provide support for it (which we will do in the build-out), but we won't rely on it for this particular application.
>
> ------
>
> a.   http://code.google.com/chrome/chromeframe/

we want to remove the boldfacing from headings and strong elements; we want to un-italicize <em> and <cite> elements.

We want all this because we don't want to take style effects for granted. This serves two purposes. First, it makes us think just that little bit harder about the semantics of our document. With the reset in place, we don't pick <strong> because the design calls for boldfacing. Instead, we pick the right element—whether it's <strong> or <em> or <b> or <h3> or whatever—and then style it as needed.

We reset these internal style sheets (or wipe them out) and then assign basic styles (or normalize them) so that we have a nice clean slate from which to work. While we like Eric Meyer's sentiment of styling each piece by hand, the reality is that the majority of the time that we are using certain elements, we are using them with some default presentation. It's easy enough to strip off the styling on the outliers as opposed to writing out every piece every time.

And that is why we are not going to use the HTML5 reset nor the original reset created by Eric Meyer for this task,[12] but a new approach that does it all at once, called Normalize.css.[13] According to its authors, it "preserves useful defaults, normalizes styles for a wide range of elements, corrects bugs and common browser inconsistencies," and more.

To see the visual difference in these, we can look at a few experiments that show the basic differences.[14] We end up with some great unified base styles and we don't have to spend as much time declaring the basics over and over again.

We want to pull the raw normalize.css from https://raw.github.com/necolas/normalize.css/ master/normalize.css and place it into our app/assets/stylesheets directory.

------

12.   http://html5doctor.com/html-5-reset-stylesheet/ or http://meyerweb.com/eric/tools/css/reset/, respectively.

13.   http://necolas.github.com/normalize.css/

14.   http://experiments.botsko.net/tests/html5-boilerplate-css/

We are also going to remove the line *= require_tree, as we want to be able to load our files in a specific order.

Let's take a moment to review the normalize.css file and see what it does. The file starts by setting up the HTML5 elements properly and then moves on to resetting and standardizing text, link colors (which we will override later), typography, lists, embedded content, figures, forms, and tables. Using this file will help us solve most of our cross-browser rendering issues and debugging nightmares. We'll look at making more targeted corrections in Section 1.8, *Testing Internet Explorer*, on page 41.

Let's get back to our layout in app/views/layouts/application.html.erb. Here's what it looks like now:

```erb
<!DOCTYPE html>
<html>
<head>
  <meta charset="utf-8">
  <title>Artflow</title>
  <%= stylesheet_link_tag    "application" %>
  <%= javascript_include_tag "application" %>
  <%= csrf_meta_tags %>
</head>
<body>

<%= yield %>

</body>
</html>
```

We need to add a require directive for our normalize style sheet to the app/assets/stylesheets/application.css manifest so that Rails includes it (see Chapter 3, *Adding Cascading Style Sheets*, on page 73, for more information on how Sprocket directives and the asset pipeline work), taking care to put it before our other files:

```css
/*
 *= require_self
 *= require normalize
*/
```

We're almost ready to build our page out, but first, let's quickly look at the preexisting boilerplates and see if there's anything we want to use in our application.

Joe asks:
Can I Use These Techniques Before Rails 3.1?

Before Rails 3.1, style sheets, JavaScripts, images, and other assets lived in the public folder. The nickname for this became the "junk drawer" of the application. The asset pipeline, which we cover in Section 3.1, *Using the Asset Pipeline*, on page 73, is such a major improvement that we're only going to work in that paradigm. If you're in an older app, there are some ways to work around this.

You can use a tool like Compass to bring in SASS and a tool like Guard or LiveReload to watch your files for changes and convert them to static assets.[a] We do this in many legacy apps that we have to maintain. We create the file structure in app/assets and then use the SASS gem to convert them as we make SCSS changes:

```
sass --watch app/assets/stylesheets/application.css:
  public/stylesheets/application.css
```

If you're adventuresome, you can also look at the Sprockets gem, which is what the asset pipeline itself uses, and attempt to bring that back to your legacy app.

a. http://compass-style.org/ and http://livereload.com/, respectively.

Borrowing from the Mega-Boilerplate

There are a few different ultimate *awesome* kick-butt HTML5 boilerplates out there that do everything under the sun. Using these arbitrarily is not smart and in many cases can add cruft to our app that we don't need. These range from tools like HTML5 Boilerplate to Twitter's Bootstrap:[15] we will use HTML5 Boilerplate here.

HTML5 Boilerplate is a collection of best practices and patterns pulled from a lot of large public-facing web projects,[16] and it covers almost everything we can think of that we may need. It's also heavily commented so that most every line has a reference to what it does and why it's included.

We are not going to use this out of the box. It is quite a complex monster and we will start at the beginning by building out the base structure of our page, including the pieces that we need as we move along. Some of the things that we are going to pull over are IE PNG fixes (to make CSS image resizing work in Internet Explorer), the normalize CSS (which we just included) and a clearfix (to help with issues related to floated elements).

---

15. http://twitter.github.com/bootstrap/
16. http://www.html5boilerplate.com

There's an argument against using resets, boilerplates, and conditional comments that says the following:[17]

> The default CSS rules are sensible and make sense (for example, they format unordered lists correctly)....There are perfectly good CSS hacks that you can use...[18] [and] at least they keep your HTML clean from those super-ugly, totally weird conditional comments, which quite mess up your code.

While this is a great approach if you're only coding for one platform or have the patience to dig everything up each time, a boilerplate (of your own creation) can save time and therefore money on projects, especially in teams where you can use the same foundation over and over again.

CSS browser-specific hacks can be problematic to maintain and only work when the *entire* development team understands them. The likelihood of this is low. Resetting and normalizing the built-in browser style sheet is the best pragmatic approach to use for both developer sanity and future-proofing our applications.

1.3 Building the Page Frame

We are now going to create our global elements: the header, the sidebar, our alerts, and the footer. These will include our application's branding (logo, taglines, and colors) as well as the primary navigation and utility navigation. Primary navigation refers to the main items, such as projects, creations, home, and other elements that help users move around the site. The utility navigation will support users logging in, logging out, and accessing their accounts.

From a process standpoint, we always want to write the minimal amount of HTML first and then add additional elements as required for layout and interactivity (JavaScript, Ajax, etc.). This helps us keep the code clean and makes us look at semantics and meaning first, as opposed to simply looking at presentation and layout.

To begin with, we are going to place some code in partials. While we normally don't want to extract things arbitrarily, putting our header and footer into partials in the layouts folder makes our layout easier to read, which makes it easier for us to focus on stepping through our build. We're going to render a partial named _header.html.erb. When we render it from app/views/layouts/application.html.erb, we refer to it with the directory name since it will be used across

---

17. http://mir.aculo.us/2010/08/10/pragmatic-html-css/
18. http://dimox.net/personal-css-hacks-for-ie6-ie7-ie8/

many controllers. If we don't specify the directory, Rails will look for the file in the current controller's view directory.

```
<!DOCTYPE html>
<html>

<head>
  <meta charset="utf-8">
  <title>Artflow</title>
  <%= stylesheet_link_tag     "application" %>
  <%= javascript_include_tag "application" %>
  <%= csrf_meta_tags %>
</head>

<body>
  <%= render 'layout/header' %>

<%= yield %>

</body>
</html>
```

Let's use one of the new HTML5 elements, <header>, to call out our first section. Headers, like most of the new HTML5 elements, need not be unique on a page and are used in various levels of a document's hierarchy. Since that's the case, we want to give it a unique ID. For this case, we'll call it page_header. Let's change app/views/layouts/_header.html.erb:

```
<header id="page_header">
</header>
```

Next, let's look at the elements within the header itself. We have a logo featuring our application name, utility navigation, application navigation, and some miscellaneous branding elements. The logo should link back to the root_url for the application. A common practice for developers is to put a logo into an <h1> tag. We will not, as it's not the headline of the page.[19] Always think of the true semantics of the content: the headline is a textual content element, not a graphic. While this may not matter on the home page, when we are inside a page, what is the main headline? Is it the logo, or, in the case of the application layout that we're currently building, is it the title of the collection (e.g., "Assets")?

The other elements should be <nav> entities with unique IDs. When we add these in app/views/layouts/_header.html.erb, it looks like this:

---

19. http://csswizardry.com/2010/10/your-logo-is-an-image-not-a-h1/

```
<header id="page_header" role="banner">
  <nav id="utility">
    <p>
      You are logged in as <strong>Sam Spade</strong>
      <%= link_to "[Your Account]", "current_user_path" %> |
      <%= link_to "[Logout]", "logout_path" %>
    </p>
  </nav>
  <%= link_to(
      image_tag("logo.png",
                alt: "Artflow",
                id: "logo"),
      root_url,
      title: "Dashboard") %>
</header>
```

We've also added an ARIA role for the header of banner. This is one of a predefined set of "landmark roles" in the ARIA specification.[20] These help with accessibility, and we should get in the habit of using them while we build, instead of retrofitting later. As for our main nav, we'll tackle the application navigation later (see Section 1.5, *Adding Navigation*, on page 28), as it's a bit more complex.

There's meaning in how we've marked up the header, and now we can use that semantic markup to style the header. Always write the minimum amount of HTML required to style the page—additional elements are the bane of our existence as view hackers. Keep it clean! The base HTML (with a reset CSS) gives us something that looks like Figure 4, *An unstyled header*, on page 17. We don't see the logo because it's white text in a 24-bit transparent PNG: white on white.

Bringing the Pretty to the Header

We'll start with the overall header itself. This will be a mix of images and CSS. Normally in the day-to-day flow, we'd either be firing up Photoshop to cut our pieces or we could have our designer send us the pieces. We've included the Photoshop file as well as the precut pieces, so you can experiment the way you prefer.

We have a bunch of elements all inline right now that we need to position to make them look like the final mockup. Our utility navigation shows up in the HTML before our logo because we are going to use a CSS property called float to have it sit on the right. float is a property that can cause a lot of headaches,

---

20. http://www.w3.org/WAI/PF/aria-practices/#kbd_layout

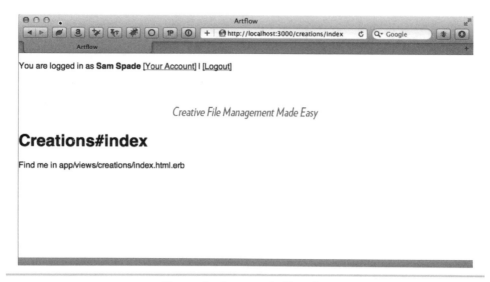

Figure 4—An unstyled header

many of which we will run into in the course of building this application. The default behavior for an element is to appear in the order in which it appears in the HTML markup. When we float an element to the right, it simply slides to the right in the same place that it would currently be. That would make the top of our element start at the bottom of the logo on the left. To get it to be equal with the logo, we need to put it in the HTML first.

Looking at the header, we see it's 78 pixels tall and has an inside padding of about 10 pixels. We would think that making the height attribute 78px would be the right solution, but we need to remember the box model.[21] The box model refers to the square space that each element takes up. It has width and height, padding, a border, and a margin. See Figure 5, *The box model*, on page 18.

So padding is *inside* the border and it gets added to the height and width of the actual element. To get our actual height attribute, we need to subtract the total padding from the measured height. So, that being said, if we want 88px in total height, and we have 10 pixels of padding on all sides, we define height at 68px in order to get the right total (68 + 10 + 10). We add some styling in a new file, layout.css.scss, taking advantage of the nesting support SCSS gives us,[22] as explained in Chapter 3, *Adding Cascading Style Sheets*, on page 73:

---

21. http://www.w3.org/TR/CSS2/box.html
22. Sassy CSS, http://sass-lang.com/.

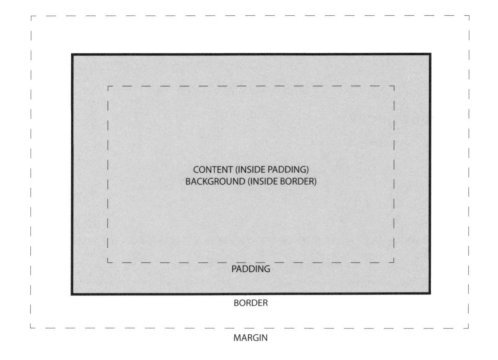

Figure 5—The box model

```
header#page_header {
  background-color: #534f4b;
  color: #fff;
  height: 68px;
  margin-bottom: 10px;
  overflow: hidden;
  padding: 10px 20px;

  a,
  a:link,
  a:hover,
  a:active,
  a:visited {
    color:#fef8e7;
    text-decoration: none;
  }

  nav#utility {
    float: right;
    font-size: 0.8em;
  }
```

```
  #logo {
    position: absolute;
    top: 15px;
  }
}
```

In order to see it, we need to call this file into the asset pipeline. Let's add our layout styling to our application.css manifest, right after the reset we added in *Getting Browsers on the Same Page*, on page 10:

```
/*
 *= require_self
 *= require normalize
 *= require layout
*/
```

Now that's starting to look like a header. We've defined link colors, determined the padding and spacing, placed our logo file, and floated our utility nav right. We just need to add the branding graphics and we'll be done. We could use an <img> tag for the logo, but since we have text overlaying it, we'll put the image in the background instead. We'll modify app/assets/stylesheets/layout.css.scss:

```
header#page_header {
➤   background: #bc471d url('/assets/brandtag.png') bottom right no-repeat;
    color: #fff;
    font-size: 0.9em;
    height: 68px;
    margin-bottom: 10px;
    overflow: hidden;
    padding: 10px 20px;
    a,
    a:link,
    a:hover,
    a:active,
    a:visited {
      color:#fef8e7;
      text-decoration: none;
    }

    nav#utility {
      float: right;
      font-size: 0.8em;
    }

    #logo {
      position: absolute;
      top: 15px;
    }
}
```

```
#tagline {
  margin-left: 20px;
}

div.container {
  overflow: hidden;
  padding: 0 20px;

}
```

We've changed background-color to simply background and used that advanced definition instead of manually specifying the background color, position, image, and repeat as four different properties. This is not some new HTML5/CSS3 trick, but what is called "CSS shorthand." This allows us to combine multiple declarations into one line and reduce the verbosity (and size) of our CSS files. In this case, background includes background-color, background-image, background-position, and background-repeat, reducing our CSS from four lines to one.

We now have our header looking correct (Figure 6, *The styled header*, on page 21). Let's move on and get our footer in place.

Setting Up Our Footer

Footers have become a whole new domain in web design. They often have multiple columns, lots of information, and lots and lots of links. One could argue that, in many cases, the old site map page has shuffled its way into the footer of every page. Links and icons abound, and the footer can end up as a junk drawer.

On this app, we're dealing with something far simpler, as there are only two elements contained inside it for our example: a <ul> and a copyright notice. Let's start with our HTML, modifying app/views/layouts/application.html.erb:

```
<!DOCTYPE html>
<html>
<head>
  <meta charset="utf-8">
  <title>Artflow</title>
  <%= stylesheet_link_tag    "application" %>
  <%= javascript_include_tag "application" %>
  <%= csrf_meta_tags %>
</head>

<body>
  <%= render 'layouts/header' %>
  <%= image_tag("tagline.png",
```

Figure 6—The styled header

```
                alt: "Creative File Management Made Easy",
                id: "tagline") %>
<div class="container">

   <%= yield %>
</div>
<%= render 'layouts/footer' %>
</body>
</html>
```

Yes, we've used a <div>. Our wrapper's job will be to center the content and sidebar <section> tags together—it's purely for presentation purposes, so the generic quality of the tag is okay. Usually we'd be the first ones to burn a <div> tag in effigy, but this isn't the time.

Here's our footer partial:

artflow/layout/app/views/layouts/_footer.html.erb
```
<footer id="page_footer">
  <ul>
    <li><%= link_to "Contact", "" %></li>
    <li><%= link_to "Help", "" %></li>
    <li><%= link_to "File a Bug", "" %></li>
  </ul>
  <p>&copy; 2011 AwesomeCo. All Rights Reserved. All Wrongs Reversed.</p>
</footer>
```

We don't need to class the <ul> or the <p>, as we can target them specifically by using the parent element's unique ID of page_footer and child selectors. If there were more elements within the footer, we would probably want to address those elements via a class or an ID directly. For now, all we need is this:

```
artflow/layout/app/assets/stylesheets/layout.css.scss
footer#page_footer {
  background-color: #807c77;
  border-bottom: 10px solid #4c2719;
  color: #fff;
  font-size: 0.7em;
  height: 100px;
  padding: 10px 20px;

  ul {
    margin-left: -10px;
    padding: 0;

    li {
      border-right: 1px solid #fef8e7;
      display: inline;
      margin: 0;
      &:last-child {
        border-right: none;
      }

      a {
        padding: 5px 10px;
        &:link,
        &:hover,
        &:visited,
        &.active {
          color: #fff;
        }
      }
    }
  }
}
```

You'll notice the :last-child pseudo-selector in here. This will select the last element that is an <li> and apply styles only to that tag. This is ideal for when you want a border between rows or columns but not on the last column. A right border works great until the end, and the :last-child lets us turn it off.

Pseudo-class selectors have been around for a while but are starting to get more support in the mainstream browsers. You can even add it into older browsers with Selectivizr.[23]

---

23. http://selectivizr.com/

A nice feature here is that SCSS's support for nesting makes the structure of our styles mirror the structure of our HTML. For more information on SCSS, see Chapter 3, *Adding Cascading Style Sheets*, on page 73. It will be easy to find what we're looking for if we need to modify the styling later.

We've built a solid header and footer that we can expand as our application grows, but what about the business in between? Next up we build out the main content portion of our page, making room for a handy sidebar that we'll use for secondary navigation and supporting content.

1.4 Adding a Sidebar

We've put together a header, and now it's time to address another important part of our layout: sidebars. A sidebar sits to the right or left of the main content and has a few potential purposes:

- Quick links, category breakouts, and other navigation

- Additional context-sensitive instructions and information

- Marketing content, advertisements, or other content on every page of the application (but which doesn't make sense in the <header> or <footer>)

- Blogrolls, references, or links to other supporting material

ArtFlow needs to display some secondary navigation, form instructions, and contact information on all its pages, so we definitely need to add a sidebar.

But is a sidebar and an aside the same thing? No. An aside is an element that supports your main content, such as a pull quote or related links from an article. It's an element that is *related* to its parent element. For a sidebar, we should use just a <section> tag and then style the content inside it accordingly. If it's a list of categories or dates, a <nav> tag might be ideal. Remember, don't overdo the semantic approach. Trying to force things into these new elements is not in the spirit of semantic markup.

Making a Place for Content

When we put together our boilerplate in Section 1.2, *Setting Up a Boilerplate*, on page 6, we just tossed a yield into the body to insert the content from the action. That worked great then, but now that we have a sidebar that needs to sit alongside, things get a bit more complex. We move our yield into a <section> in our app/views/layouts/application.html.erb, adding a secondary <section> to boot.

```
<!DOCTYPE html>
<html>
<head>
  <meta charset="utf-8">
  <title>Artflow</title>
  <%= stylesheet_link_tag    "application" %>
  <%= javascript_include_tag "application" %>
  <%= csrf_meta_tags %>
</head>
<body>
  <%= render 'layouts/header' %>
  <%= image_tag("tagline.png",
                alt: "Creative File Management Made Easy",
                id: "tagline") %>
  <div class="container">
➤    <section id="content">
➤      <%= yield %>
➤    </section>
➤    <section id="sidebar">
➤    </section>
  </div>
  <%= render 'layouts/footer' %>
</body>
</html>
```

Getting the sidebar in place is simple enough: we'll put it to the right of our content and center our wrapper. This belongs along with the general layout styling we added in Section 1.3, *Building the Page Frame*, on page 14:

artflow/layout/app/assets/stylesheets/layout.css.scss
```
section#content {
   float: left;
 }
section#sidebar {
   margin-right: -20px;
   width: 300px;
 }
```

We'll also create a sidebar.css.scss for the sidebar-specific content. For now, let's give sections inside the sidebar a light gray background and a bit of padding:

artflow/layout/app/assets/stylesheets/sidebar.css.scss
```
section#sidebar {
  background-color: #edeae6;
  -webkit-border-top-left-radius: 10px;
  -webkit-border-bottom-left-radius: 10px;
  -moz-border-radius-topleft: 10px;
  -moz-border-radius-bottomleft: 10px;
  border-top-left-radius: 10px;
  border-bottom-left-radius: 10px;
```

```
      color: #666;
      font: {
        size: 0.8em;
        weight: normal;
      }
      line-height: 1.3em;
      padding: 10px;
      a,
      a:link,
      a:visited {
        color: #666;
        text-decoration: underline;
      }

      a:hover,
      a:active {
        color: #bc471d;
      }

      section {
      }

      #functional_nav {
        ul {
          list-style-type: none;
          margin: 0;
          padding: 0;
        }
      }

      #recent_activity {
        header {
          background-color: #bc471d;
          border-bottom: 5px solid #807c77;
          margin: 10px -10px;
          padding: 5px 10px 0 10px;
          h1#recent {
            background: transparent url('/assets/txt_recent-activity.png')
                        no-repeat scroll top left;
            margin: 5px 0 0 0;
            padding: 0;
            text-indent: -999px;
          }
        }
      }
    }
```

We need to add a require directive for the sidebar to our application.css manifest to make sure it's included (for more information on how this works, see Chapter 3, *Adding Cascading Style Sheets*, on page 73):

```
/*
 *= require_self
 *= require normalize
 *= require layout
 *= require sidebar
 */
```

Now that we have an empty sidebar in the right place with a basic style for its content, let's figure out how we can add markup to the sidebar from our action templates.

Filling in the Layout with content_for

From our design, we see that we need a listing of recent creation activity displayed in the sidebar on every page. After putting the list in a partial, we simply render it from a new <section> tag in app/views/layouts/application.html.erb:

```
<!DOCTYPE html>
<html>
<head>
  <meta charset="utf-8">
  <title>Artflow</title>
  <%= stylesheet_link_tag    "application" %>
  <%= javascript_include_tag "application" %>
  <%= csrf_meta_tags %>
</head>
<body>
  <%= render 'layouts/header' %>
  <%= image_tag("tagline.png",
                alt: "Creative File Management Made Easy",
                id: "tagline") %>
  <div class="container">
    <section id="content">
      <%= yield %>
    </section>
    <section id="sidebar">
➤     <section id="recent_activity">
➤       <header><h1 class="ir" id="recent">Recent Activity</h1></header>
➤       <%= render partial: 'activity_items/recent' %>
➤     </section>
    </section>
  </div>
  <%= render 'layouts/footer' %>
</body>
</html>
```

This is great, but we also need to support actions adding more content to the sidebar for context-sensitive information. How do we get additional content from the action's rendering process?

If you'll remember, we're already pulling content rendered by our actions in the layout for the main content. This really isn't any different; the trick here is to use yield, but this time indicate *which* content rendered by the action we want inserted. yield without an argument will retrieve the main content, but we want the content for the sidebar, so we modify our app/views/layouts/application.html.erb:

```erb
<!DOCTYPE html>
<html>
<head>
  <meta charset="utf-8">
  <title>Artflow</title>
  <%= stylesheet_link_tag    "application" %>
  <%= javascript_include_tag "application" %>
  <%= csrf_meta_tags %>
</head>
<body>
  <%= render 'layouts/header' %>
  <%= image_tag("tagline.png",
                alt: "Creative File Management Made Easy",
                id: "tagline") %>
  <div class="container">
    <section id="content">
      <%= yield %>
    </section>
    <section id="sidebar">
      <%= yield :sidebar %>
      <section id="recent_activity">
        <header><h1 class="ir" id="recent">Recent Activity</h1></header>
        <%= render partial: 'activity_items/recent' %>
      </section>
    </section>
  </div>
  <%= render 'layouts/footer' %>
</body>
</html>
```

From a layout perspective, we're done now. We just need to wire in any actions that would like to provide content for the sidebar. We do this with a helper named content_for(), which we can use to add a listing of designers assigned to a project when viewing the project's page:

```erb
artflow/layout/app/views/projects/show.html.erb
<% content_for :sidebar do %>
  <section id='assigned_designers'>
    <header><h1>Assigned Designers</h1></header>
    <ul>
      <%= render @project.designers %>
    </ul>
```

```
    </section>
<% end %>

<article>
  <header>
    <h1><%= @project.name %></h1>
  </header>
  <!-- Project information -->
</article>
```

We can add as much (or as little) sidebar content as we'd like, and it will be inserted exactly where we've put our yield. We can even check to see if there's sidebar content using content_for?(:sidebar), which would be helpful if we wanted to add a CSS class to the <body> to support easily styling both sidebar and sidebar*less* layouts.

We can use the same trick to change the contents of the <title> tag for a page, which is useful for search indexing. Let's update the layout in app/views/layouts/application.html.erb:

```
<title>
  <% if content_for?(:title) %>
    ArtFlow: <%= yield :title %>
  <% else %>
    Artflow
  <% end %>
</title>
```

With this in place, we can add text to our title from any page just by using content_for :title. Neat!

Now we have a sidebar, and actions can insert content into it (and our title), but how do we move between actions? Next we tackle a more complex topic: adding navigation.

1.5 Adding Navigation

Our application would be pretty useless if we didn't offer our users a way to move around, wouldn't it? ArtFlow has a few important sections that our users need access to, and we've identified them as Home, Creations, Campaigns, Designers, and Projects. We've been tasked with adding these navigation items as a series of simple tabs at the top of the application.

Building the Tabs

First, we add an element with the list of links we'll need in the <header> we created in *Bringing the Pretty to the Header*, on page 16.

We modify app/views/layouts/_header.html.erb:

```erb
<header id="page_header" role="banner">
  <nav id="utility">
    <p>
      You are logged in as <strong>Sam Spade</strong>
      <%= link_to "[Your Account]", "current_user_path" %> |
      <%= link_to "[Logout]", "logout_path" %>
    </p>
  </nav>
  <%= link_to(
      image_tag("logo.png",
                alt: "Artflow",
                id: "logo"),
      root_url,
      title: "Dashboard") %>
  <nav id="main_nav" role="navigation">
    <ul>
      <li><%= link_to 'Home', root_path %></li>
      <li><%= link_to 'Creations', creations_path %></li>
      <li><%= link_to 'Campaigns', campaigns_path %></li>
      <li><%= link_to 'Projects', projects_path %></li>
    </ul>
  </nav>
</header>
```

A <ul> tag is the natural choice here, as our main navigation really is just a list of places to visit in the application. Now we just need to make this list look like tabs running horizontally across the screen. This is a pretty classic style, so we know exactly what CSS to add to our style sheet. We create a navigation.css.scss file:

```scss
artflow/layout/app/assets/stylesheets/navigation.css.scss
nav#main_nav {
  li {
    background: #555;
    display: inline-block;
    margin: 0 2px;
    padding: 4px 6px;

    a,
    a:link,
    a:visited {
      color: #fff;
      text-decoration: none;
    }
  }
}
```

Then we add a require directive to our application.css manifest (for more informa-tion on how this works, see Chapter 3, *Adding Cascading Style Sheets*, on page 73):

```
/*
*= require_self
*= require normalize
*= require layout
*= require sidebar
➤ *= require navigation
*/
```

We now have our inactive tabs styled and ready to go, and we use inline-block so they sit side by side. We use this instead of float since it's a bit less erratic across browsers, and we use it instead of inline because our <li> tags have content. We want to have control over the margins around this content, and inline elements don't always support dimension attributes. inline-block makes the most sense because they're blocks; they're just sitting next to each other. The end result looks like this:

Now users know where they can go, but how can they tell where they are?

Providing Context

An important piece of feedback that our application's main navigation needs to give our users is *context*, something we're not providing yet. We need to visually differentiate the active tab (where they are) from the inactive tabs (where they can go). We need to define what the active tab looks like; we'll do this by changing the tab background color to the inverse of the rest of the tabs—light on dark instead of dark on light:

```
artflow/layout/app/assets/stylesheets/navigation.css.scss
nav#main_nav {
  li {
    background: #555;
    display: inline-block;
    margin: 0 2px;
    padding: 4px 6px;
    a,
    a:link,
    a:visited {
      color: #fff;
      text-decoration: none;
    }
➤   &.active {
```

```
➤        background: #fff;
➤        margin-bottom: -1px;
➤        a,
➤        a:link,
➤        a:visited {
➤          color: #555;
➤          font-weight: bold;
➤        }
➤      }
➤    }
    }
```

So we've added a definition for an active CSS class, which is an inverse of the inactive tabs and sits a pixel lower so it looks like it's "connected" to the content below it (just like a real tab). We nested this inside the li selector by using the SCSS & parent selector (for more information on SCSS syntax, see Chapter 3, *Adding Cascading Style Sheets*, on page 73).

Now we just need to add the class to the correct tab, which raises a question: How does the navigation know what page the user is looking at and which tab to activate?

Let's take a step back and remember something important when it comes to rendering views in Rails: what the user sees is the result of a single action's view being rendered. It stands to reason, then, that when we're editing that view, we know which tab should be active, right? Why not just have the action's view tell the navigation which tab to show as active?

In Section 1.4, *Adding a Sidebar*, on page 23, we discussed the ability of templates to define content that is then used in the surrounding layout (using content_for() and yield). It's a handy trick that will serve us well with navigation, too, since we'd like the main template for an action to be able to render the navigation, but for the navigation to show up where it belongs.

To do this, we extract the navigation and put it into its own partial and wrap it in a content_for(). We stick the partial in the views/layouts/ directory, since it's in direct support of the layout. Let's add app/views/layouts/_main_nav.html.erb:

```erb
➤ <% content_for :main_navigation do %>
     <nav id="main_nav" role="navigation">
       <ul>
         <li><%= link_to 'Campaigns',   campaigns_path %></li>
         <li><%= link_to 'Creations',   creations_path %></li>
         <li><%= link_to 'Assignments', assignments_path %></li>
       </ul>
     </nav>
➤ <% end %>
```

Then we replace the hole we've just put in our app/views/layouts/_header.html.erb with a yield that will insert the navigation in the <header> no matter where it's rendered.

```erb
<header id="page_header" role="banner">
  <nav id="utility">
    <p>
      You are logged in as <strong>Sam Spade</strong>
      <%= link_to "[Your Account]", "current_user_path" %> |
      <%= link_to "[Logout]", "logout_path" %>
    </p>
  </nav>
  <%= link_to(
        image_tag("logo.png",
                  alt: "Artflow",
                  id: "logo"),
        root_url,
        title: "Dashboard") %>
➤ <%= yield :main_navigation %>
</header>
```

At this point we can render the navigation from our action view, but we don't handle adding the active CSS class yet. We'll fix that by having the navigation partial look for a current_tab local variable and use a simple helper, nav_tab() to build our <li> tags for us, checking whether each should be activated.

artflow/layout/app/helpers/navigation_helper.rb
```ruby
def nav_tab(title, url, options = {})
  current_tab = options.delete(:current)
  options[:class] = (current_tab == title) ? 'active' : 'inactive'
  content_tag(:li, link_to(title, url, options))
end
```

Render the partial with the right current_tab, and the navigation will be added to the <header> with the right tab activated:

artflow/layout/app/views/layouts/_main_nav.html.erb
```erb
<% content_for :main_navigation do %>
  <nav id="main_nav" role="navigation">
    <ul>
➤     <%= nav_tab 'Campaigns',   campaigns_path,   current: current_tab %>
➤     <%= nav_tab 'Creations',   creations_path,   current: current_tab %>
➤     <%= nav_tab 'Assignments', assignments_path, current: current_tab %>
    </ul>
  </nav>
<% end %>
```

Since we'll be rendering this partial from each action and since passing a local is a bit verbose, we'll give ourselves a handy little helper, currently_at() that we can use to make things a bit easier to understand:

```
artflow/layout/app/helpers/navigation_helper.rb
def currently_at(tab)
  render partial: 'layouts/main_nav', locals: {current_tab: tab}
end
```

Now adding context-aware main navigation is only a currently_at() away. Our creations index, for instance, is easy to wire up:

```
artflow/layout/app/views/creations/index.html.erb
<h2>Creations</h2>
```

➤ `<%= currently_at 'Creations' %>`

`<%= render @creations %>`

That single line adds our navigation exactly as it should be, and it's always that simple, no matter how complex the workflow or how deep the page.

Main navigation is just the beginning of the story, as it only provides us with the starting point for each area of the application. How do we support users digging deeper?

Secondary Navigation

Designers using ArtFlow need the ability to add a creation quickly from anywhere in the application. Looking at the design, we know we're supposed to have a functional, secondary set of navigation at the top of the sidebar, so we'll add a link there. First we need to set aside a place within our sidebar. Let's put the navigation at the top of our app/views/layouts/application.html.erb:

```
<section id="sidebar">
  <nav id="functional_nav">
    <ul>
      <% if current_user.designer? %>
        <li><%= link_to 'Add Creation', new_creation_path %></li>
      <% end %>
      <%= yield :functional_nav %>
    </ul>
  </nav>
  <%= yield :sidebar %>
  <section id="recent_activity">
    <header><h1 class="ir" id="recent">Recent Activity</h1></header>
    <%= render partial: 'activity_items/recent' %>
  </section>
</section>
```

We've taken the extra step of adding a yield inside our navigation list so that we can add additional items from actions that need them using content_for.

Joe asks:
Why Not Use controller_name and action_name?

The controller_name() and action_name() helpers provide an easy way for us to determine which action the user is currently looking at, so why isn't the navigation using these to determine the active tab? Why aren't we just keeping the navigation in the layout and adding in some logic that figures out which page we're on?

While it's true that in small applications there may be a simple mapping between tabs and controllers, things can get messy pretty quickly in larger applications—when a controller's actions are spread across different tabs, when the user workflow requires more complex rules, or when the way code is broken up within the application falls out of sync with the way users navigate through it.

To prevent our navigation degenerating into a snarl of conditionals to guess the current page, we simply tell the navigation which tab is active. It's explicit, it's easy to find and modify, and it never gets more complex than that.

Sure, we can add a heuristic for determining the current page, but is that the simplest solution, or merely the "cleverest?" Sometimes the best way to fix a problem is to avoid it entirely.

Speak of the devil—when we're looking at a creation, we'd like to quickly update its details, so we provide a link to the edit action:

artflow/layout/app/views/creations/show.html.erb

```erb
<% content_for :functional_nav do %>
  <li><%= link_to 'Edit this creation', @creation %></li>
<% end %>
```

Using this pattern, we can easily add context-sensitive functional links that make navigating laterally within a section of ArtFlow easy for our users (and for us to develop, too).

Don't Forget the Breadcrumbs

Just like Hansel and Gretel, our users run the risk of getting lost in our application (except the witch eats *us* in this version of the folktale). While our main navigation gives users immediate feedback on which section of the application they're viewing, it's not enough. We need a simple technique to lead them back out of the forest—and it's no surprise the classic user-interaction solution is named "breadcrumbs."

Our ArtFlow product manager is concerned about the feedback that he's been getting from customer service since our beta release. Our users want to be able to navigate from deeper parts of the application back to shallower waters, especially since many of the workflows we need to support deal with people jumping into a creation, changing something, then moving on to new creations.

One of the popular features with our enterprise users is fine-grained control of creation permissions used to support their more "robust" quality controls and approval processes. The permissions options are sizable, so we've extracted it from our standard creation form and put it on its own page with additional instructions to make configuration less cluttered. The path from the creation listing to the permissions form looks something like this:

Our users need to be able to jump back from any point in this path. Here's how we model the breadcrumbs for the permissions page:

```
artflow/layout/app/views/creations/permissions.html.erb
<nav id="breadcrumbs" itemtype="http://schema.org/WebPage" itemprop="breadcrumb">
  <li><%= link_to 'Creations', creations_path %></li>
  <li><%= link_to truncate(@creation.name), @creation %></li>
  <li><%= link_to 'Edit', edit_creations_path(@creation) %></li>
  <li>Permissions</li>
</ul>
```

Nothing new here, except for the fact that we don't make the final (current) location a link. We've also added in some optional microformat data for breadcrumbs, which is part of the WebPage microformat.[24] This doesn't look like breadcrumbs yet, so let's fix that with a sprinkling of CSS:

```
artflow/layout/app/assets/stylesheets/navigation.css.scss
nav#breadcrumbs {
  background: #ddd;
  li {
    display: inline-block;
    margin: 0 2px;
    padding: 4px 6px;
    a,
    a:link,
    a:visited {
      padding-right: 12px;
      color: #000;
    }
    &:after {
      content: " » ";
    }
```

---

24. http://www.schema.org/WebPage

```
    &:last-child {
      &:after {
        content: "";
      }
    }
  }
}
```

The secret here is using the :after pseudo-class selector with the content property to add our "double greater than" (») characters between the items. We do
this by typing the real character, because the content property doesn't allow
HTML entities (in this case, raquo) and because the plain numerical form, \00bb,
is a bit esoteric. The result looks like this:

Assets » **Print Ad** » **Edit** » **Permissions**

Thankfully we don't need to worry about IE6 and IE7 (which don't support
:after) because ArtFlow is a product for internal use, and we've long since gone
through the trouble of convincing our IT director to upgrade the company to
more modern browsers.

If we did have to worry about older browsers, we'd be relegated to using a
plain <p> tag with links and character separators between them; we wouldn't
be able to accomplish the same separation of style and content.

More Feedback

Navigation is important not only because it allows users to move around our
application but also because it provides them with important feedback on
where they are within the application. Now we'll look at providing a different
kind of feedback: how we give them a well-earned pat on the back—or how
we tell users that something has gone horribly wrong.

1.6 Displaying Notifications

In the course of users interacting with ArtFlow, we will often need to tell them
whether or not an action was successful. In Rails we conventionally do this
by displaying values stored in the flash object. We add values to the flash object
from our controller actions and display them later in our views.

When a creation is successfully created in ArtFlow, for instance, we add a
notice to flash before we redirect:

artflow/layout/app/controllers/creations_controller.rb
```
flash[:notice] = "Creation added!"
```

Likewise, we add an alert when things don't go as planned right before we re-render the form in question:

```
flash.now[:alert] = "Could not save creation!"
```

When we add a value to flash, we can decide whether or not that value should be kept until the next request. In the case of the notice above, persisting the value across requests is exactly what we want; we're redirecting, so if it wasn't persisted, the notice would just disappear. In the case of the alert, however, we're not redirecting—we're simply re-rendering the form. If we persisted the alert, it would live one request too long and cry wolf unnecessarily. The form will display additional details about any errors that occurred. We'll learn more about this in *Displaying Errors*, on page 131.

Since we don't want the alert to persist, we specify that it be added to flash.now instead of just flash, since the default holds on to the value. Thankfully, our views don't have to care how the values are set or how long they'll live—they just need to display them, which we do by using the appropriately named notice() and alert() helpers.

We set up the basic HTML to show these notifications in our layout file:

artflow/layout/app/views/layouts/application.html.erb
```erb
<% if notice %>
  <p class="notification notice">
    <%= notice %>
  </p>
<% end %>

<% if alert %>
  <p class="notification alert">
    <%= alert %>
  </p>
<% end %>
```

We're using some conditionals here to make sure we don't add empty <p> tags to our pages when there's nothing to report. We'll give the tags a generic style that will be shared between both alerts and notices and add them to a new file, notifications.css.scss:

artflow/layout/app/assets/stylesheets/notifications.css.scss
```scss
.notification {
  background-position: 10px 9px;
  background-repeat: no-repeat;
  color: #fff;
  font-size: 14px;
  font-weight: bold;
  line-height: 1.6em;
```

```
  margin: 0 auto 20px;
  padding: 0.75em 0.75em 0.75em 45px;
}
```

That gives us the overall shape and size of the elements. We add a require directive for our new style sheet to our application.css manifest (as described in Chapter 3, *Adding Cascading Style Sheets*, on page 73):

artflow/layout/app/assets/stylesheets/application.css

```
/*
 *= require_self
 *= require normalize
 *= require layout
 *= require sidebar
 *= require navigation
➤ *= require notifications
*/
```

Now we get fancy:

artflow/layout/app/assets/stylesheets/notifications.css.scss

```
.notification {
  background:{
    position: 10px 9px;
    repeat: no-repeat;
  }
  color: #fff;
  font: {
    size: 14px;
    weight: bold;
  }
  line-height: 1.6em;
  margin: 0 auto 20px;
  padding: 0.75em 0.75em 0.75em 45px;

  .notice {
    background: {
      color: #006302;
      image: url("assets/notification_check.png");
    }
  }

  .alert {
    background: {
      color: #920202;
      image: url("assets/notification_x.png");
    }
  }
}
```

The spacing on the left is created to give our icon a place to sit as a background image. Mixing this with color changes on each creates notifications that look like this:

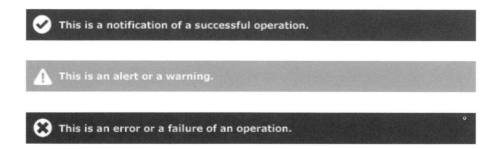

We can use any icons we'd like to match our overall application branding. In these two examples, we've used icons from Drew Wilson's Pictos icon set.[25] By providing a consistent style to notifications, we improve the user experience with a common expectation of how success and failure are communicated. Now we just need to finish the footer element.

1.7 Validating Our Code

We've spent a lot of time writing our code in this chapter and we are now going to make sure that it is valid HTML and CSS. Why do we bother to validate HTML? As long as it renders, isn't it okay? Not necessarily.

When we validate our HTML, we are looking to use it as our first line of debugging. If it's not valid HTML, we really can't fault the browser for rendering it in an odd way. We fed it something wrong and it did not like the taste.

While many browsers have been built to handle this malformed HTML (or "tag soup," as it's sometimes called[26]), in some cases they were not. HTML5 acknowledges that there's a lot of bad code out there, and it takes the stance that browsers should try to interpret this code for a better user experience. As nice as that may be, we are going to write well-formed, valid HTML5 for our application.

While some would say that we should just know this stuff, the reality is that HTML can be quite complex, and pages—when rendered from many different partials and helpers—can sometimes get broken up. Requiring validation as

25. http://pictos.drewwilson.com/
26. http://en.wikipedia.org/wiki/Tag_soup

you work helps our teams write better view code and teaches developers new and old how to write properly formatted markup.

We are also future-proofing our views in the sense that any future browser will more than likely render old versions of properly formatted HTML correctly. In the early days of the browser wars, we might have used a cool proprietary (and not valid) tag or technique only to find it deprecated or removed from the next version of the browser.

Let's get our tools in place. First, we need to download the Total Validator Basic application.[27] This runs on Windows, Mac OS X, and Linux (requiring the Java framework) and works in conjunction with a Firefox extension. Figure 7, *Starting up a test in Total Validator*, on page 41 shows an examploe of the application window.

Not only will Total Validator take care of HTML validation, it will also look at web accessibility and the WCAG, or Web Content Accessibility Guidelines and its various levels of support. This may not seem like an important thing to some of us, but we are professionals, and accessibility and valid code are important parts of good code craftsmanship. Also, as professionals, we should be providing the best quality experience to as many people as possible. You never know who may have a visual impairment that affects the way that user interacts with the Web.

A nice side benefit of this is that search engine robots, such as Google bot, see many pages in a manner that is very similar to how a screen reader will see a web page. By using these best practices, we get an easy double win of helping our search engine results as well.

We can run a page at a public url (http://www.artflowme.com) or a local URL (such as *http://localhost:3000/* or *http://dev.artflowme.com*) through the tool. Since we're focused on our application right now, we'll run our localhost:3000 URL.

Let's turn our creations/index into this and see how we've fared through the course of today's build. We get a result back that looks something like Figure 8, *Our validation results*, on page 42, and we find that we only have one major error:

```
[WCAG v2 3.1.1 (A)] Use the 'lang' or 'xml:lang' attribute to denote the
primary language of the document
```

Since we were checking for accessibility as well as HTML validation, we were advised that we need to give a lang attribute to denote the primary language

---

27. http://www.totalvalidator.com/downloads/extensiontool.html

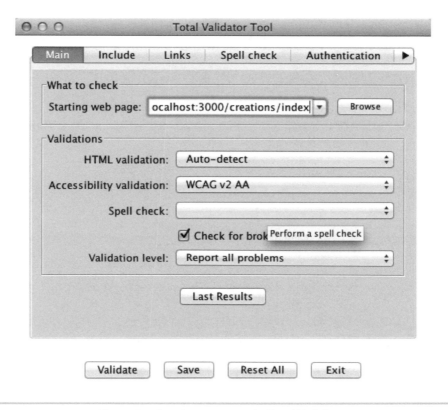

Figure 7—Starting up a test in Total Validator

of the document. Since we're not looking at internationalization yet, we'll add lang="en" to our <html> tag and we're good to go (for now).

At the end of the day, validating our code is something that we, as professionals, should do. It helps future-proof our sites and lets us write better, more consistent markup. So, validate early and often, and the world will be a better place.

1.8 Testing Internet Explorer

There are few things more frustrating while working in the view layer than having a project ready to go except for one bug that seems unsolvable in an older version of Internet Explorer. We all run into this situation at one point or another in a development process, and while solving any given bug is beyond the scope of this book, we can talk about the process used to ensure that your code works well in as many browsers as you care to try to support.

Figure 8—Our validation results

Our process involves starting with clean, valid HTML markup and CSS and then debugging older browsers based on that baseline. We just looked at this in Section 1.7, *Validating Our Code*, on page 39, so it should be fresh in your mind.

To aid in the task of browser testing, we keep a browser library of old versions around in order to be able to replicate bugs when they come in. In most cases, it's as easy as duplicating the application bundle (on OS X) or exe and renaming it. For Safari, we can even download old binaries from the MultiSafari project.[28]

---

28. http://michelf.com/projects/multi-safari/

> ## Joe asks:
> # Why Support Older Browsers in the First Place?
>
> Truthfully, we might not need to. The first thing we should do is to take a look at our target market (as well as our existing traffic) and ask ourselves some questions. Do we have people visiting us in IE6? How about newer versions of IE? How much support is good enough?
>
> If your traffic doesn't justify the work, then perhaps you should consider dropping support for older browsers. Google has recently dropped support for both IE6 and IE7 for their Apps product. If Google can do it, maybe you can too.
>
> Other sites continue to support IE6 and IE7. At LivingSocial, we have enough traffic to make it worthwhile. If 1 percent of our traffic is using a browser, it's generating enough revenue that we need to make sure that the site is at least functional. We don't spend a lot of time on anything below IE7, but we do take a look from time to time.

Internet Explorer is the one browser that causes a problem with keeping a library of standalone browsers for testing, as it is so intertwined with the Windows operating system. If you have a physical machine you can have one version of IE, but how do you get beyond that? Here are a few options to explore.

Multiple IEs with a Virtual Machine

It's nearly impossible to run different versions of MSIE executables on the same Microsoft system due to numerous conflicts with DLLs and other issues related to integrating the browser into the Windows operating system. While the newer versions of IE (9 and 10 previews, as of this writing) have emulation modes built in for older versions, they don't behave exactly as the originals do, especially with regard to JavaScript. Since a lot of our work is now with dynamic sites, we need to look at some other options.

Our first option is to create a virtual partition (with Parallels, Virtual Box, etc.) and use a program called IETester.[29] This application includes versions of Internet Explorer from 5.5 through 10 and will let you have multiple tabs open at the same time.

This option requires that we have a valid Windows install DVD and a license for our virtual machine host. This is the simplest setup, as we only need one drive image and one application in order to run the software.

---

29. http://www.my-debugbar.com/wiki/IETester/HomePage

While IETester is pretty decent at rendering, the intrinsic difficulties that come with attempting to sandbox browsers will sometimes raise their ugly heads, and we'll end up looking at a screen in IETester (or its cousin, Multiple IE) that looks different than the actual browser. They also exhibit issues with certain conditional comments and can crash on a regular basis (especially the IE7 tabs).

The next step is to move into the high-sweat-equity, low-cost solution proposed by Andrew Ordi.[30] Microsoft offers limited disk images that have the operating system and a browser. They cannot be validated as "genuine" in the Microsoft system and have a time limitation on them, but they are provided by Microsoft specifically for testing websites. These are available on Microsoft's site for those who want to roll their own.[31]

Andrew's technique, which uses these images, has been codified for us in a script by xdissent on github.[32] It saves us a lot of the sweat equity pain of setting all this up. The downside to this script is the sheer size of these images. Each one is in multiple images and they total many gigabytes in size—twelve gigabytes and then some, to be exact. If you have the space and patience, this is as close as you can get to the real thing without setting up actual machines for each browser.

One of the best software solutions is to use a combination of dedicated virtual machines and a sandboxed browser tool called IE Collection.[33] This collection goes all the way back to IE1 (if you happen to have a copy of Windows NT lying around on which to run it) and has the original JavaScript engines as well as the IE developer toolbar and Firebug for IE.

IE Collection has a compatibility chart on its site, which shows us that IE7 doesn't work right in Windows 7, so we'll need at least two VMs to make this work. We'll use Windows 7 for most everything except IE7. For that we'll use Windows XP running Service Pack 3. If that's not doable, we can run IE8 with an IE7 compatibility mode that will give us a pretty close view of what the IE7 user would see.

From here, we can get far more complex if the need arises by creating standalone environments for each version of IE that we need to target, as well as even setting up permanent boxes or VMs that are always running and accessible to our development network for people to test their sites on. These

---

30. http://blog.affirmix.com/2009/04/01/ie6-ie7-and-ie8-on-mac-os-x-step-by-step/

31. http://www.microsoft.com/download/en/details.aspx?displaylang=en&id=11575

32. https://github.com/xdissent/ievms

33. http://utilu.com/IECollection/

solutions are generally better used for serious QA applications rather than for development, so for now we'll stick with IE Collection.

Using a Testing Service

There are many online software solutions to help us test our browser options as well. These tools can help identify early problems but can be time-consuming when iteratively beating against the code in an attempt to shake loose a CSS bug in one browser.

Most of these are software-as-a-service offerings and therefore have a recurring cost associated with them. The systems take a URL and create snapshots of that page. It doesn't give us interactive power (as a tool such as Firebug would), but it lets us see a wide variety of browsers in relatively short order.

The first of these that we'll examine is Adobe's recent Browser Lab offering. It delivers not only MSIE versions from 6 through 9 but also Chrome 11 and 13 on Windows, Firefox 4 and 5 (on Windows and OS X), and Safari 5 on OS X as of this writing.

Browser lab has the benefit of a Firefox plugin and ease of integration into our workflow with Firebug and other Firefox extensions and tools (e.g., Selenium). The downside, as with any hosted service, is that we can't use it unless we're connected to the Net.

Another option for a hosted service is Litmus, which we look at in the Email Testing section of Chapter 8, *Working with Email*, on page 189. If the team is already using this for email testing, we might be able to get what we need out of the web testing portion of the application without an additional cost.

Targeting and Fixing the Issues

Now that we can look at our site in all the various versions of Internet Explorer, we can start figuring out what problems we have and then target them. While there are many CSS hacks that allow us to target these browsers, they are arcane and difficult to remember. A developer who doesn't know better might clear them out while refactoring and cause our site to break.

Likewise, having a separate CSS file for each version of Internet Explorer causes readability problems. As developers, we're constantly jumping back and forth between files to see what we had to hack.

While we could attempt to force IE to bow to our will through threats, bribes, and using the Force, the best solution is to expressly target the version of the browser that is misbehaving with a CSS class.

```
nav#mainbar {
  /* base styles for this element */
}

.ie7 nav#mainbar {
  /* Styles that will only apply to IE7 */
}
```

This uses the power of CSS with the cascade to override our declarations and fix the rendering problem in whatever version we target. But how do we get the class detected?

We're going to use a gem called ie_conditional_tag by our very own Bruce Williams. This uses IE conditional statements to detect the version of Internet Explorer and apply a class to the <html> tag.

We are going to add the gem to our gemfile, as follows:

```
gem 'ie_conditional_tag'
```

Then we run bundle install to get it pulled in. To implement it, we open up our application layout file and change two lines, replacing the <html> and </html> tags with a do block.

```
<!DOCTYPE html>
<%= ie_conditional_tag :html do %>
  <head>
    ...
  </body>
<% end %>
```

This generates a series of conditional statements:

```
<!DOCTYPE html>
<!--[if lt IE 7]><html class="ie ie6"><![endif]-->
<!--[if IE 7]><html class="ie ie7"><![endif]-->
<!--[if IE 8]><html class="ie ie8"><![endif]-->
<!--[if IE 9]><html class="ie ie9"><![endif]-->
<!--[if gt IE 9]><html class="ie"><![endif]-->
<!--[if !IE]><html><![endif]-->
  <head>
    ...
```

Now that we have this in place, we can start fixing our issues. Some of the common problems are related to floats and the box model. We also might run into issues with browser support on certain tags and elements. A great place to research what is supported in which browser is quirksmode.org.

This approach is different than the HTML5 Boilerplate approach that we saw earlier, since we target MSIE versions explicitly here. Internet Explorer 10 (in preview version) removes conditional statement support,[34] so we may have to resort to JavaScript or some other technique to target that browser in the future. IE 10 seems to be close to standards compliance, so we may be in the clear.

Regardless of support, remember that many different browsers will be hitting our applications, and every one of them is being used by a potential customer. We should provide some experience or help if the browser can't support our application, and we should encourage people to upgrade to newer browsers. But let's be nice about it.

1.9 Wrapping Up

We've accomplished a lot this chapter, including building a strong foundation for our application and picking up some important patterns and tools we'll use as we continue to build it out in the next few chapters.

In the next chapter, we will set a few ground rules to head off an all-too-common problem: letting our views become an unreadable quagmire that no one wants to touch. We'll get acquainted with some habits to avoid and some straightforward approaches to fixing and refactoring hard-to-read view code.

---

34. http://www.sitepoint.com/microsoft-drop-ie10-conditional-comments/

If you can, help others; if you cannot do that, at
least do not harm them.

> ➤ *The Dalai Lama*

CHAPTER 2

Improving Readability

Our templates often become unreadable and unmaintainable messes that make applications that we'd otherwise describe as simple and elegant turn into complex, unapproachable projects that are resistant to change.

We can reduce this complexity by simplifying our display logic, carefully structuring our templates, and using some common sense Rails tactics to make the source of our templates as beautiful as the interface it presents to our users and as elegant and expressive as the controller and model parts of our application. In this chapter we'll learn how do just that and improve the readability and maintainability of our templates by introducing some helpful tips and techniques.

Let's start with the basics, such as how we lay out the syntax of our templates and what we can do to standardize and improve their flow. Later we'll look at how we can use helpers and partials to restructure and condense our templates and catch up on some standards we should be baking into our markup from the beginning.

2.1 Choosing a Templating Language

It's tempting to lay the blame for ugly, unreadable templates entirely at ERB's feet. It's the default. There's no doubt that the format is more verbose than some other alternatives, especially the popular HAML language, which trades end tags for whitespace sensitivity and gains a measure of succinctness in the bargain.[1]

In our experience, changing template languages has only a minor effect on readability when compared to other factors. While markup structure may be

---

1. http://haml-lang.com/

Some Text Editors to Try

Text editor choice can be as deep as religion to some developers. Regardless of the tool, everyone needs to work with the same agreed-upon conventions. At LivingSocial, many of our developers use TextMate with the Whitespace bundle installed.[a] This strips out trailing whitespace and converts tabs to spaces on every save. The reasoning behind that has been explained well at http://blogobaggins.com/2009/03/31/waging-war-on-whitespace.html

Here are some other editors to try:

- *Emacs*: A highly extensible, customizable editor, with Lisp at its core (http://www.gnu.org/s/emacs). Many variants are available, including one for OS X,[b] and Ruby support is available. Much of this book was written with it, as it's Bruce's favorite.

- *Vim*: A highly configurable text editor built to enable efficient text editing (http://www.vim.org/). Ruby is supported, and it is available in many system-specific versions, including OS X.[c]

- *Sublime Text*: Another editor that has some nice features. We recommend version 2, with updated Ruby support (http://www.sublimetext.com/2).

- *BBEdit*: Probably one of the most powerful and long-running editors for the Mac. John used to use it extensively before switching to TextMate. Available at the App Store or http://www.barebones.com/products/bbedit/.

It doesn't matter what editor you use, as long as it's sufficiently configurable and you know how to use it. As *The Pragmatic Programmer: From Journeyman to Master* [HT00], by Andy Hunt and Dave Thomas, suggests, "the editor should be an extension of your hand." Pick the one that catches your fancy and learn it inside and out.

---

a. https://github.com/vigetlabs/whitespace-tmbundle
b. http://emacsformacosx.com/
c. http://code.google.com/p/macvim/

shorter to describe in HAML, a readable ERB template and a readable HAML template have one thing in common: a developer who cared enough to keep the markup clean and simple. Without that basic element, it doesn't matter what we're using. No templating language is a silver bullet for bad practices.

We use the templating language that works for our team, and use it where it makes sense. After all, it doesn't need to be an all-or-none decision; one approach is to use HAML for complex layout files (full of stock markup) and ERB elsewhere.

For ArtFlow, we're using ERB from top to bottom. Now let's put down some ground rules for our team, and quick!

2.2   Standardizing Coding Practices

It's important that teams follow consistent, sane rules when it comes to writing templates and style sheets, from indentation standards to the ordering of CSS properties.

Say we've been away on vacation for the past week, soaking up the sun somewhere suitably tropical and devoid of Internet access. We've come back and found a *mess*. Our team has been working furiously on new features, and the templates look like a bowl of half-cooked spaghetti.

What does half-cooked spaghetti look like in code? Avoiding ASCII art, it's really what happens when we've let our code go during development. Line length is all over the place, indents are haphazard, tags are not balanced, and we don't know what we're closing when we have a closing </div>. It's hard to read, hard to maintain, and hard to extend. Obviously we need to do something.

Indenting Without Hard Tabs

One of the first things we discover is that some members of our team are using hard tabs ("hard" refers to using tab characters, as opposed to "soft" tabs, which are spaces that emulate tabs). This causes portability problems across editors and other tools and is inconsistent with the way Ruby developers write code.

Tabs vs. spaces is somewhat of a holy war in programming circles. We at ArtFlow Industries Inc. use spaces because we have many programmers, some of whom prefer tab stops of differing sizes. This becomes a major issue when we agree on, say, a four-space indent per line. Each individual has tab stops set differently. For example, Frank uses two-space tabs. So each time he indents a line with tabs, he inserts two tab characters to achieve the required four-space indent. Sam likes four-space tab stops, so he only tabs once. When Frank opens Sam's recent commits, the indentation is all wrong in his text editor because it renders tabs as two spaces. Likewise, when Sam opens Frank's commits, things are overindented, like in Figure 9, *Indenting going horribly wrong*, on page 52.

This gets really bad when Sam decides to reflow his code to make it look better on his editor. He then commits this to our source code repository, and when we try to discover who has made specific changes to the file, it looks as if Sam's modified the entire file (because, well, he has), as we see in Figure 10, *Minor whitespace changes can look like major modifications*, on page 53.

```
class AssetsController < ApplicationController

    def create
        if @asset.valid?
            flash[:notice] = "Asset created!"
        else
            flash.now[:alert] = "Could not save asset!"
        end
        # Redirect
    end
end
```

Figure 9—Indenting going horribly wrong

This causes a big problem; let's fix it. We replace all tabs with standard two-space indentation, and we make sure our team members are using editors that transparently support soft tabbing.

Indenting for Logic and Markup

For our ArtFlow app/views/clients/index.html.erb template we have a listing of clients that breaks an important rule on page 233:

```
<ul>
<% @clients.each do |client| %>
<li><%= link_to client.name, client %></li>
<% end %>
</ul>
```

The contents of *any* pair of tags—either HTML opening and closing tags or the start and end tags for an ERB block—should be indented a level to indicate hierarchy. Things inside a pair of tags are effectively children of the parent tag. The purpose of indentation is to visually indicate hierarchy and nesting, no matter which types of tags are involved.

Here it would be helpful to immediately see that our ERB loop is *inside* the <ul> tag merely by scanning the template. At first glance here, it appears to be a sibling. Let's change the indenting to be cleaned up the way we want it.

artflow/readability/app/views/clients/index.html.erb
```
<ul>
  <% @clients.each do |client| %>
    <li><%= link_to client.name, client %></li>
  <% end %>
</ul>
```

```
 ● ● ●                    Terminal — bash — 77×38
          bash
Soho:flash jathayde$ svn diff
Index: assets_controller.rb
===================================================================
--- assets_controller.rb          (revision 89783)
+++ assets_controller.rb          (working copy)
@@ -1,16 +1,16 @@
 class AssetsController < ApplicationController

-  def create
-    if @asset.valid?
-      flash[:notice] = "Asset created!"
-    else
-      flash.now[:alert] = "Could not save asset!"
-    end
-    # Redirect
-  end
+        def create
+                if @asset.valid?
+                        flash[:notice] = "Asset created!"
+                else
+                        flash.now[:alert] = "Could not save asset!"
+                end
+                # Redirect
+        end

 end
Soho:flash jathayde$ █
```

Figure 10—Minor whitespace changes can look like major modifications

A good way to think about this is to imagine that the ERB tags are *inserted* into the hierarchy between the <ul> and its child <li> tags. Following this simple rule will help make the logical and physical structure of templates more obvious.

Don't worry about how the generated HTML looks. Browsers are the ones that do the reading (or during debugging, Firebug and the Chrome developer tools are the ones that clean things up[2]).

Policing Line Length

As developers, we've all had the experience where we see code go off the right edge of the editor screen.

---

2. http://getfirebug.com/ and http://code.google.com/chrome/devtools/, respectively.

Joe asks:

But My Whole Team Has Massive Monitors. Why Can't We Use Line Lengths More Than 80 Characters Wide?

Even with extra-large monitors in many development environments, the reality is that we still hit code from a variety of devices and with a variety of preferences. Many users bump up the font size so that while it may be 1600 pixels wide, it's still only 80–100 characters wide.

Using 78–80 characters is a standard for editing that will work on almost any system, because that is the default width of terminals, including older VAX systems. Your team can decide to go longer, but our rule for this team will be 80.

For more guidance on line length (and many other concepts in this chapter), we recommend *Clean Code: A Handbook of Agile Software Craftsmanship* [Mar08], by Robert C. Martin.

Anything over eighty characters will potentially float off in the ether if someone views it from a terminal window, and scrolling horizontally (either physically in the window or with our eyes on a high resolution screen) back and forth makes for slow reading. It's easier to read a narrow block of text than one that stretches across the width of the screen. If we break it into multiple lines, we can see everything at once much easier.

Soft wrapping might sound like a solution, but it's a Band-Aid that makes line editing more difficult and doesn't work well when our developers use command-line utilities.

Some text editors, such as TextMate, have a column counter and a wrap column setting so you automatically know when you hit your determined character limit. They also have macros and other tools to help with reformatting large blocks of text.

Lining Up Tags and Attributes

When tag contents span multiple lines, take care to line up the opening and closing tags horizontally and indent the contents one level. Working on the marketing copy for ArtFlow, you can see our <p> and <em> tags are lined up correctly and their contents set a level deeper.

Let's look at a snippet from ArtFlow's homepage as an example:

Joe asks:

A New Line for Every Element?

If there's an inline markup tag, such as <b>, <i>, <strong>, <em>, <abbr>, <dfn>, and similar tags, we do not always kick them to a new line. It's about improving readability. If putting one word on a new line doesn't improve readability, don't do it.

artflow/readability/app/views/pages/home.html.erb

```
<p>
  Have a file, store a file.
  Then change it, tag it, and share it or send it.
  <em>
    This isn't your father's asset management application.
  </em>
</p>
```

When we stack lots of classes or have long ID and class names, we can end up with a long line just for one HTML element. We fix this with a newline between attributes (and some care to line them up):

```
<p id="product-description"
   class="important blurb rounded">
  Have a file, store a file.
  Then change it, tag it, and share it or send it.
  <em>
    This isn't your father's asset management application.
  </em>
</p>
```

We can add ERB comments to our template for TODOs, placemarkers, or short descriptions for complex markup. They look like normal ERB tags and start with a # character, just like Ruby comments do:

```
<%# TODO: Add list of articles. -BW 2011-11-01 %>
```

While adding ERB comments can clarify and illuminate, at some point they can also make a page messy and more cluttered, and just like code comments, it's easy to let them get out-of-date. Less is more!

Now that we have some basic formatting rules to serve as our foundation, let's dig into the way we're actually building up our markup to see if we can simplify things and make our template more readable.

> **Joe asks:**
> ## Why ERB Comments Instead of HTML Comments?
>
> HTML comments are present in your generated markup and visible to users of your application (if they're curious and click View Source). ERB comments get stripped out long before your page ever gets to a browser. This doesn't matter so much for smaller apps, but a few kilobytes here and there can start to add up over millions of users (just ask Twitter).
>
> Use ERB comments unless you really want to whisper something to the geekiest of your users—or as a *temporary* debugging technique.

2.3 Simplifying Complex Output

While the Rails view is the place where model attributes get echoed for the users to see, we get into a bit of a tight spot when we are asked to cobble together bits from various attributes and display them in a specific way.

Clean Up ArtFlow Filenames

Throughout ArtFlow, we've been referring to creations with a combination of their given names, revision numbers, and file formats (e.g., FooCo Wireframe (Draft, r0004, PDF). This makes for some pretty ugly templates, like our listing of creation records in app/views/creations/index.html.erb:

```
<ul>
  <% @creations.each do |creation| %>
    <li>
      <%= creation.name %>
      (<%= creation.stage %>,
       r<%= "%04d" % creation.revision %>,
       <%= creation.format.upcase %>)
    </li>
  <% end %>
</ul>
```

That's a lot of ERB concat tags, isn't it? Open, close, open, close... We can use a couple of techniques to remove low-level string formatting and interpolation from this view to support a more fluid and less distracting reading experience. Anything that complicates the flow and affects readability is your enemy.

Helpers vs. Model Methods

There's an argument to be made for adding methods that return display-related information about a model directly to the model. It's tempting to do (after all, this *is* model information), but we need to keep in mind where we plan to use the information and what we want to display.

The model layer doesn't support link_to() or other routing-related methods, and since it doesn't have access to the request or session, customizing output for the user is also out of the question. Add to this that littering a clean data model with string manipulations like capitalization, snippets of HTML, and other modifications that support requirements only needed from the view just doesn't make sense, and a helper is usually the right option—except in cases where what we need to display is constrained and not request-specific (e.g., for interactive use in the Rails console or for output by Rake tasks).

Sometimes we want to go further and use presenters. We'll learn more about them in Chapter 6, *Using Presenters*, on page 143.

Using Helpers

It looks like we've decided to pull this out of our template just in time—we've been asked to add links to the file, and our product manager hinted that we'll probably need to add links to individual revisions sometime in the near future.

Let's extract the file information from our list and create a new helper method in app/helpers/creations_helper.rb:

```ruby
module CreationsHelper
  # The standard reference line for a creation
  # Includes name, stage, revision, and format
  def creation_reference(creation)
    padded_revision = 'r%04d' % creation.revision
    raw("#{link_to(creation.name, creation)} (#{creation.stage},
        #{padded_revision}, #{creation.format.upcase})")
  end
end
```

It's so fresh and so clean. That looks a lot better without all of those ERB tags, doesn't it? The raw() method we're using makes sure Rails doesn't escape the tags we're generating inside the string; we know the contents don't include any cross-site scripting (XSS) opportunities.[3] Now all we need to do is fill in the hole we left in our app/views/creations/index.html.erb template by an invocation of our new helper:

---

3.   http://guides.rubyonrails.org/security.html#cross-site-scripting-xss

```
<ul>
  <% @creations.each do |creation| %>
    <li><%= creation_reference(creation) %></li>
  <% end %>
</ul>
```

That is much more readable and straightforward.

And Just a Little Accessibility

link_to() is just one of the many helpers that come with Rails, and it generates an anchor tag with an href attribute. Anchors can have various attributes, including a title attribute. The title attribute could be spoken by a user agent or shown as a tool tip in your browser. We can add this to our app/helpers/creations_helper.rb helper by passing a :title symbol to link_to(). It creates a title attribute in the rendered HTML.[4]

```
module CreationsHelper
  # The standard reference line for a creation
  # Includes name, stage, revision, and format
  def creation_reference(creation)
    padded_revision = 'r%04d' % creation.revision
➤   link = link_to(creation.name,
➤                   creation,
➤                   title: "More info on #{creation.name}")
➤   raw("#{link} (#{creation.stage}, #{padded_revision},
➤       #{creation.format.upcase})")
  end
end
```

Most browsers render this as the nice yellow box, the tooltip, that shows up when you hover over a link for a certain amount of time. This isn't difficult, taking just a few moments to implement, and our users will thank us later. This can help to provide more contextual information for users; sometimes JavaScript popups are too much and the link by itself isn't enough.

The next thing to add comes directly out of feedback from our clients, who think it would be great if they could see a thumbnail of the creation (if one exists). The suggestion makes sense; a thumbnail would help clients more easily browse and navigate to the creation they want to look at. Let's add it.

For the sake of sanity, we'll just say that there's a creation.default_image that exists and is created by the file upload and processing method of your choice. So we can just use an image_tag() helper to put this in, right? Let's use it from app/views/creations/_creation.html.erb:

---

4.   http://www.w3.org/TR/html4/struct/links.html#h-12.1.4

```
<%= image_tag(@creation.default_image) %>
```

But wait! Frank got this working, and then, while testing it with our client, we hit the case of a new user without an image and, well, that wasn't a pretty exception error. We need to provide some logic to provide a default "no thumbnail" image. Putting this straight into the app/views/creations/_creation.html.erb template presents an ugly if/else construct for us to read over every time we open this view.

```
<% if @creation.default_image? %>
  <%= image_tag(@creation.default_image) %>
<% else %>
  <%= image_tag("missing_creation.png")%>
<% end %>
```

We've got that fixed now, but it's a lot of conditional code in the view. Using a helper to handle this immediately makes sense. So let's extract that code and put it in app/helpers/creations_helper.rb:

```
def creation_thumbnail(creation)
  if creation.default_image?
    image_tag(creation.default_image)
  else
    image_tag("missing_creation.png")
  end
end
```

Now we can get to that by calling creation_thumbnail, and all is well with the world. Not so fast. We have a user with visual impairment that uses a screen reader sometimes. There's nothing worse than listening to a screen reader say "image, image, image," and knowing that those are critical to interaction. We'll add an :alt attribute to our image_tag helper in the same way we added :title to our link_to(). This is actually required for Web Accessibility Initiative (WAI) Level 1 and Section 508 compliance.[5]

```
artflow/readability/app/helpers/creations_helper.rb
def creation_thumbnail(creation)
  if creation.default_image?
    image_tag(creation.default_image, alt: creation.name)
  else
    image_tag("missing_creation.png",
              alt: "No image for this creation")
  end
end
```

---

5.   http://www.section508.gov

Web Accessibility Initiative and Section 508

Web accessibility is optional for many of us working on web apps, but it is required for any federal government site due to the Section 508 amendment to the Rehabilitation Act of 1973. This bill requires that federal programs (including those on the Web) do not discriminate or limit access to individuals with disabilities.

For those of us who need to develop in this space, this means that we need to follow Section 508 guidelines,[a] which are similar to the W3C Web Accessibility Initiative.[b] While private sector apps are not required by law to be accessible, it helps us write better code and serve a broader segment of the population.

With the advent of AI tools like Apple's Siri and others, there will be more screen reading employed outside of the traditional visual-impaired user space, and we need to support all of our users. Also, search engine robots are effectively the equivalent of a blind user. It's not only good business and good stewardship, it's good SEO, too.

---

a. http://section508.gov
b. http://www.w3.org/WAI/

Time and time again we've seen that users click images more than links, so in the spirit of defensive design we will make the image a link as well.[6]

We modify creation_reference in app/helpers/creations_helper.rb, adding our thumbnail:

```ruby
def creation_reference(creation)
  padded_revision = 'r%04d' % creation.revision
  link = link_to(creation_thumbnail(creation),
                 creation,
                 title: "More info on #{creation.name}")
  raw("#{link} (#{creation.stage},
      #{padded_revision}, #{creation.format.upcase})")
end
```

That's some serious cleanup right there. So far we've improved our code's readability with whitespace and line length management, moved a bunch of conditional code into helpers, and added much-needed accessibility. Next we take a look at some of Rails's built-in helpers for number formatting.

Formatting Numbers

Management approved this ArtFlow so they could have better reporting on media campaigns in which the creations were used. After all, once they know

---

6. *Defensive design* is a term coined by 37signals before it became the inventor of Ruby on Rails. As a usability shop, it put forth that developers should plan for users to break applications and websites in every way possible and should ensure that the website/application responds appropriately in turn.

> ## It's About More Than Avoiding Repetition
>
> A common argument for leaving poor, complex view code in place goes like this:
>
> > It only happens in one place!
>
> You'll quickly discover something about views: complexity here is more expensive than in pure Ruby code. You're not running against Don't Repeat Yourself principles,[a] but this is poor consolation when you (and others) still can't read and reason about your code. Here's why once is too much:
>
> - More people have to read it, and many of those people may not have the programming chops to understand the backflips you're doing. This is especially true in mixed teams of developers, designers, and occasionally even copy editors.
>
> - Complex code should be tested. It's easier to test helpers in isolation than in templates.
>
> - Complexity should be documented. While ERB comment tags are useful for marking TODOs, method comments that can be processed by RDoc and other *real* documentation generators can be useful, especially in large, professional projects that may have team turnover and need long-term continuity.
>
> ---
>
> a.   http://pragprog.com/the-pragmatic-programmer

the best performing creations, they can then use them over and over and over again—until our design staff starts burning effigies of them on the balcony.

While there are whole books dedicated to reporting and we have lots of other things to fix right now, we're going to punt and just touch on the display of the numbers. We know that formatting and presenting numbers in a meaningful way will be critical in our reporting features.

The first "Oh, no!" we run across is on the campaign page. An advertising campaign has_many :creations, runs for a certain amount of time, and has a cost associated with it. In our app/views/campaigns/show.html.erb template we find this:

```
<h1><%= @campaign.name %></h1>
<p>
  Costing $<%= @campaign.cost %>
  and running from <%= @campaign.start_date %>
  to <%= @campaign.end_date %>
</p>
```

While this isn't horrible, we are expanding our e-commerce operation within the year. Before our next trip to the Caribbean, we'll be dealing in pounds and euros. How will we handle the differences in formatting, such as when to use periods, commas, and the currency symbol? The good news is that there's an existing Rails helper already built for us, number_to_currency():

artflow/readability/app/views/campaigns/show.html.erb
```
<h1><%= @campaign.name %></h1>
<p>
  Costing <%= number_to_currency(@campaign.cost) %>
  and running from <%= @campaign.start_date %>
  to <%= @campaign.end_date %>              .
</p>
```

Once we've reached global domination, we can look at some of the other attributes available in this helper, including :locale and :unit.[7]

We also see that back on our awesome creation index of joy and wonder that we have a display of the physical size of the file—the only problem is that it is in bytes, and while that worked in the early computing days, our basic files are typically in megabytes.

What solutions exist here? Well, part of the NumberHelper methods is something called number_to_human_size(), which handles file size changes.[8] We use it when we add the file size to our creation_reference() helper:

artflow/readability/app/helpers/creations_helper.rb
```
def creation_reference(creation)
  padded_revision = 'r%04d' % creation.revision
  link = link_to(creation_thumbnail(creation),
                 creation,
                 title: "More info on #{creation.name}")
➤ size = number_to_human_size(creation.filesize)
  raw("#{link} (#{size}, #{creation.stage},
      #{padded_revision}, #{creation.format.upcase})")
end
```

This will display a size of 45444 bytes as 44.3 KB or a size of 97398597 as 92.8 MB. That whole base-1024 system of measurement really messes with the multiplier if you're just truncating it, especially as sizes get larger.

There are so many ways to clean up numbers, and our attention to detail here will have a big payoff for ArtFlow users. Who wants to divide by 1024?

Now that we have some tools for formatting model attributes, we'll dig into how to deal with the challenges that come in the view with traversing model records and rendering templates for those records.

---

7. http://api.rubyonrails.org/classes/ActionView/Helpers/NumberHelper.html#method-i-number_to_currency
8. http://api.rubyonrails.org/classes/ActionView/Helpers/NumberHelper.html

2.4   Working with Models

In Chapter 1, *Creating an Application Layout*, on page 1, we looked at how models in ArtFlow are interrelated (see Figure 1, *ArtFlow models*, on page 2).

Creations are shared across users through groups and various roles and rights. It's a tangle of associated data that we constantly need to mine for information to show in our views.

Simplifying Access to Associations

In ArtFlow, we use ActiveRecord for our models, and we frequently need to traverse the associations from record to record to get at the data. Here in app/views/creations/show.html.erb, we show the client name for a creation we're viewing:

```
<dl>
  <dt>Client</dt>
  <dd><%= @creation.project.client.name %></dd>
</dl>
```

It's neat that we can get to the information, but this makes for some pretty verbose view code, and it can be brittle—as tightly coupled with the model as it is, changes there may cause exceptions to occur anywhere data is accessed in templates.

Here's one approach we could use to protect our templates from changes: setting an instance variable in the controller action. This is easier to track down and modify in the event of changes to our modeling.

artflow/readability/app/controllers/creations_controller.rb
```
@client = @creation.project.client
```

This works great—it goes a long way toward decoupling the view from the model, and it's easier to test. However, there is a complication. It adds a requirement that templates that need the client name always have a @client instance variable defined, which is problematic if the templates are being rendered from other actions and controllers. There's also the possibility that in trying to provide all the instance variables needed for a view we'll end up querying the database unnecessarily; due to some condition in the view, the data may not be needed!

Another option is going to the class file; we could add a client_name() method to our Creation model (avoiding Law of Demeter violations[9]), but you can

---

9.   http://c2.com/cgi/wiki?LawOfDemeter

imagine how crowded and muddled our models could become if we did that often enough, even if we were just delegating. We'd be polluting our models with "shortcut" methods that are only needed from the view. For now, we'll opt for a lighter, more flexible approach using a helper to at least decouple our templates somewhat:

artflow/readability/app/helpers/creations_helper.rb
```ruby
def creation_client_name(creation = @creation)
  creation.project.client.name
end
```

This makes our template code very simple, hiding away excessive method chaining (which we may reduce later by adding methods to our models):

artflow/readability/app/views/creations/show.html.erb
```erb
<dl>
  <dt>Client</dt>
  <dd><%= creation_client_name %></dd>
</dl>
```

Since we've also allowed a creation to be passed as an argument to the helper (but haven't required it, instead defaulting to the @creation instance variable if one isn't provided), we can also use the helper from views that show more than one creation.

We'll use the helper as we build our CreationsController index action template to show multiple creations.

Displaying Multiple Items

When you're showing a list of things, it's easy to let it get ugly; there's a lot going on, from the actual mechanics of the iteration itself to stateful, UX-heavy issues like pagination. Sometimes we just need to go back and simplify, removing code that doesn't really matter so that the code that does is more obvious to the reader.

We've been building the markup we use to display a creation in the creation listing we started in *Using Helpers*, on page 57. It's a perfectly serviceable, if verbose and procedural, approach. We'll just use the creation_client_name() helper from earlier to show the client for each creation in app/views/creations/index.html.erb:

```erb
<ul id='creations'>
  <% @creations.each do |creation| %>
    <li class='creation'>
      <p>
        <%= creation_reference(creation) %>
        <span class='client'><%= creation_client_name(creation) %></span>
      </p>
```

```
    </li>
  <% end %>
</ul>
```

While this is fine and dandy, we end up with a lot of code in the middle of our view that deals with what just one creation looks like and has nothing to do with the listing itself. That doesn't seem right. One approach we might take would render the creation with a partial, hiding that logic in another file, _creation.html.erb. Here's what our index.html.erb looks like now:

```
<ul id='creations'>
  <% @creations.each do |creation| %>
    <%= render creation %>
  <% end %>
</ul>
```

Here we're using a partial to render each creation. Rails automatically determines that we want to render the creation partial based on the class of model we're rendering. We go a level further and let render() handle the iteration for us, merely passing it an array of objects to render:

artflow/readability/app/views/creations/index.html.erb
```
<ul id='creations'>
  <%= render @creations %>
</ul>
```

This cuts it down to one line in our view; the boilerplate iteration code is removed and only the important part—the fact we're rendering our creations—remains. That one line can move an awesome amount of logical and structural complexity to the individual item partial, where it belongs, and doesn't even have a procedural loop taking up space in the listing. It's a nice benefit to conventional partial naming, which is one of our rules, on page 233.

Now with a single line, we can render the entire listing! Next we'll deal with conditional content; mixing logic and presentation sure can make a mess—let's see what we can do to clean it up.

2.5 Displaying Conditional Content

One of the most ugly but common patterns you find in templates is large if/elsif/else clauses used to display alternate sets of content based on different conditions. This is especially common when handling different visibility rules based on roles and rights.

In ArtFlow we have a few roles and rights that we need to pay attention to when we're displaying ways that a user can interact with a creation. Currently

> ## Joe asks:
> ## What If My Partials Aren't Named Conventionally?
>
> If you're sitting on top of record-related partials that aren't named based on the model with which they're associated, you have a couple of options:
>
> 1. Rename them.
>
>   No, we're not joking. You should be working with tools like source control that make changes less painful and should have fostered a relationship with your team that lets you do things like rename files (and methods, classes, etc.) when it makes sense to do so. Naming things correctly matters, both philosophically and, in this case, because keeping to Rails conventions makes your code shorter and more maintainable. Shortcuts, especially officially supported shortcuts, are a good thing.
>
> 2. In cases where this isn't possible—or if you have several different "flavors" of partials for a model you'll want to use the :partial and :collection options to render().[a]
>
> _____
>
> a. For more about available render() options, see the guide at http://guides.rubyonrails.org/layouts_and_rendering.html#using-render.

in our _creation.html.erb partial (which we render from the listing on the index template), we use a standard series of conditions to render the appropriate management controls for a creation:

```erb
<% if current_user.manages?(creation) %>
  <ul class='controls'>
    <% if current_user.admin? %>
      <!-- stuff for admins -->
    <% elsif current_user.editor? %>
      <!-- stuff for editors -->
    <% elsif current_user.authored?(creation) %>
      <!-- stuff for the author -->
    <% elsif current_user.shares?(creation)%>
      <!-- stuff for everyone else -->
    <% end %>
  </ul>
<% end %>
```

Wow, that's a mess. If our controls are complex, it would be very easy to glance over this partial and lose track of who sees what. This is a partial that's trying to be everything to everybody.

Replacing Clauses with Partials

Let's rip the logic out of the view and put it into our CreationsHelper, using separate, focused partials to display the alternate content.

```
artflow/readability/app/helpers/creations_helper.rb
def controls_for_creation(creation)
  if current_user.manages?(creation)
    partial = controls_partial_for_creation(creation)
    contents = render(partial: partial,
                      locals: {creation: creation})
    content_tag(:ul, contents, class: 'controls')
  end
end
def controls_partial_for_creation(creation)
  if current_user.admin?
    'creations/controls/admin'
  elsif current_user.editor?
    'creations/controls/editor'
  elsif current_user.authored?(creation)
    'creations/controls/author'
  elsif current_user.shares?(creation)
    'creations/controls/collaborator'
  end
end
```

Let's create a subdirectory, controls, under the creations view directory to keep our partials nicely grouped; this has a side benefit of letting us see what roles and rights we're supporting merely by looking at the file listing.

With this in place, we can clean up our app/views/creations/_creation.html.erb partial by removing a lot of cruft that isn't necessary anymore.

```
<%= controls_for_creation(creation) %>
```

Look at that, a simple partial; the tangle of ERB tags has been extracted to leave a single, descriptive line.

By removing the logic and alternate sets of content from our creations/creation partial, we make reading easier and future modifications less complicated and error-prone. Peace of mind is knowing an enterprising coworker won't accidentally show admin controls to an author because that designer accidentally deleted an elsif while updating a <button> CSS class.

Naming Your Conditions

Throughout ArtFlow we need to keep a user's permissions and personal preferences in mind when showing creations. A good example is how we handle creation previews for images. Here's some old code we've just dug up in app/views/creations/_preview.html.erb. It displays a thumbnail after verifying that a thumbnail exists, it's viewable by the current user, and the current user wants an expanded view:

```erb
<% if creation.thumbnail? && current_user.can_view?(creation) %>
  <% if session[:view] == 'expanded' %>
    <%= image_tag creation.file.url(:thumbnail), class: 'thumbnail' %>
  <% end %>
<% end %>
```

This is a bit gnarly, isn't it? It's a set of Russian nesting doll–style if statements wrapping the lone line of actual markup to be shown. We collapse these down to a meaningfully named helper, show_preview?(), that verifies all the conditions with an all?() trick:

artflow/readability/app/helpers/creations_helper.rb
```ruby
def show_preview?(creation)
  creation.thumbnail? &&
    current_user.can_view?(creation) &&
      expanded_view?
end

def expanded_view?
  session[:view] == 'expanded'
end
```

This makes for much better reading; as in the story of Rumpelstiltskin, a name is a powerful thing to know. We change our app/views/creations/_preview.html.erb partial:

```erb
<% if show_preview?(creation) %>
  <%= image_tag creation.file.url(:thumbnail), class: 'thumbnail' %>
<% end %>
```

We could even skip the if entirely by using a helper that conditionally yields to a block:

artflow/readability/app/helpers/creations_helper.rb
```ruby
def previewing(creation)
  yield if show_preview?(creation)
end
```

This gives our template a distinctly DSL-like feel:

artflow/readability/app/views/creations/_preview.html.erb
```erb
<%= previewing creation do %>
  <%= image_tag creation.file.url(:thumbnail), alt: creation.title %>
<% end %>
```

We follow a similar pattern any time we run into long conditions that are hard to read and that distract from the real content of the template.

We've worked hard to make our template shorter, easier to read, and more obvious at a glance. Next we'll work on how to stop the identifiers we add to our markup that support client-side code and asynchronous requests from muddling up our templates.

2.6   Adding Model DOM IDs for JavaScript

In ArtFlow our users are frequently looking at and modifying data for multiple creations at once; when making a change to a creation in these batch views, we can't switch the users' context (and lose their progress) by sending them to a new page—we need to asynchronously update the creation and leave everything else intact.

Adding In-place Editing

While we were sipping piña coladas, our team added a neat feature to the listing of creations in ArtFlow: the ability to quickly modify creation attributes in place, just like we needed. Here's how it works:

1. The user clicks an Edit button next to the creation.
2. A form for the creation's attributes replaces the creation information.
3. When the form is submitted, the updated creation information replaces the form.

To do this (with some unobtrusive JavaScript and Ajax), our team has associated an <li> with each creation on the page by assigning an HTML ID attribute based on the record id. Let's modify our app/views/creations/_creation.html.erb partial:

```
➤ <li id='creation-<%= creation.id %>' class='<%= creation.file_type %>'>
    <% if @creation.default_image? %>
      <%= image_tag(@creation.default_image) %>
    <% else %>
      <%= image_tag("missing_creation.png")%>
    <% end %>
    <%= controls_for_creation(creation) %>
  </li>
```

Using the content_tag_for() would have been a better option:

```
➤ <%= content_tag_for :li, creation, 'class'  => creation.file_type,
➤                                    'data-id' => creation.id do %>
    <% if @creation.default_image? %>
      <%= image_tag(@creation.default_image) %>
    <% else %>
      <%= image_tag("missing_creation.png")%>
    <% end %>

    <%= controls_for_creation(creation) %>
➤ <% end %>
```

> **Joe asks:**
> ## What About div_for?
>
> div_for() is a specialized version of content_tag_for() that specifically generates a <div>. While there's nothing wrong with using a <div> for truly generic, display-related purposes—like wrapping two child elements together to achieve a certain visual effect —using semantic elements makes our code easier to read and style.
>
> Since div_for() is used to wrap the information for a record in a generic <div>, it's almost always the wrong choice. If we have domain data to display, surely we can figure out a better, more descriptive semantic element to use!

Doing it this way gives us a few nice benefits:

- We don't need to figure out a scheme for the ID attribute. Rails automatically selects an ID (based on the Ruby class and id). Since we don't care what is used—we just need to have a consistent way to refer to the tag elsewhere—we don't need to manually create an ID ourselves.[10]

- Attributes that include characters that could be interpreted badly just inserted as-is are escaped safely.

- We're not putting one type of tag inside another type of tag. Not only is this just plain ugly, but it can cause problems with editor/IDE syntax highlighting and formatting.

We took the extra step of adding a data-id attribute to our tag as well. This will let JavaScript extract the ID of our creation more easily without having to parse the tag ID attribute. We'll learn more about custom data attributes later, on page 105.

We have enough for now, and since we have a pretty Ruby-savvy team working on ArtFlow, we're comfortable distilling this into a nice, clean helper that we can reuse in the editing partial that JavaScript switches out, too. We give it a name that describes exactly what it's for:

artflow/readability/app/helpers/creations_helper.rb
```ruby
def switching_creation_tag_for(creation, &block)
  content_tag_for(:li, creation, class: creation.file_type, &block)
end
```

---

10. We can just use dom_id() where we need it elsewhere: http://api.rubyonrails.org/classes/ActionController/RecordIdentifier.html#method-i-dom_id.

Our templates end up having a minimum of eye-distracting boilerplate; the behavior and style nuts and bolts (the id attribute for JavaScript and class attribute for CSS) are tucked away in our helper.

artflow/readability/app/views/creations/_creation.html.erb

```erb
<%= switching_creation_tag_for creation do %>
  <% if creation.default_image? %>
    <%= image_tag(creation.default_image) %>
  <% else %>
    <%= image_tag("missing_creation.png")%>
  <% end %>
  <%= controls_for_creation(creation) %>
<% end %>
```

2.7 Cleaning Up

One of the last things we can do to keep our code in check is to do some manual inspection of our CSS and HTML and look for opportunities for refactoring and cleanup. Many features are added separately, and over time more efficient means of writing various things arise.

One of the first things to look for in large codebases is declarations of the same selector two or three times in CSS. When this happens once, it's not that big a deal, but if it happens a lot, it adds up to hundreds of lines of redundant and overridden declarations.

We also want to identify where we have different class names that have the same styles or have styles that we could abstract to a generic class and use specific overrides. We see this show up a lot when JavaScript show/hide wizard setups are involved. Each "page" in this instance has a unique ID, and let's say they share the same page look and feel. You will often find each selector declared individually.

If you don't want to add another class, at least collect them together and write your declarations once:

```css
#id_number_1,
#id_number_2,
#id_number_3 {
  // declarations for all 3 IDs
}
```

Likewise, look for places where extra, superfluous HTML has entered the mix, and be a stringent editor. Take out that which is not critical and leave the cleanest, best-performing code in place.

Always make time for this kind of work. It's not as glamorous as launching a new feature or as exciting as playing with the most cutting-edge new CSS3 techniques, but it is paramount to having healthy code over the long term.

2.8 Wrapping Up

We've nearly recovered from the aftermath of our vacation to the Caribbean, with some of the worst of the view smells scrubbed from our templates. We'll need to keep an eye out in case these problems reappear. Be vigilant!

Now we have a semantic page structure, and we've cleaned up some messy view code that got away from us. That's a pretty good day! Tomorrow we'll take a deeper look at our CSS assets and discover some new techniques to keep things on the right track as we build out the application.

On matters of style, swim with the current. On
matters of principle, stand like a rock.
➤ *Thomas Jefferson*

CHAPTER 3

Adding Cascading Style Sheets

Rails makes a lot of decisions for us; from the beginning we've had a default ORM (ActiveRecord), template engine (ActionView with ERB), and support for testing, so it should come as no surprise that this emphasis on "convention over configuration" has grown to include the way we handle assets in the view layer too.

Rails 3.1 introduced the *asset pipeline*, a set of built-in features that includes concatenation and compression of our CSS and JavaScript files and support for alternate syntaxes.

We'll discuss JavaScript in Chapter 4, *Adding JavaScript*, on page 101, but right now let's look at Cascading Style Sheets, or CSS. Even in mixed teams with well-defined roles, knowing how to read and edit a CSS file is a skill that every developer should have, since often missing or badly implemented design can stop development in its tracks. It doesn't have to be about making things *pretty*. Sometimes in a pinch what we really need to do is just add enough basic styling to make things *work*, and we should do so responsibly.

We've been adding style sheets to our ArtFlow application, but to build them more easily and effectively we need to dig a little deeper into how Rails uses Sprockets, the library at the core of the asset pipeline, to find and process our asset files.[1] Sprockets lets us use a tool that will make our jobs easier— Sass—which is a more dynamic alternate syntax for CSS than just plain CSS.

3.1 Using the Asset Pipeline

Let's take a look at how Sprockets works, starting with some changes to where our assets need to be placed.

---

1. http://getsprockets.org/

Where to Put Files

Sprockets introduces new locations for our asset files. Instead of a single, mixed directory for each type of asset under public, Sprockets is configured in Rails to look for assets in subdirectories of app/assets for application-specific assets like page styles, lib/assets for assets you wrote but that may be used across several applications (like company branding), and vendor/assets for assets we didn't create but we're using from the wider community. This separation makes it easier to determine which things we should be modifying and which we should leave alone.

Conventionally, the main style sheet for an application is located at app/assets/stylesheets/application.css. In building the views for our ArtFlow application, we've already added a few new lines:

```
/*
 *= require_self
 *= require normalize
 *= require text
 *= require buttons
 *= require layout
 *= require sidebar
 *= require navigation
 *= require notifications
 *= require forms
 *= require formtastic
 *= require media
*/
```

The require lines we've added in comments aren't technically CSS: they're examples of what Sprockets calls *directives*—instructions that describe the dependencies of the CSS file, telling Rails which files to combine when serving the file.

Sprocket Directives

Sprocket directives are placed within CSS comments and must be located at the top of the file.

The require directive should feel very familiar to Ruby developers. It directs Rails to treat the file named as a dependency and to pull it into this file when creating the generated copy. This will kick off any processing necessary to generate the final content of the dependency, which we'll see more details about in *Dynamically Building CSS*, on page 76.

The require_tree directive is similar but allows us to define an entire directory of CSS files to recursively combine and include, which it does in alphabetic order. Since this can have unintended consequences and to make it more obvious what our CSS includes, it's usually best to avoid require_tree and use require directions with explicit filenames.

The require_self directive takes the styles defined in the file itself and inserts them at this point. We can use this to add ad hoc styles to our application.css that we don't necessarily want to rip out into a separate file. The fact that we can put require_self before or after the other directives gives us the flexibility to control in exactly what order the content is inserted, which is important when it comes to the precedence of the CSS rules.

How Sprockets Finds Files

All of the files referenced from our style sheet don't need to be in app/assets/stylesheets. Rails will also search in lib/assets/stylesheets and then in vendor/assets/stylesheets if a file isn't found. We can see the full list of paths using the runner command and use the y() method to pretty-print the assets.paths configuration setting:

```
% rails runner "y Rails.configuration.assets.paths"
---
- /path/to/artflow/app/assets/images
- /path/to/artflow/app/assets/javascripts
- /path/to/artflow/app/assets/stylesheets
- /path/to/artflow/lib/assets/images
- /path/to/artflow/lib/assets/stylesheets
- /path/to/artflow/lib/assets/javascripts
- /path/to/artflow/vendor/assets/images
- /path/to/artflow/vendor/assets/javascripts
- /path/to/artflow/vendor/assets/stylesheets
```

We also see image and JavaScript asset directories listed here, but for style sheets Rails is only interested in finding files including a .css extension. The first matching file wins and will be used when generating our CSS. We'll see similar behavior when we talk about JavaScript assets in Chapter 4, *Adding JavaScript*, on page 101.

We can also reference files in subdirectories; in this case we want to use a specific set of typography styles in typography.css under vendor/assets/stylesheets/blueprint:

artflow/css/app/assets/stylesheets/application.css
```
/*
 *= require_self
 *= require normalize
 *= require layout
 *= require sidebar
```

```
    *= require navigation
    *= require notifications
➤   *= require blueprint/typography
   */
```

So we can build larger CSS files out of smaller CSS files, but what dynamic tools do we have to build the CSS content itself?

Dynamically Building CSS

We're used to dynamically generating HTML; we work with .html.erb files (HTML preprocessed by the ERB template engine) in our views all the time. A little library called Tilt, shipped with Rails 3.1 alongside Sprockets, generalizes and expands this concept for other file types.[2] The secret lies in the file extension.

Want to generate CSS with ERB? Use the .css.erb suffix. How about SCSS (which we'll learn more about next in Section 3.2, *Learning SCSS*, on page 76)? Use .css.scss. Want to mix the two? A .css.scss.erb extension will run the content through ERB, then SCSS; it starts at the end of the filename and works backward, extension by extension, until it reaches the final format we want to generate.

With a little configuration, we can add more preprocessors or even write our own, but let's focus on Sass, the default CSS processor for Rails, and on the format it provides, SCSS, which is uniquely suited to help make our lives easier when building style sheets.

3.2 Learning SCSS

The Sassy CSS language is provided by Sass, a project by Hampton Catlin and numerous contributors. It has been included as a default since Rails 3.1.[3] SCSS extends the CSS language to include a number of features that include variables, functions, file imports, nested selectors, mixins, and inheritance. Let's look at how this has made writing our CSS easier.

Simplifying Advanced Selectors

On the homepage for our application, we have some marketing content that needs to be styled. It's a <section> with some optimistic descriptions of our product features and links to supporting pages:

---

2. https://github.com/rtomayko/tilt
3. http://sass-lang.com/

The Asset Pipeline in Production

You'd be right to get a little nervous hearing about dynamically generating assets if it meant you'd be forced to build them in a live production environment, as requests are being served.

Don't fret. Rails ships with an assets:precompile Rake task that will handle generating static files for you.[a] You can either run this locally (if you don't want to go through the bother of installing some dependencies on your server) and ship the files during deployment, or you can have the task run on the server immediately after deployment (e.g., for Capistrano, after "deploy:update_code").

Check with your host to determine the best course of action. Some, like Heroku, may handle this automatically for you.[b]

---

a.   http://guides.rubyonrails.org/asset_pipeline.html#precompiling-assets
b.   http://heroku.com

artflow/css/app/views/pages/home.html.erb

```erb
<section id='features'>
  <p>
    You're in charge! Our flexible, advanced
    <a href='/features/approval'>approval process</a> gives
    you the final say on the designs created for your
    advertising campaigns.
  </p>
  <p>
    Access the service from the <a href='/features/mobile'>mobile</a>
    device of your choice. We support them all!
  </p>
</section>
```

Now we need to select the elements we're going to style. We do this with selectors, a key part of CSS syntax. If we were going to style a <section> element, its <p> elements, and any <a> elements inside of them, we'd do it with three separate statements:

css/flat_selectors.css

```css
section {
  /* section styles go here */
}
section p {
  /* p styles go here */
}
section p a {
  /* a styles go here */
}
```

These are *descendant* selectors; the spaces between section, p, and a indicate depth. If we read the selectors backward, we can substitute the word *inside* for each space; we're styling anchors inside paragraphs inside sections.

CSS forces us to keep our selectors "flat"; even though we're describing a deep markup structure, we have to describe individual, narrow slices to connect our styles with the elements we want to affect. This is one of the most frustrating constraints of the CSS syntax. Sass gives us a better option, allowing us to structure our styles to mirror the structure of the markup. We can nest our selectors! Here's a refactoring of our styles to make use of this:

```
css/nested_selectors.scss
section {
  /* section styles go here */
  p {
    /* p styles go here */
    a {
      /* a styles go here */
    }
  }
}
```

Now descendant selectors are much more obvious; they're implicit in the structure of our styling. This makes the rules easier to find and harder to lose, misorder, or accidentally override since they're not just lying around. It also makes it easier to show related groupings of rules without the need for large comment banners marking off different parts of the file.

Let's revamp a more complex page. In ArtFlow we have a list of parties that are interested in being notified when changes are made to a creation. This list includes the designer, project manager, and the client, at a minimum. It looks something like this:

```
artflow/css/app/views/creations/_interested.html.erb
<ul id='interested'>
  <li class='client'>
    <a href='/clients/10/people/233'>Joe Thrower</a>
  </li>
  <li class='staff designer'>
    <a href='/staff/12'>Jack Johnson</a>
  </li>
  <li class='staff pm'>
    <a href='/staff/3'>James Monsanto</a>
  </li>
  <%# Other people here... %>
</ul>
```

In our old CSS, we had styles for each type of person à la carte:

Joe asks:

What's the Difference: SASS vs. SCSS?

SASS and SCSS are two different dialects of the same thing. They are both present in the Sass gem. Rails versions since 3.1 default to the SCSS syntax as the preferential way to write CSS. We also prefer to use SCSS because it allows users to also write regular CSS while getting the benefits of mixins, includes, and more.

css/interested.css

```
ul#interested {
  list-style: none;
}
ul#interested a {
  text-decoration: none;
}
ul#interested a:hover {
  text-decoration: underline;
}
ul#interested li.staff a,
ul#interested li.staff a:visited {
  font-style: bold;
}

ul#interested li.staff.designer a {
  color: #000;
}
ul#interested li.client a {
  color: #000;
  font-style: italic;
}
```

It could be worse, of course; these could be missing the ul#interested prefix or be strewn across the file haphazardly, but you get the idea. Let's modify this to use nesting to tell the story a bit more clearly:

```
ul#interested {
  list-style: none;
  li {
    a {
      text-decoration: none;
    }
    a:hover {
      text-decoration: underline;
    }
  }
  li.staff a {
    font-style: bold;
  }
}
```

```
  li.staff.designer {
    a, a:visited {
      color: #000;
    }
  }
  li.client {
    a, a:visited {
      color: #000;
      font-style: italic;
    }
  }
}
```

Now at least these look like a related group of styles. The nesting isn't quite complete, and there's still a bit of duplication, though; the styles for staff, designer, and client are really extending the style for the li, aren't they? How can we put these styles inside the li definition, considering these aren't descendants of li but modifications? Easy—SASS has added an & selector. Let's see it in action:

artflow/css/app/assets/stylesheets/interested.css.scss
```
ul#interested {
  list-style: none;
  li {
    a {
      text-decoration: none;
➤     &:hover {
        text-decoration: underline;
      }
    }
➤   &.staff {
      a {
        font-style: bold;
      }
➤     &.designer {
        a, a:visited {
          color: #000;
        }
      }
    }
➤   &.client {
      a, a:visited {
        color: #000;
        font-italic: italic;
      }
    }
  }
}
```

What does this mean? Let's dig in. When Sass compiles the file and sees &, instead of adding the selector as a child of the enclosing selector, it replaces the & with the name of the enclosing selector. So, for instance, &.client becomes li.client.

In practice it's easier to forget about all this and just read the & as "with": "an <li> *with* a client class's <a> tag should look like..." You can chain & selectors, too, as you can see with our designer class, an additional modification to the staff class.

Defining and Using Variables

Our first pass at writing our styles for ArtFlow included a conspicuous legend in comments we used to try to keep our team on the same page.

```
/*
 * Fonts
 * -----
 * Verdana, Arial, Helvetica, sans-serif (Heading)
 * Georgia, Times New Roman, serif (Accent)
 * Times New Roman, Times, serif (Body)
 *
 * Colors
 * -------
 * #333    Near Black
 * #d4f2ff Light Blue
 * #436ca7 Dark Blue
 * #ffc    Highlight
 * #50B450 Dark Green
 *
 */
```

Since our legend was just a comment, we needed to copy and paste the settings whenever we needed to use them, as we did for our basic text and heading styles:

```
body {
  font-family: 'Times New Roman', 'Times', serif;
}
h1, h2 {
  color: #333333;
  font-family: 'Verdana', 'Arial', 'Helvetica', sans-serif;
}
h3 {
  color: #50B450;
  font: italic bold 20px 'Georgia', 'Times New Roman', serif;
}
```

These values are pretty much like constants, aren't they? Let's convert our "merely descriptive" legend into a set of SCSS variables we can reuse and then turn this into text.css.scss:

```
$heading-font: 'Verdana', 'Arial', 'Helvetica', sans-serif;
$accent-font: 'Georgia', 'Times New Roman', serif;
$body-font: 'Times New Roman', 'Times', serif;

$near-black: #333;
$light-blue: #d4f2ff;
$dark-blue: #436ca7;
$highlight: #ffc;
```

Now we can reuse the settings easily across our selectors by applying them to our properties:

```
body {
  font-family: $body-font;
}
h1, h2 {
  color: $near-black;
  font-family: $heading-font;
}
h3 {
  color: $dark-green
  font: italic bold 20px $accent-font;
}
```

It turns out our $dark-blue setting isn't quite right, since we just eyeballed it in a color picker. We'd like it to be exactly 25 percent darker than $light-blue, but doing the math ourselves is just silly. Sass ships with a set of ready-to-use utility functions for colors. We'll let Sass figure it out:

```
$dark-blue: darken($light-blue, 25%);
```

We don't need to know the exact color code for $dark-blue; Sass calculates it, and we've assigned it to a variable for later use. So now that we have these settings in one SCSS file, how do we share it?

File Imports

CSS has an @import rule that allows it to load CSS files; a basic use looks something like this:

```
artflow/css/app/assets/stylesheets/text.css.scss
@import "brand";
```

The @import rule exists in SCSS as well—it's just been extended to allow including .scss files, too. We use @import in our Rails SCSS when the contents of an SCSS file need definitions provided elsewhere, commonly for variables and mixins (which we'll cover in *Mixins*, on page 84). For example, we could define our brand colors in a separate SCSS partial, _brand.scss:

```scss
$heading-font: 'Verdana', 'Arial', 'Helvetica', sans-serif;
$accent-font: 'Georgia', 'Times New Roman', serif;
$body-font: 'Times New Roman', 'Times', serif;

$near-black: #333;
$light-blue: #d4f2ff;
$dark-blue: darken($light-blue, 25%);
$highlight: #ffc;
```

We can use these mixins in our .css.scss files elsewhere simply by adding an @import. Now that we've extracted our variables, we'll import it to use in our headings:

artflow/css/app/assets/stylesheets/text.css.scss
```scss
@import "brand";

body {
  font-family: $body-font;
}
h1, h2 {
  color: $near-black;
  font-family: $heading-font;
}
h3 {
  color: $dark-green
  font: italic bold 20px $accent-font;
}
```

It's important to remember that the Sprockets require directive and the @import rule that SASS provides occur at different times and serve two completely different purposes.

The Sprockets require directive just pulls in the final, processed result for the file named into the current document (usually application.css). While it kicks off the processing by asking for the file, it doesn't care about what the internal semantics of the file are; it's just concatenating.

The @import rule in SCSS files is quite a bit different, since it is loading and parsing the related file to use those mixins as SCSS language definitions. This happens while processing the document, and since each SCSS file is processed separately, each file should @import the definitions it needs.

Use require when you just want to shove content together and @import when you want to use the definitions present in the dependency in the current file.

Mixins

In our ArtFlow application there are a number of UI components that have a similar look and feel. One common pattern we're using pops an element off of the gray background by setting the top border to white and the bottom border to a dark gray, as you can see here:

This doesn't have enough semantic meaning to sprinkle as CSS classes in our HTML markup, but we don't want to have to type this for a bunch of CSS selectors either:

```
css/popout.css
border-top: #fff 1px solid;
border-bottom: #bbb 1px solid;
```

Let's pull this out into a SCSS mixin instead, which will let us mix this purely presentation-related feature into the style definition for our semantically named classes. We put this in _popout.scss:

```
@mixin popout {
  border-top: #fff 1px solid;
  border-bottom: #aaa 1px solid;
}
```

We put this into an SCSS partial so that we can @import it elsewhere, as we do for our sidebar, where the section headers are designed as bars:

```
@import "popout";

section#sidebar {
  section {
    header {
      @include popout;
      background: #ccc;
      font-family: $heading-font;
      font-size: 18px;
    }
  }
}
```

We need to make our popout mixin a bit more flexible, though, since it turns out we need it to work with a variety of surrounding backgrounds (the page body is a light gray, but we have other background colors elsewhere) and internal backgrounds. Let's update the mixin to handle this for us and calculate a light top border and dark bottom border from the options we give it.

artflow/css/app/assets/stylesheets/_popout.scss

```scss
@mixin popout($inside: #ccc, $surrounding: #ddd) {
  background-color: $inside;
  border-top: lighten($inside, 80%) 1px solid;
  border-bottom: darken($surrounding, 20%) 1px solid;
}
```

This gives us the flexibility to use the popout style regardless of the background of the element or its surroundings. If our sidebar was dark blue and we wanted light blue bars, we could simply @include our mixin with additional arguments:

artflow/css/app/assets/stylesheets/sidebar.css.scss

```scss
@import "popout";

$sidebar-bg: #003366;
$bars-bg: #97d4fe;

section#sidebar {
  background: $sidebar-bg;
  section {
    header {
      @include popout($bars-bg, $sidebar-bg);
      font-family: $heading-font;
      font-size: 18px;
    }
  }
}
```

As we can see in the following graphic, the mixin now automatically compensates for the darker background.

The sky's the limit with mixins. We could go further, defining default font styles, a border radius, and box shadows—anything CSS can do, Sass mixins can do dynamically.

Selector Inheritance

Mixins are great, but there's an even simpler way to add common styles to a selector—if there's another selector we can inherit from, we can just pull it in.

In ArtFlow we used to have separate button and modifier classes (like red), but we'd like to combine the more generic button class with the different styles so we don't have to remember to compose button styles using multiple classes.

We took the à la carte approach:

```
css/buttons.css
.button {
  display: inline-block;
  padding: 5px 10px;
  font: small-caps bold 14px/21px "Arvo", "Courier New", serif;
  background: #ddd;
  -moz-box-shadow: 0 1px 2px #888;
  -webkit-box-shadow: 0 1px 2px#888;
  box-shadow: 0 0 1pxpx #888;
}
.red {
  background: #f00;
  color: #fff;
}
```

In our latest revision, we've named our buttons for the purpose they serve
instead and pulled in the settings from our generic button class with @extend:

```
artflow/css/app/assets/stylesheets/buttons.css.scss
.button {
  display: inline-block;
  padding: 5px 10px;
  font: small-caps bold 14px/21px "Arvo", "Courier New", serif;
  background: #ddd;
  -moz-box-shadow: 0 1px 2px #888;
  -webkit-box-shadow: 0 1px 2px#888;
  box-shadow: 0 0 1pxpx #888;
}
.cancel-button {
  @extend .button;
  background: #f00;
  color: #fff;
}
.ok-button {
  @extend .button;
  background: #16A000;
  color: #333;
  text-shadow: 0 -1px 1px #fff;
}
```

This lets us use simpler, single classes (cancel-button and ok-button) on elements
we want to style without having to manually copy over attributes. We keep
the generic .button style, too, for simple gray buttons—which is why we didn't
use @mixin, the definition of which is always abstract.

Referencing Images from SCSS

We need to take special care when we reference other assets, such as images, from our style sheets. Because Rails adds "fingerprints" to the asset filenames during compilation (which helps prevent stale client-side caches across deployments without invalidating caches for assets that haven't changed), we can't "guess" the correct filename by ourselves.

Instead, we can use a few convenient Sass functions that Rails has added for us. In our notifications.css.scss we can look up the correct path for our alert notification image using the asset-path() function:

```
artflow/css/app/assets/stylesheets/notifications.css.scss
.alert {
  background: {
    color: #920202;
➤   image: url(asset-path("notification_x.png", image));
  }
}
```

We have to tell Rails that this is an image by passing a second argument. There's a handy shortcut for images we can use instead, image-path(). Let's use that to add the checkmark image we use for our notice notifications. Don't worry, we'll change the alert notification too.

```
artflow/css/app/assets/stylesheets/notifications.css.scss
.notice {
  background: {
    color: #006302;
➤   image: url(image-path("notification_check.png"));
  }
}
```

Just as with the path-suffixed route helpers in Rails, there are url versions of image-path() and asset-path(), too, but for our purposes path is fine (and saves us a few bytes).[4]

We've learned a lot about Sass—from useful missing syntactic features of CSS like nested selectors to dynamic functions and inheritance mechanisms. For more information, check the project website or see the *Pragmatic Guide to Sass* [CC11].[5]

Now that we know where to put files for the asset pipeline and understand the format we should be using, let's focus on some specific CSS techniques we can use as we build out our application's look and feel.

4. http://edgeguides.rubyonrails.org/asset_pipeline.html#css-and-sass
5. http://sass-lang.com/

Adding the Power of Bourbon

Bourbon is a powerful extension to SASS that lets us simplify many of the cutting-edge CSS3 calls. Normally when we write a new feature call (e.g., border-radius), we end up with four or five lines to target each vendor-specific switch (-moz or -webkit). Bourbon lets us easily use includes to only call one line and pass it a parameter. We'd simply call the following:

```
@include border-radius(5px);
```

And that will output all the relevant browser-specific CSS. This keeps our development style sheets much cleaner and easier to maintain. You can find out more about Bourbon at https://github.com/thoughtbot/bourbon.

3.3 Adding Sprites

Some of ArtFlow's users have complained that the application is loading too slowly for them. After some analysis, we discover that the amount of time spent requesting individual images for pages is completely unreasonable. We have a lot of little images and icons, and every one of these results in another request sent to the server. While this isn't much of a problem on a low traffic site, high traffic sites can get hammered into oblivion by too many assets.

One approach here is to hand off delivery to a content delivery network, or CDN, such as Akamai or Amazon's CloudFront. But, of course, there's a financial cost associated with delivering assets from someone else's fast servers, and the core problem is that there's overhead for the client with every file request.

Instead, we are going to cut down the number of requests and get rid of lots of extraneous overhead by combining these images into one image. This is a process taken from the days of low processing (8-bit) gaming, when computers built complex scenes out of a series of images, or sprites.[6] Sprites are combined into a grid of images that use basic CSS properties of clip and background-position to display the right piece of the overall image in the UI. Then our client only downloads the single image instead of several smaller ones.

Working the Images

Building a set of sprites takes time and attention to detail. Pieces must be spaced correctly and not show up when other adjacent sprites are called from the same image.

---

6. http://www.alistapart.com/articles/sprites

Let's look at the icons we've currently got in ArtFlow. As we see below, there are about twenty different images that we use, all of which are licensed from Drew Wilson's Pictos set.[7]

We've created a sprite (as seen in the following graphic) by lining up our icons on a grid. Since the icons are 32 pixels square, we used a 40 pixel grid to make it easier for us to write the CSS for these. Our background position on the image will always be a multiple of 40 in the x and y dimensions. That makes things easier for us to work with compared to constantly measuring the original file to find out where things start and stop.

Now we add a helper to build the HTML for our icons:

artflow/css/app/helpers/icons_helper.rb
```ruby
module IconsHelper

  def icon_to(text, icon, destination)
    link_to(text, destination,
            class: "#{icon}-icon sprite-icon",
            title: text)
  end

end
```

To make this a sprite, we're going to use what amounts to image replacement, substituting the text for the pretty icon we define through the specific icon CSS class, which will be displayed in the background.

---

7. http://pictos.drewwilson.com/

There are various image replacement techniques that have been tested over the years, but they all come down to taking an element, setting its height and width, and setting an image background. If the element previously had content, such as a headline tag, we'll move that out of frame with a negative text-indent property. Our CSS in app/assets/stylesheets/icons.css.scss looks like this:

```
a.email-icon {
  background: transparent url(image-path("iconsprite.png")) top left no-repeat;
  background-position: 40px 80px;
  height: 32px;
  text-indent: -5000px;
  width: 32px;
}
```

This works great, but with this many icons, we'll be repeating a lot of the same CSS and only changing the background position. Let's use the sprite-icon class on our link to extract some of this to one place.

```
a.sprite-icon {
  background: transparent url(image-path("iconsprite.png")) top left no-repeat;
  background-position: 0 0;
  height: 32px;
  text-indent: -5000px;
  width: 32px;
}

a.email-icon { background-position: 40px 80px; }
```

Now for each new icon, we only need to add one line of CSS. That simplifies things and also lets us handle alternate cases with an override.

Let's use our helper to add an icon to approve an ArtFlow creation:

artflow/css/app/views/creations/show.html.erb
```
<% if @creation.approvable?
  <p>
    <%= icon_to("Approve Creation",
                :approve, approve_creation_path(@creation)) %>
  </p>
<% end %>
```

Now for the magic: some CSS to handle the image replacement. Since there's no such thing as an "abstract" icon, and since we don't want to use multiple classes on our elements, we define a @mixin as follows:

artflow/css/app/assets/stylesheets/icons.css.scss
```
@mixin icon($x-offset: 160px, $y-offset: -160px) {
  background-image: url("iconsprite.png");
  background-position: $x-offset $y-offset;
  background-repeat: no-repeat;
```

```
height: 0;
width: 40px;
padding: 40px 0 0;
overflow: hidden;

/* half transparent */
-khtml-opacity:.50;
-moz-opacity:.50;
-ms-filter:"alpha(opacity=50)";
filter:alpha(opacity=50);
opacity:.50;

/* more opaque on hover */
&:hover {
  -khtml-opacity:.80;
  -moz-opacity:.80;
  -ms-filter:"alpha(opacity=80)";
  filter:alpha(opacity=80);
  opacity:.80;
}
}
```

The mixin supports passing the *x*- and *y*-coordinate offsets needed to "move" the image so that the icon we'd like is in our 40 x 40 pixel window. The default offset is currently a white background (no icon) taken from the bottom right of our sprites image. We add a few icon definitions overriding this default with the correct offsets for each icon:

artflow/css/app/assets/stylesheets/icons.css.scss
```
.approve-icon  {
  @include icon(80px, -40px);
}
.person-icon {
  @include icon(0, 0);
}
.star-icon {
  @include icon(0, -40px);
}
```

It's worth mentioning that while this works great on sites with a lot of sprite usage, the fancy hover behavior we've added can cause performance issues, especially with the -ms-filter and filter directives. Since these target Internet Explorer, the relevance of this depends on IE usage by our users.

The solution is to actually make the images grayed out and either have two different sprite collection images (at different color levels) or place them all into one and have the CSS set the background to a different area of the image on hover.

This can get a bit tedious if we have a lot of images. If the overhead of handling sprites becomes a major concern, another approach we can take is to build Compass, a comprehensive Sass framework, into our Rails application.[8] Compass has built-in support for sprites in addition to layout, typography, and other tools.[9]

Remember, we don't want to *start* with sprites. Sprites are a technique we use when image downloads become a performance problem. We're careful not to make these sprite collections just because we can. When we get to a critical point where images start to become a problem, then we can turn to this method to help cut down connection requests and improve render times and user-side caching.

Now that we've tackled images, we're going to move on to see what we can do to improve the look and selection of the fonts we're using for our design.

3.4 Using Web Fonts

Over lunch we start talking about our app with our designers. We invariably end up in a discussion about the state of web fonts. One of our designers complains that there's no good web fonts for headlines and that she's limited to ugly or more ugly when choosing fonts.

Traditionally, we have been limited to a certain number of fonts that exist by default on the majority of systems. These are Times New Roman and Georgia for serif fonts and Verdana, Helvetica, and Arial for sans-serif fonts. There are a handful of other fonts available, but those are the ones most used.

Since we could not always ensure that the browser being used would have our font of choice, the concepts of font stacks started to be used to provide fallbacks. We use a font stack to specify the font we'd like to see first, and if that's not available, it gives us the next one. A traditional font stack for a sans-serif font would look like this, put in app/assets/stylesheets/fonts.css.scss:

```
body {
  font-family: Verdana, Helvetica, Arial, sans-serif;
}
```

The browser will first ask the system for Verdana, then Arial, and so on down the list. Fonts that have a space in the name need to be placed in quotes, like "Trebuchet MS".

---

8. http://compass-style.org/
9. http://compass-style.org/help/tutorials/spriting/

We'll be building on the old approach to integrate a new font served from our application because we always want to provide a fallback for browsers that may not support the newest techniques or if there's an issue with the font. And we always want to provide a fallback to a generic font in any font stack (e.g., ending with "sans-serif") to make sure that the text is rendered correctly even on browsers and devices that have small user bases (or that we simply can't test). If we don't define a fallback font such as sans-serif, the font will be rendered in whatever the default font is for the browser. This is more than likely a serif font in 16px height.

There is an alternate technique called @font-face that lets us embed fonts into our web pages and render text in all sorts of new ways.

@font-face first arrived in the CSS2 specification, but it was removed in CSS2.1. It has come back in the CSS3 spec, and it's been supported by Firefox 3.5+, Opera 10, Chrome 4+, Safari 3.2+, and Internet Explorer since version 5.

Unlike tools like sIFR or Cufon,[10] these font files are downloaded with the page and then rendered like any other text. This is good, because you typically don't have the jump after a screen renders with the new font. This is bad, because if you have too many nonstandard fonts, you have a much higher initial page load time.

Like many web standards, each browser has taken a different approach to fonts. Firefox likes the WOFF font format. iOS needs SVG. Microsoft has supported this technology since Internet Explorer 5.5 but only using the EOT file format. Some newer browsers support TTF (TrueType) and OTF (OpenType) formats. There are also licensing issues with just the formats (same reason we have OGG video vs. MP4). We will use the possible formats in a cascading order of preference and end up with a solution that works for most browsers.

Creating a Font to Serve

In the design mockups he provided earlier, our designer specified a free font that we can use on the Web called Museo Sans. It is distributed with a license that allows us to use it for web embedding from the exljbris Font Foundry.[11]

We have our font file, which is in OpenType (.otf) format. While we can serve this file, we won't see our fonts in many browsers, as they don't all support OTF. We're going to use a free online tool at FontSquirrel.com to generate our web font kit, which will include EOT, WOFF, OTF, and SVG formats.

---

10. http://www.mikeindustries.com/blog/sifr or http://cufon.shoqolate.com/generate/, respectively.

11. http://www.exljbris.com/museosans.html

For fonts, we should create a separate fonts folder in the app/assets directory and place our font files in there. The asset pipeline will put these into the public/assets folder when it processes everything.

We type this in our shell:

```
% cd app/assets
% mkdir fonts
```

And we're ready to build our custom @font-face font.

We could have purchased a piece of software (e.g., FontLab) and done this ourselves, but Font Squirrel's online tool is simply too good *not* to use. We choose the font(s) we want in the kit and upload them, and it generates the various file types we need to provide coverage to almost every browser.

Looking at the Font Squirrel interface, we just need to upload a font file and then let it do its processing. We could get really specific on the Expert mode, but since we're not trying to achieve some great typographic solution, we can just use the Optimal setting.

Optimal helps us ensure that we don't include parts of the font we aren't likely to use, such as odd characters. This technology is great, but overusing it can kill our initial page load times. Not only will that make our clients frustrated, but it can affect page rank and other factors as well. If we are only using this on an internal network, we can be more lenient with large font sets, but for public facing sites, optimization is paramount.

Google now uses page load time to affect the page rank of a site.[12] It's not critical for an internal facing app, but it's a best practice to not keep users waiting for the initial site load.

We may be forced to look at a close, web-friendly font instead of our ideal font selected from legal sources. Always weigh the end user in determining if embedded fonts are right for our website or application.

After the font generator is done processing, it will let us download the fonts, an example HTML and CSS file, and some other notes. We will need to put the @font-face declaration into our CSS file and adjust the paths to be relative to where we actually placed our fonts using the construct we looked at earlier in this tip.

Next, we can add this font name into our font-family declarations, and if the browser supports it, we will see our text rendered in a lovely font:

---

12. http://searchengineland.com/google-now-counts-site-speed-as-ranking-factor-39708

What a Headline!

Let's add it to the _brand.scss file we created in *File Imports*, on page 82, to specify our brand-level styles:

```
➤ $heading-font: "Museo Sans", 'Verdana', 'Arial', 'Helvetica', sans-serif;
  $accent-font: 'Georgia', 'Times New Roman', serif;
  $body-font: 'Times New Roman', 'Times', serif;

  $near-black: #333;
  $light-blue: #d4f2ff;
  $dark-blue: darken($light-blue, 25%);
  $highlight: #ffc;
```

Now that we have our font files ready, let's integrate them into our application.

Serving a Font File

To serve this font file via @font-face, we add this in the beginning of our app/assets/stylesheets/fonts.css.scss CSS file:

```
@font-face {
  font-family: 'Museo Sans';
  src: url('MuseoSans.eot');
  src: url('MuseoSans.eot?iefix') format('eot'),
       url('MuseoSans.woff') format('woff'),
       url('MuseoSans.otf') format('opentype'),
       url('MuseoSans.svg') format('svg');
}
```

We use a declaration that starts with an @ symbol. In this case, we tell CSS that we are defining a font face. The second line names the font and how we will access it later when we apply it to elements. We then start with an .eot file, which is the format supported by Internet Explorer.

The second line specifies a local font, since Internet Explorer can't understand the local() value. But why the declaration again for the EOT format? Well, we want to make sure that browsers that *do* understand the local() value won't pull an actual font from the local machine. The ?iefix switch on the path to the file makes IE stop right there. In this way, we can almost guarantee that we will always display the font we serve as opposed to a user's local font.

As mentioned earlier, we have multiple formats to support multiple browser types: WOFF will be read by Firefox. SVG is the favorite of iOS. And OTF (or TTF) works nicely in Safari and Chrome. If you don't have all of these, you can go back and use the Font Squirrel service to convert a font into these formats.

Font Services

Sometimes fonts we want aren't available for us to embed but are available through a software-as-a-service provider such as TypeKit, Google Webfonts, or Fontspring. These have benefits and drawbacks. First, they handle encoding and provide tools for creating and optimizing font bundles for our site. They also handle serving of the font bundle, which is a benefit but can be problematic on rare occasions. Once in a while, we've seen a page load delay because of an externally served font.

We'll need to weigh the benefits and the drawbacks as well as look at other options, such as image replacement for static text, in order to provide the best implementation of the designer's mockup.

We now have awesome typography, and our designer and design staff are happy and all will be well with the world. But we need to provide attribution on this font as per the license instructions. We're going to add this line right before our @font-face declaration in app/assets/stylesheets/fonts.css.scss:

```
/* A font by Jos Buivenga (exljbris) -> www.exljbris.nl */
```

Now we're ready to move on. We want to call this font, so we simply add it to our body font stack. If it downloads and the browser recognizes it, we'll see it rendered in our interface.

```
body {
  font-family: 'Museo Sans', Verdana, Helvetica, Arial, sans-serif;
}
```

After the afternoon coffee run, our designer stops by to see how things are going and notices that the italics aren't quite right. We're using a system-faked italicization, but this font has different characters for actual italics. So how can we use the actual italic font provided by the font foundry?

We need to define a different @font-face declaration. We can use the font-style attribute to group the fonts together, like this:

```
/* A font by Jos Buivenga (exljbris) -> www.exljbris.nl */
@font-face {
  font-family: 'Museo Sans';
  src: url('MuseoSans.eot');
  src: url('MuseoSans.eot?iefix') format('eot'),
       url('MuseoSans.woff') format('woff'),
       url('MuseoSans.otf') format('opentype'),
       url('MuseoSans.svg') format('svg');
}
@font-face {
  font-family: 'Museo Sans';
  font-style: italic;
```

> ### Joe asks:
> # Can I Use Any Font?
>
> No. Fonts, like many creative products, are licensed. Some fonts are licensed for use as included files (many of them available at the League of Movable Type website), but for most fonts, your license does not allow you to include them in a web page that you serve to other computers. If it's not clear in the license, you need to contact the typographer and clarify. Ignorance of the law is not a defense to break it.
>
> Be wary of "free" fonts from large collection sites, as many of these are actually copies of fonts requiring licenses.

```
  src: url('MuseoSansItalic.eot');
  src: url('MuseoSansItalic.eot?iefix') format('eot'),
       url('MuseoSansItalic.woff') format('woff'),
       url('MuseoSansItalic.otf') format('opentype'),
       url('MuseoSansItalic.svg') format('svg');
}
```

We change our HTML to handle it like this:

```
body {
  font-family: 'Museo Sans', Verdana, Helvetica, Arial, sans-serif;
}

em {
  font-style: italic;
}
```

We check our browsers, and the italic font now looks correct in Safari, Firefox, and Chrome. Internet Explorer, however, does not recognize the font-style attribute here, and we will not have italicized text in MSIE. Opera 10 also has issues with italics. To work around this, we're going to create two separate @font-face names in our CSS.

```
artflow/css/app/assets/stylesheets/fonts.css.scss
/* A font by Jos Buivenga (exljbris) -> www.exljbris.nl */
@font-face {
  font-family: 'Museo Sans';
  src: url('MuseoSans.eot');
  src: url('MuseoSans.eot?iefix') format('eot'),
       url('MuseoSans.woff') format('woff'),
       url('MuseoSans.otf') format('opentype'),
       url('MuseoSans.svg') format('svg');
}
@font-face {
  font-family: 'Museo Sans Italic';
  src: url('MuseoSansItalic.eot');
```

```
src: url('MuseoSansItalic.eot?iefix') format('eot'),
     url('MuseoSansItalic.woff') format('woff'),
     url('MuseoSansItalic.otf') format('opentype'),
     url('MuseoSansItalic.svg') format('svg');
}
```

We've given the italic form a unique name. This requires that we define the font-family attribute for any element that we want to be italicized in the proper font. This may not be an issue for you, but many italic fonts have different character styles that differ greatly from the guessed italics (or oblique) font that the system can generate on the fly.

```
artflow/css/app/assets/stylesheets/fonts.css.scss
body {
  font-family: 'Museo Sans', Verdana, Helvetica, Arial, sans-serif;
}

em {
  font-family: 'Museo Sans Italic', Verdana, Helvetica, Arial, sans-serif;
  font-style: italic;
}
```

If we didn't have to support MSIE, we would have skipped this step and gone with the cleaner grouping of fonts that respect the font-style: italic declaration. As with most of these techniques, it's best to know what you need to support up front and target those devices and browsers.

Font faces can help reduce images and provide a closer level of control for design staff, especially on internal-facing apps. It's important that we not overuse this tool and that we optimize our fonts to be as small as possible for the task required.

There are so many exciting things coming down the pike with the CSS3 Fonts Module that have not yet been implemented.[13] While these things may take a while to get into all browsers, we can start using them today and marking up our code properly. Good typography starts with familiarizing yourself with typographic rules, such as those found in Robert Bringhurst's *The Elements of Typographic Style*, which is being translated to the Web.[14]

3.5 Wrapping Up

As we've learned in this chapter, CSS can be a pretty deep topic, but it's surmountable given Rails's improved asset tools and some attention to detail.

---

13. http://www.w3.org/TR/css3-fonts/
14. http://webtypography.net/

Even if we don't have a design bone in our body and think that bright green and violent purple are completely reasonable choices for a pair of background and body text colors, we can edit a CSS file responsibly and even use some neat SCSS shortcuts to cut down on the drudgery.

Next we look at another arena where Rails has made significant improvements to ease the tasks of the developer, and we look at another dark art of the front end developer, JavaScript.

A different language is a different vision of life.

➤ *Federico Fellini*

CHAPTER 4

Adding JavaScript

Sometimes we need to add client-side behavior to our Rails applications to support a more interactive user experience, adding features like custom form controls and asynchronous requests (Ajax). This is where Ruby stops being useful and it's time to rely on our JavaScript. Today, knowledge of JavaScript is necessary to being effective as a user interface developer. Luckily (and not surprisingly), Rails developers have an advantage. Out of the box, we can use CoffeeScript, a cleaner, more concise language that compiles into JavaScript.[1]

In this chapter we'll focus on making our ArtFlow application user interface easier to use by adding some client-side behavior and improving the creation-commenting interface and messaging systems. While we do this, we'll pick up some CoffeeScript and learn how we can make our code shorter, cleaner, and more expressive by letting it write JavaScript for us. (Bid the curly braces adieu!)

4.1   Using JavaScript from Rails

The way Rails developers have used JavaScript from Rails has changed over the years; in the early days of Rails we commonly dropped JavaScript directly into our templates in <script> tags, inline in onclick attributes, and even generated JavaScript by interacting with Ruby object proxies, an approach termed Ruby JavaScript (RJS). While all of these approaches worked in a general sense, they involved dirtying our template code with yet another language (aren't HTML and Ruby enough?), and things got messy very quickly.

Let's look at an example. In ArtFlow we display a list of comments on each creation's page. This is how our designers and clients discuss the work being

---

1.   http://jashkenas.github.com/coffee-script/

done. By default, we only show the last three comments, but we support displaying all of the comments with a link at the top of the comment stream. Users can click the link to toggle the expanded view.

In the past, we implemented this control with JavaScript directly inserted into the template, setting the link's onclick attribute. Here's what our code in app/views/creations/show.html.erb looked like:

```
<p>
  <%= link_to 'View All Comments', '#comments',
          onclick: "var comments = $('#comments li');
                  if ($(this).text() == 'View All Comments') {
                    comments.show();
                    $(this).text('Collapse Comments');
                  } else {
                    comments.slice(3).hide();
                    $(this).text('View All Comments')
                  }
                  return false;" %>
</p>
```

This isn't the easiest code to read. In just a few lines we have to switch languages from HTML to Ruby (via ERB) and then to JavaScript. The code itself is fairly basic DOM querying and manipulation using jQuery, the default JavaScript framework (read: handy box of tools) that ships with Rails. We used jQuery's $() function to change the link text and find all the comment <li> tags to change their visibility.[2]

Let's figure out how we can make this code a bit easier to read and maintain. While we could shorten this up by extracting the code into a function and invoking it from our onclick, what if we could take the JavaScript out of the template entirely, attaching the behavior to our element just like we apply CSS styles to a selector? This technique is called *Unobtrusive JavaScript*, it's the leading best practice for adding client-side behavior to a web page, and it's one of the rules we follow, on page 233.

Coding Unobtrusively

Let's put Unobtrusive JavaScript, or UJS, into practice by converting our expander link. The first step is to give the element we'd like to add our behavior to some identifying feature, like an id or a class, just as we would if we wanted to style the element with CSS:

---

2.   http://jquery.com

```
artflow/js/app/views/creations/show.html.erb
<% if @creation.comments.any? %>
  <p><%= link_to 'View All Comments', '#comments', id: 'comment_expander' %></p>
<% end %>
```

OK, so we have an id we can use. Let's define and attach our behavior. We'll do this in a separate file under app/assets/javascripts (this is similar to how we handled style sheets in Chapter 3, *Adding Cascading Style Sheets*, on page 73). Instead of using plain, vanilla JavaScript, we'll use CoffeeScript instead. When we originally created our Comment (using rails generate resource), Rails created a stub at comments.js.coffee, so we'll use that.

CoffeeScript syntax is more concise than JavaScript for a number of reasons. Since anonymous functions are used so frequently in JavaScript, it supports a shorter syntax for defining them: -> instead of function. It also uses indentation rather than curly braces to denote code blocks, doesn't use semicolons (unless, like Ruby, you want more than one statement on a line), and has a host of other features like string interpolation and iterators that will feel familiar to Rubyists.

We add the expander link code to our CoffeeScript file with a few small modifications:

```
artflow/js/app/assets/javascripts/comments.js.coffee
$(document).ready ->

  $('#comment_expander').click (e) ->
    comments = $('#comments li')
    if $(this).text() == 'View All Comments'
      comments.show()
      $(this).text('Collapse Comments')
    else
      comments.slice(3).hide()
      $(this).text('View All Comments')
    e.preventDefault()
```

The first difference is that we wrap our code in a function we pass to $(document).ready() (everything indented is the function body). This delays execution of the code until the DOM has been completely put together by the browser. Next, we use jQuery's $() function to find an element with the id we're looking for. If it finds one, a click event handler is attached using the click() function. The only difference to the function body is that we call preventDefault() on the click event rather than using return false, as it's more explicit (and doesn't have any event propagation side effects). We're replacing the default behavior of the link, which would take users to the list of comments farther down the page, but only for browsers that support JavaScript.[3]

Let's talk about how this is an improvement over inlining the JavaScript. First of all, look at the template code—a single, easily readable line that only does one thing! We use Rails and HTML to *configure* the JavaScript behavior, rather than define it in place. Since the code itself is in a separate file, managed by the asset pipeline (as explained in Section 3.1, *Using the Asset Pipeline*, on page 73), we get to use the flavor of JavaScript we want, too—CoffeeScript— and make use of detailed comments with nice tools like Docco to make teaching and maintaining our client-side code easier in the long term.[4] If this was a consulting project, this would help us build a more polished deliverable for our client, too.

Now we need to make sure our comments.js.coffee gets loaded by the browser. We used javascript_include_tag() to pull in our application.js:

artflow/js/app/views/layouts/application.html.erb
```
<%= javascript_include_tag "application" %>
```

Now it's just a matter of adding a Sprockets require directive (see *Sprocket Directives*, on page 74) in application.js for comments:

artflow/js/app/assets/javascripts/application.js
```
//= require modernizr-1.7.custom
//= require jquery
//= require jquery_ujs
➤ //= require comments
```

Now our code will be included in application.js, and after the DOM is completely loaded by the browser, our expander behavior will be automatically attached to the link for our comment list.

We need to use JavaScript in several other places in our ArtFlow user interface. We'll see that in many cases adding client-side behavior in Rails is even easier than the custom control we just built; often it doesn't require even a single line of JavaScript. This is thanks to Rails's inclusion of *jQuery UJS*, a library that automatically adds some common client-side features purely based on hints we leave in our HTML.

Using jQuery UJS

The automatic inclusion of the jQuery UJS library, an "Unobstrusive Java-Script adapter" for Rails and jQuery, gives us a lot of JavaScript power for

---

3. http://fuelyourcoding.com/jquery-events-stop-misusing-return-false/
4. http://jashkenas.github.com/docco/

free. Just by providing a special option or two to standard Rails helpers, we can add client-side behavior without writing any JavaScript (or CoffeeScript) ourselves.[5]

Rails puts the jQuery UJS library into our application.js automatically:

`artflow/js/app/assets/javascripts/application.js`
```
//= require jquery_ujs
```

Let's try using it. One thing that the adapter can handle for us is adding confirmation dialogs for links. This would be nice for our Remove Creation control in ArtFlow. Rather than needing the screen real estate for a confirmation checkbox on the page (we don't want people to remove their hard work by accident), we can just ask the user for confirmation when clicking the control. We just need to pass a :confirm option to link_to():

`artflow/js/app/views/creations/show.html.erb`
```
<p>
  <%= link_to "Remove Creation", @creation, method: 'delete',
              confirm: "Are you sure you want to remove this creation?" %>
</p>
```

Clicking the link in our browser yields a nice little modal dialog box with our question, as seen in Figure 11, *A JavaScript confirmation dialog*, on page 106.

How does JavaScript know it should pop up the confirmation dialog? Well, let's look at the HTML our link_to() generated:

`js/confirm.html`
```
<p>
  <a href="/creations/1"
     data-method="delete"
     data-confirm="Are you sure you want to remove this creation?">
    Remove Creation
  </a>
</p>
```

The thing to notice here is the addition of a data-confirm attribute to our <a> tag. We also have a data-method attribute to support sending an HTTP DELETE request (which the adapter also sets up for us). Custom data attributes are a part of the HTML5 specification and are meant to be used by a site's own scripts to add behavior.[6]

These data attributes are the hints that Rails leaves behind for the jQuery UJS adapter to look for. When the page loads, it automatically finds the

---

5. https://github.com/rails/jquery-ujs
6. http://www.w3.org/TR/html5/elements.html#embedding-custom-non-visible-data-with-the-data-attributes

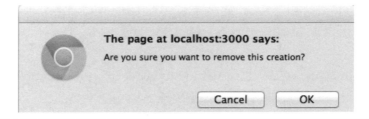

Figure 11—A JavaScript confirmation dialog

elements containing these special attributes and attaches the appropriate behavior, all without a single line of custom JavaScript. In this case, the data-confirm attribute tells the adapter to check the user's intention with a confirmation dialog before following through and sending the request. The request itself is also handled by the adapter; since it found a data-method attribute, it will help the browser put together the request as needed for Rails to route it to the CreationsController destroy() action.

This unobtrusive approach, prepackaged and behind-the-scenes, is so decoupled that in many cases we can ignore the details and just use the Rails helpers to get the behavior we want. Now let's look at a more advanced example by building an asynchronous form and adding some special behavior of our own to the page with a bit of jQuery.

Building a Remote Form

In *Coding Unobtrusively*, on page 102, we looked at the creation commenting system that our designers and clients use when discussing the progress of a Creation. Let's continue to improve that portion of our ArtFlow user interface. The comment list is at the bottom of our show.html.erb:

```
artflow/js/app/views/creations/show.html.erb
<ul id='comments'>
  <%= render @creation.comments %>
</ul>
```

Since we're passing the creation's set of comments to render(), it will render each one of them with the _comment.html.erb partial:

```
artflow/js/app/views/comments/_comment.html.erb
<li>
  <%= raw textilize(comment.body) %>
  <p class='meta'>
    <%= link_to comment.user.name, comment.user %>,
    <%=l comment.created_at %>
  </p>
</li>
```

Now let's create our comment form. We don't allow comment editing, so we'll hardcode in Comment.new as the object for the semantic_form_for() we learned about in *Formtastic*, on page 138. Let's edit app/views/comments/_form.html.erb:

```
<%= semantic_form_for [@creation, Comment.new] do |f| %>
  <%= f.inputs :body, label: false %>
  <%= f.buttons do %>
    <%= f.commit_button 'Add Comment' %>
  <% end %>
<% end %>
```

Passing in the creation and the comment together as an array will make sure the form submits to the nested route for the comments that we've defined in our config/routes.rb:

artflow/js/config/routes.rb
```
resources :creations do
➤   resources :comments
    member do
      get 'permissions'
    end
end
```

Our form will submit to POST /creations/:creation_id/comments, which is created by this route. We insert the form partial at the bottom of our comment listing:

artflow/js/app/views/creations/show.html.erb
```
<ul id='comments'>
  <%= render @creation.comments %>
</ul>
<h3>Add Comment</h3>
<%= render 'comments/form' %>
```

Our CommentsController create() action is pretty simple; it merely creates the comment and redirects back to the comment listing:

artflow/js/app/controllers/comments_controller.v1.rb
```
class CommentsController < ApplicationController
  before_filter :find_creation

➤   def create
➤     @comment = @creation.comments.new(params[:comment])
➤     @comment.user = current_user
➤     @comment.save
➤     redirect_to @creation
➤   end
  private
  def find_creation
    @creation = Creation.find(params[:creation_id])
  end
end
```

Right now this form is synchronous, which means when we submit a new comment, the browser changes location; it does a POST to our controller, and we're redirected back. We want people to be able to submit comments and see those comments pop up in place immediately without leaving their place on the page.

Let's change this to an asynchronous operation by modifying comments/ _form.html.erb and telling Rails that the form is remote.

artflow/js/app/views/comments/_form.html.erb

```
<%= semantic_form_for [@creation, Comment.new], remote: true do |f| %>
  <%= f.inputs :body, label: false %>
  <%= f.buttons do %>
    <%= f.commit_button 'Add Comment' %>
  <% end %>
<% end %>
```

When Rails sees the remote option, it adds a data-remote attribute to the <form> tag it outputs, just as it added a data-confirm attribute when we used a confirm option for the link_to() for Figure 11, *A JavaScript confirmation dialog*, on page 106. The behavior that the jQuery driver attaches this time is a bit more complex; it intercepts user submission of the form and stops the browser from sending a normal, synchronous HTTP POST. Instead, an asynchronous request is sent by JavaScript and the browser stays put while it waits for a response.

All of this happens without us having to do anything special except make sure the controller is sending a JavaScript response that tells the script what to do next.

Right now, our controller will respond to all requests with a redirect. That's not going to work for the asynchronous request JavaScript will send; we want to send back JavaScript code to be evaluated, not send the browser back to this page—that's the whole point of the asynchronous request in the first place! Let's edit our create() action in our CommentsController to differentiate between HTML and JavaScript requests:

artflow/js/app/controllers/comments_controller.rb

```
class CommentsController < ApplicationController
  before_filter :authenticate_user!
  before_filter :find_creation

  def create
    @comment = @creation.comments.new(params[:comment])
    @comment.user = current_user
    @comment.save!
    respond_to do |format|
      format.html do
```

```
➤           redirect_to comments_url
➤         end
➤       format.js
➤     end
    end

    private

    def find_creation
      @creation = Creation.find(params[:creation_id])
    end
  end
```

By not passing a block to format.js, we're indicating that the template for this action and format should be rendered. This will be the JavaScript code we'd like evaluated. Let's have our create.js.erb template insert the new comment at the bottom of the comment list on the page:

artflow/js/app/views/comments/create.js.erb
```
$('#comments').append("<%=j raw(render(@comment)) %>");
```

This is just an ERB template that generates JavaScript instead of the HTML we're used to. It's just a single line, so it's tempting to use render :inline from the CommentsController, but we don't! The brevity isn't an excuse to get messy and inconsistent. We keep *all* of our templates in files, where they belong, and other developers on our team will know where to find them.

In create.js.erb we're finding the comments list with a CSS selector using jQuery's $() function and then appending content to it with append(). The content we're adding is the result of rendering the comment's _comment.html.erb partial. But what's with the raw() and j() we're wrapping it in?

Whenever we insert content into an ERB template with a concatenation tag (that is, a <%= %>), Rails will automatically escape any embedded HTML inside the string, unless we tell it we're sure the content is safe to insert by using the raw() helper. We don't want to see the HTML itself, do we?

The j() helper is a bit of syntactic sugar for escape_javascript(), which takes a string and cleans it up so that it can be safely inserted into JavaScript. If the result of our render() includes any quotes, we don't need them causing a JavaScript syntax error by prematurely closing the string. This little j() handles escaping these quotes for us.

Let's review how this all works from end to end. First, our user fills in a comment and submits the form. The form submittal is intercepted by Java-Script, which kicks off an asynchronous request to the server. The server responds with a chunk of JavaScript code that appends a new comment <li>

(our comment partial) to our <ul> of comments. When JavaScript receives the response, it evaluates it, and a new comment is added to the bottom of the list. With just a touch of JavaScript, we've made the interface feel more responsive.

So far we've been content letting Rails and the jQuery UJS driver add behavior to the page by looking for custom data attributes. Let's go a step further and figure out how we can manipulate the DOM and add our own events.

We've seen that with jQuery (which we can learn more about in *jQuery in Action* [BK10] by Bear Bibeault and Yehuda Katz) and Rails's powerful jQuery UJS driver we can quickly build Ajax interfaces and even easily attach our own custom behavior to the page, all while using a new, cleaner syntax for JavaScript and CoffeeScript.

As more and more of our application's interaction code moves out of traditional requests and into asynchronous requests with JavaScript, we should ensure that our code has test coverage to prevent breakage when we push to production servers and our users. Let's take a look at adding a layer of tests to make sure our interface is built correctly and will keep working as our system grows.

4.2 Testing Ajax

While our web browser will notify us of errors in the console (and sometimes also through popup alerts), we need a more automated solution that will help us track down problems quickly and with less effort and won't be completely constrained to the JavaScript bits of code. We'd like to test how our JavaScript and Ruby parts work together. We'll install a couple libraries to help us out.

Cucumber is a framework that lets us define how we expect our user interface to work using an easy-to-read, domain-specific language (Gherkin) and then lets us verify our system against that definition.[7] To do this, Cucumber can use Capybara, a library of test drivers ranging from the simple and lightweight to full-blown control of a browser session complete with JavaScript support.[8]

Testing with Cucumber and Capybara

Together, Cucumber and Capybara make an impressive acceptance testing framework that will help us make sure all the pieces of our application work correctly for our users. Surprisingly, getting such an advanced system up and running is remarkably straightforward. Let's do it now.

---

7. http://cukes.info/
8. https://github.com/jnicklas/capybara

Getting our testing environment starts in our Gemfile, where we add capybara, cucumber-rails, launchy (used to launch the browser for debugging, as explained in *Show Me the Page*, on page 114), and database_cleaner (used for resetting our database between tests):

artflow/js/Gemfile
```
group :test do
➤   gem 'capybara'
➤   gem 'cucumber-rails'
➤   gem 'launchy'
➤   gem 'database_cleaner'
    gem 'turn', :require => false
    gem 'factory_girl'
end
```

After installing the new libraries with Bundler, we need to run the cucumber:install generator to configure our application to run Cucumber.

```
% rails generate cucumber:install
    create  config/cucumber.yml
    create  script/cucumber
     chmod  script/cucumber
    create  features/step_definitions
    create  features/support
    create  features/support/env.rb
     exist  lib/tasks
    create  lib/tasks/cucumber.rake
      gsub  config/database.yml
      gsub  config/database.yml
     force  config/database.yml
```

Once the generator has finished its work, we test run Cucumber to make sure everything's configured correctly. We'll use the handy cucumber Rake task that's been set up for us:

```
% rake cucumber
0 scenarios
0 steps
0m0.000s
```

Great! The zeroes here are good news: Cucumber runs! Let's start our first scenario by creating a new file in the features directory and write out how we expect the interface to behave.

Scenarios consist of multiple lines, or *steps*, written in Cucumber's extensible Gherkin language.[9] We'll start with making sure a designer can sign in, then we'll build on that later to verify the designer can add a comment.

---

9.   https://github.com/cucumber/cucumber/wiki/Gherkin

```
artflow/js/features/session.feature
```
```
Scenario: Designer can sign in
  Given I am designer "Lindsay Bluth" with an account
  And I sign in
  Then I should see "Welcome, Lindsay Bluth"
```

Let's try running Cucumber again:

```
% rake cucumber
...
1 scenario (1 undefined)
3 steps (3 undefined)
0m0.005s
```

Cucumber ran our scenario line by line...or it would have, if it understood what we wanted the first step to be. Thankfully Cucumber told us exactly what it needs: new step definitions added. Let's copy the first chunk of Ruby code it output and paste it into a new file, features/step_definitions/common_steps.rb. We replace pending with what we want the step to do:

```
artflow/js/features/step_definitions/common_steps.rb
```
```ruby
Given /^I am designer "([^"]*)" with an account$/ do |name|
  email = "#{name.downcase.gsub(' ', '.')}@artflowme.com"
  @user = Designer.create!(name: name, email: email, password: 'testtest')
end
```

Step definitions consist of a pattern and a block to execute when run. Matches for groups in the regular expression are automatically yielded as arguments to the block. In this step we capture the name of the designer, then in the body of the step definition we create the designer record with a simple password and an email address we generate so that validations pass. We assign the record to an instance variable, @user, so we can reference it in later steps.

Let's put in our other two step definitions now:

```
artflow/js/features/step_definitions/common_steps.rb
```
```ruby
Given /^I sign in$/ do
  visit new_designer_session_path
  fill_in('Email', :with => @user.email)
  fill_in('Password', :with => 'testtest')
  click_button('Sign in')
end

Then /^I should see "([^"]*)"$/ do |text|
  has_content?(text)
end
```

As we implement these steps we dive more fully into Capybara's DSL.[10] Not surprisingly, it feels like we're giving instructions to a browser. We will be!

In our first step, we use visit() to request a URL. We go to the sign-in page for designers, then we use the fill_in() method to fill in our form fields. We wrap up the sign-in process by pressing the "Sign in" button. It's exactly what we would do with a browser in front of us.

We verify that the page contains the welcome message by using the has_content?() method. Running Cucumber again, we see everything's passing. Success!

```
% rake cucumber
...
1 scenario (1 passed)
3 steps (3 passed)
0m0.005s
```

Now we *know* our sign-in process works, and we've built up step definitions that we'll need to use in future scenarios. We can use them now to check our comment form. Let's add features/comments.feature.

Since all of our comment scenarios require a signed-in user, we'll add our first two sign-in steps (we don't need to check the welcome message) as a background. This will will make them run before each scenario automatically.[11]

artflow/js/features/comments.feature
```
Background:
  Given I am designer "Lindsay Bluth" with an account
  And I sign in
```

We also want to make sure there's a creation around for us to add comments to. Let's add a new step to our background:

artflow/js/features/comments.feature
```
  Background:
    Given I am designer "Lindsay Bluth" with an account
➤   And a creation
    And I sign in
```

This is a step that's around purely to set up some data for us, just like when we created our designer. Its implementation is a bit more complex, though, because we need to create the ecosystem of associated records for the creation and make sure it belongs to our designer! We add the step definition in features/step_definitions/creation_steps.rb:

---

10. http://rubydoc.info/github/jnicklas/capybara/file/README.md
11. https://github.com/cucumber/cucumber/wiki/Background

> ### Show Me the Page
>
> Sometimes when we encounter an error or an unexpected step failure, we may want to see what the content of the actual page that Cucumber is interacting with looks like.
>
> We can do this by adding a step definition that calls the Capybara method save_and_open_page(), for instance:
>
> ```
> Then /^show me the page$/ do
>   save_and_open_page
> end
> ```
>
> When Cucumber executes this step (and the Launchy library is installed), Capybara will pop up a browser window, showing the page content. We won't be able to interact with the page (since our application isn't running), but we can view the source and verify that the page looks as expected or fix our step definitions to suit.[a]
>
> ---
>
> a.   http://rubygems.org/gems/launchy

artflow/js/features/step_definitions/creation_steps.rb

```ruby
Given 'a creation' do

  # Create client record
  client = Client.create!(name: 'TestClient',
                          email: 'client@test.artflowme.com',
                          password: 'testtest',
                          password_confirmation: 'testtest')
  campaign = client.campaigns.create!(name: 'National 1')
  project = campaign.projects.create!(name: 'Pamphlet')
  # Add current user to project
  project.designers << @user
  # Add creation
  sample = File.open('test/fixtures/creation.png')
➤ @creation = project.creations.create!(name: "Logo",
➤                                        designer: @user,
➤                                        description: "Test",
➤                                        file: sample)
end
```

Now we'll add our first scenario to the file, verifying that the comment form is visible to our user before any comments have been added. This is important: the user needs the form to add the first comment!

artflow/js/features/comments.feature

```
Scenario: Designer sees form when comments empty
  When I go to the creation's page
  Then there should be 0 comments
  Then the comment form should be visible
```

We'll put the step definitions in features/step_definitions/comment_steps.rb.

artflow/js/features/step_definitions/comment_steps.rb
```
When /^I go to the creation's page$/ do
  visit creation_path(@creation)
end

Then /^there should be (\d+) comments?$/ do |number|
  assert_equal Integer(number), all(:css, '#comments li').size
end

Then /^the comment form should be visible$/ do
  assert has_selector?(:css, 'form#new_comment')
end
```

The visit() method has made another appearance here by taking us to the creation's page. We kept around the creation we generated earlier just so we could figure out the right URL to go to.

To check the number of comments, we match a count in our step and compare it to the number of <li> tags we can find inside our comment list using Capybara's all() method.

The has_content?() method we used earlier has a brother, has_selector?(), that we use in our third step to make certain our comment form is present in the document.

Running rake cucumber shows we're on track; our designer can reach the creation page and see the form. Now let's see if we can get a comment submitted! It's time to run a browser.

By default, when Capybara runs our Cucumber steps, it uses the Rack::Test driver, which is very fast since it doesn't need to drive a browser session, but it doesn't support JavaScript.[12] We can tell it to use the Selenium driver (and Firefox) instead by adding a Cucumber tag, @javascript, to our scenarios.[13]

We'll use that tag in our next scenario, testing the comment form we created in *Building a Remote Form*, on page 106:

artflow/js/features/comments.feature
```
@javascript
Scenario: Designer adds comment
  When I go to the creation's page
  Then there should be 0 comments
  When I enter a comment and submit it
  Then there should be 1 comment
```

---

12. https://github.com/brynary/rack-test
13. http://seleniumhq.org/

We only need to add one custom step definition for this scenario to run, which is to add some text to the comment form and then submit it:

```
artflow/js/features/step_definitions/comment_steps.rb
When /^I enter a comment and submit it$/ do
  fill_in('comment_body', with: 'Test Comment')
  click_button('Add Comment')
end
```

We told Capybara to fill_in() the form field that matched comment_body. Earlier when we used fill_in(), on page 113, we could rely on the name of the associated label() tags, but here we can't, since our <textarea> doesn't have one. Thankfully Capybara's flexible enough to handle either case.

Now that we have everything in place, we can run our new, JavaScript-enabled scenario with rake cucumber.

This time things work a bit differently. The other scenarios run just as before, but when Cucumber hits our new scenario, a browser window opens and, guided by Cucumber, acts out our scenario, testing our full user interface.

Now that we know how to automate a battery of tests against our user interface, let's look at how our team can use Selenium to manually test our application without having to know a line of code.

Manual Testing with Selenium IDE

There are tools out there to make manual testing a reasonable choice, too, especially for team members without access to our application code and test suite. One favorite of our quality assurance team is the Selenium IDE, which allows them to record the tests while browsing the site in Mozilla Firefox, as shown in Figure 12, *The Selenium IDE in Firefox*, on page 117.

To install the Selenium IDE, we simply visit the Selenium website with Firefox and install the extension.[14] After it's in, we visit our ArtFlow application in Firefox and start the Selenium IDE.

When we click Add Creation, it calls a function called clickAndWait(), which does exactly what a user would do: it clicks a link and waits for it to load. The parameter of link= is what is called a *locator*, and it lets us select a block of text and act upon it, in this case, by clicking it.

Once we've followed a particular flow or a UI flow that we want to test, we can stop recording and save the test by selecting Save Test Case from the File menu in the IDE.

---

14. http://www.seleniumhq.com/download/

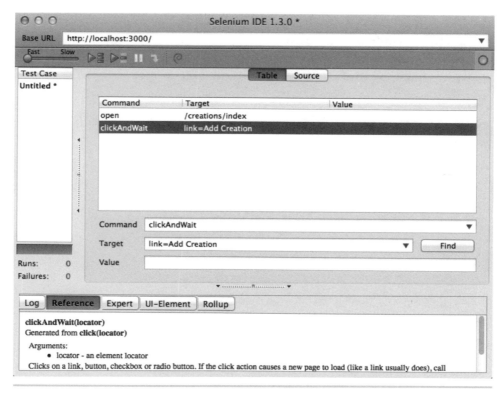

Figure 12—The Selenium IDE in Firefox

One of the other powers of Selenium is its ability to work with a third-party solution, like SauceLabs' OnDemand offering,[15] which uses Selenium Remote Control and Selenium Grid,[16] to test multiple browsers at once. This will let us address these browsers and find out if our JavaScript is breaking or if there are other UI issues that may haunt us.

You can find out more about Selenium testing and driving it with Ruby and Cucumber in *Web Development Recipes* [HWWJ12] and *Scripted GUI Testing with Ruby* [Dee08], both published by The Pragmatic Bookshelf.

4.3 Wrapping Up

In this chapter we've dug into JavaScript and CoffeeScript and how we can use them from Rails unobtrusively. We learned how to wire Ruby and Java-Script together to make asynchronous requests that keep our users on task

15. http://saucelabs.com/ondemand
16. http://selenium-grid.seleniumhq.org/

and in one place, and we've discovered we can use Cucumber and Selenium to test our user interface to make sure it works correctly. Next up, we tackle one of the most complex aspects of view development (and one of Rails's greatest strengths): building usable, maintainable forms.

If I want your opinion, I'll ask you to fill out the
necessary forms.

> ➤ *Unknown*

CHAPTER 5

Building Maintainable Forms

Forms, in many ways, are the core interface that users rely on to interact with the applications we write. Forms allow us to get input from the user and to support users signing in, submitting content, and searching for data —really, to do just about anything meaningful. Keeping our form code clean and easy to read, maintain, and extend means we can react to user feedback more quickly and produce consistent input UI changes across our application more easily.

There's a lot going on in a good form—labels and field layout, hints, placeholders, default values, validation errors—but all of this complexity is manageable using the tools that Rails provides.

In this chapter we'll build the creation form for the creation management application we've been developing, ArtFlow. First we'll build the form using standard Rails helpers, then we'll clean it up by creating our own custom form builder (a powerful but underused feature of Rails), and finally we'll learn how some tools the Rails community has developed can take us even further. When we're done, the form used by designers, clients, and managers to upload and annotate creations will feel simple and intuitive to everyone— even us! We'll lay the groundwork for that form first.

5.1 Using Semantic Form Tags

When we build forms to create or update records in Rails, we use the form_for() helper. This helper does a lot of work for us, including automatically determining which HTML action and method to use for the record based on Rails and REST conventions.

We start the form for our ArtFlow creation using form_for() in app/views/creations/_form.html.erb:

```
<%= form_for @creation do |f| %>
<% end %>
```

That's as basic as a form gets, though this is quite a bit less than what's actually useful! What we can see, though, is that our form_for() helper accepts a block (everything between the do and the end) and yields a form builder instance (which we call f).[1] We'll use methods on this form builder instance to generate our fields themselves. We start with name and description, plus a submit button for good measure:

```
<%= form_for @creation do |f| %>
  <%= f.label :name %>
  <%= f.text_field :name %>

  <%= f.label :description %>
  <%= f.text_area :description, cols: 40, rows: 4 %>

  <%= f.submit %>
<% end %>
```

We added labels to our fields with label(); this form builder method generates <label> HTML tags, which tell our users the name of the field and provide an easy way to focus the related form control (by letting users click the labels). We associated our labels to the name and description form controls by passing their names as arguments to label().

The form controls themselves are pretty easy to understand too. The name form control uses text_field(), which produces an <input> element with type="text" suitable for single-line entry. Our description is a more substantial form control, a <textarea>, generated with the text_area() method.

We can't forget our file_field, can we? This would be a pretty poor creation form if we couldn't actually upload a creation!

```
➤ <%= form_for @creation, html: {multipart: true} do |f| %>
    <%= f.label :name %>
    <%= f.text_field :name %>
    <%= f.label :description %>
    <%= f.text_area :description, cols: 40, rows: 4 %>

➤   <%= f.label :file %>
➤   <%= f.file_field :file %>

    <%= f.submit %>
<% end %>
```

---

1. We'll go into detail about form builders in Section 5.2, *Building Custom Form Builders*, on page 132.

Joe asks:
What About form_tag Instead of form_for?

form_tag() is the generic form tag helper and can be used to create ad hoc forms. Because form_tag() doesn't have the model-related smarts of form_for(), we don't use it when the form's subject is a model: we'd rather let Rails do the extra work for us. Why figure out which URL to send the form results to and what the current value of every field is if we don't have to?

One case where it makes sense to use form_tag() is when we'd just like a parameter or two sent to an action: for instance, a search form that submits a parameter named q entered in a text_field_tag().[a]

When your form is backed by a model, use form_for(). When it's not, use form_tag().

---

a.   For an example of a search form that has been implemented with form_tag(), see http://guides.rubyonrails.org/form_helpers.html#a-generic-search-form.

Notice we modified our form_for() invocation to pass multipart: true. This option tells Rails to generate the <form> tag with an enctype attribute that will force the request to be encoded as multipart/form-data. If we forgot this, we'd only be sending the filename, so we're glad we caught it!

Right now the form is just a loose bag of mixed labels and form controls. We add some structure to more clearly define how these elements are related so it makes a little more sense when we read it (and so we can style it more easily). Let's start by adding a <fieldset>.

The Case for Fieldsets

There is an HTML element ignored by Rails scaffolding (and unknown to many developers) called <fieldset>. It is, as the name would imply, a group of fields that are somehow associated. In the wilds of static HTML, you might see an example like this:

```
<fieldset>
  <legend>Label for this Fieldset</legend>
  <!-- inputs, etc -->
</fieldset>
```

The <legend> here is, in effect, the label for the <fieldset>. A standard browser rendering of this looks something like this:

⌐Label for this Fieldset────────────────────────
│
│
└

Using a <fieldset> is great for things like address blocks and credit card blocks in e-commerce systems, not to mention grouping a series of checkboxes or radio buttons into a single input. We use <fieldset> to group related fields in our forms and rely on it for styling. Even when there's one group of fields in a form, it's a good habit to get into, so we'll add it to our creation form, skipping the optional <legend>:

```
<%= form_for @creation do |f| %>
  <fieldset>
    <%= f.label :name %>
    <%= f.text_field :name %>

    <%= f.label :description %>
    <%= f.text_area :description, cols: 40, rows: 4 %>
  </fieldset>
  <%= f.submit %>
<% end %>
```

Let's get these fieldsets lined up.

Laying Out Fields

The layout of the form isn't quite right yet; we have our labels and their related form controls in a <fieldset>, but since they're all inline elements, everything is placed in one long horizontal line!

We'd like a vertical form with each label above its form control, which turns out to be more readable than side-by-side pairings[2]—and definitely more usable than the mess we have now!

We could add some CSS to force each element to display: block, but that won't give us the level of control we'd like for styling, plus it feels a little like a dirty hack. Since it's pretty safe to say that a <fieldset> consists of a *list* of fields, let's use a list to break this up; we'd like a tag around each field that groups the label and form control for styling anyway.

```
<%= form_for @creation, html: {multipart: true} do |f| %>
  <fieldset>
    <ol>
      <li>
        <%= f.label :name %>
        <%= f.text_field :name %>
      </li>
      <li>
        <%= f.label :description %>
```

---

2. See the extensive usability testing by Luke Wroblewski at http://www.lukew.com/resources/ articles/web_forms.html.

```
      <%= f.text_area :description, cols: 40, rows: 4 %>
    </li>
    <li>
      <%= f.label :file %>
      <%= f.file_field :file %>
    </li>
  </ol>
</fieldset>
<%= f.submit %>
<% end %>
```

Now we add a little CSS to give each label its own line by default; we want that vertical form! Let's add a style to app/assets/stylesheets/forms.css.scss:

artflow/forms/app/assets/stylesheets/forms.css.scss
```
fieldset label {
  display: block;
}
```

We can't forget to add a require directive for this style sheet to our application.css manifest so that it's included:

```
/*
 *= require_self
 *= require reset
 *= require layout
 *= require sidebar
➤ *= require forms
 */
```

Things are really coming together; as we can see in the browser, our labels and form controls are perfectly stacked against the left side of the form:

Name

Description

File

(Choose File) No file chosen

(Create Asset)

This is a good start on our form, but what happens when things get more complex?

Wrapping Fields in Tags

There's a lot of conflicting opinions about which tag (or tags) is most suitable for grouping labels with their form controls. Persuasive arguments can be made for using <li> inside ordered and unordered lists, going the ultra-semantic route with description (formerly "definition") lists (whose <dt> and <dd> pairs sadly don't provide an easily stylable grouping) and treating the fieldset as a normal flow of paragraph tags. Some might even claim that, as a purely display-related issue, generic <div> tags are the best fit.

We picked an ordered list (<ol>) because it most resembles how we see the natural structure and purpose of a form: a list of fields our users fill in one by one. The fact that we could come up with a reasonable semantic choice ruled out using a <div> from the very beginning.

Side-by-Side Fields

If only our form could stay this simple, but in reality sometimes we need to support side-by-side labels and form controls.

For our creation form we've been tasked to add a secondary fieldset with some printing-related metadata for our creations (since our designers have the good fortune of being tasked with print design, too):

```
<fieldset id='creation-print' class='inline'>
  <ol>
    <li>
      <%= f.label :color_space %>
      <%= f.select :color_space, %w(CMYK RGB Other) %>
    </li>
    <li>
      <%= f.label :bleed, "Bleed size (in.)" %>
      <%= f.text_field :bleed, size: 5 %>
    </li>
  </ol>
</fieldset>
```

This new fieldset needs to look a bit different, with a smaller font size and side-by-side labels and form controls. Easy enough—with a bit of CSS we can make sure our labels sit to the left of the form controls and line up correctly:

```
artflow/forms/app/assets/stylesheets/forms.css.scss
fieldset#creation-print {
    font-size: 0.9em;
}
fieldset.inline label {
    display: inline;
    width: 240px;
}
```

We normally don't want to use a class named "inline," as it confuses style with markup. For this purpose, we'll show it, but we would want to replace that name with something more meaningful—for example, the contents of the fieldset or some other designator. With this in place, a horizontal layout pops into view for our print-related fields:

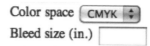

Supporting inline fields on a case-by-case basis isn't difficult either. For instance, in our creation form's main fieldset we need to include a form control designers can toggle to indicate if the creation is visible to the client. It's a checkbox, and it looks a bit weird placed below its label instead of next to it. We'll fix that by switching the order of the label and the field, then adding a more focused CSS selector for the <li>:

```
artflow/forms/app/assets/stylesheets/forms.css.scss
fieldset.inline label,
➤ fieldset li.inline label {
    display: inline;
    width: 240px;
}
```

We can even switch the order of the label and the checkbox (so the checkbox is to the left) without having to edit the CSS, since we're just using inline and don't need to deal with floats:

```
<li class='inline'>
  <%= f.check_box :visible %>
  <%= f.label :visible, 'Visible to client?' %>
</li>
```

Our use of .inline for both <fieldset> and <li> brings up an important point: CSS specificity.

The Important of Being Explicit

Imagine if we had multiple developers/designers working on this form (and others in our application), and they all had ideas on different tags that could be used to define content that should be shown inline. What would happen if, instead of using specific CSS selectors, they decided to use a more generic selector like .inline? What if someone else modified it later to match how his/her tag should look? They'd step all over each other, especially in cases where a tag itself wasn't inline but contained elements that should be (like our <fieldset> above). In CSS, context (and specificity) is everything; to prevent unexpected styling elsewhere, we need to make our selectors a little more explicit.

> **Joe asks:**
> ## What About CSS Frameworks?
>
> There are a bevy of CSS frameworks out there, and many have extensive definitions loaded up from the get-go (some of them very useful in laying out forms). While this can help jump-start your work in certain instances, it can also be a chain around your neck as your forms become more complex. We looked at some of these in Chapter 3, *Adding Cascading Style Sheets*, on page 73.

Generic classes can cause nightmares for developers; CSS is hard to document clearly, and tracking down unexpected display behavior (someone else's idea of how everyone else's inline class should look) can be time-consuming and frustrating.

While providing more specific selectors may seem verbose and can create longer style sheets, it can also reduce nightmares of views breaking left and right when development is moving at a good clip. Why slam on the design brakes?

We don't *start* with generalized CSS classes; we work *toward* them as we notice commonalities appear in various places throughout our application. It's an interactive refactoring process that developers will be familiar with elsewhere.

Getting specific is easy to accomplish when using CSS selectors. There is a variety of selectors in the CSS2 and CSS3 references at the W3C.[3]

Now that we've tackled the basics of single-column form layout and have some solid CSS selector practices to follow, we'll look at how usability can become more complicated when our form grows another column.

Tabbing Order

Time passes and requirements change. Now we've been told our little fieldset of print-related metadata, which had been languishing at the bottom of our form, needs to be placed at the top right of our form so print designers see it immediately.

Up to the top it goes:

```
<%= form_for @creation, html: {multipart: true} do |f| %>
➤   <fieldset id='creation-print' class='inline'>
➤     <legend>Print Details</legend>
```

---

3. http://www.w3.org/TR/CSS2/selector.html and http://www.w3.org/TR/css3-selectors/, respectively.

```
➤      <ol>
➤        <li>
➤          <%= f.label :color_space %>
➤          <%= f.select :color_space, %w(CMYK RGB Other) %>
➤        </li>
➤        <li>
➤          <%= f.label :bleed, "Bleed size" %>
➤          <%= f.text_field :bleed, size: 5, placeholder: "Inches" %>
➤        </li>
➤      </ol>
➤    </fieldset>
    <fieldset>
      <ol>
        <li>
          <%= f.label :name %>
          <%= f.text_field :name %>
        </li>
        <li>
          <%= f.label :description %>
          <%= f.text_area :description, cols: 80, rows: 4 %>
        </li>
        <li>
          <%= f.label :file %>
          <%= f.file_field :file %>
        </li>
      </ol>
    </fieldset>
    <%= f.submit %>
<% end %>
```

We've also added a <legend > tag to describe these fields as "print details," and we've set the size and placeholder HTML attributes of bleed to give our users a hint as to the value that's expected (we might as well do things right). Now we float the fieldset to the right with a little CSS:

artflow/forms/app/assets/stylesheets/forms.css.scss
```
fieldset#creation-print {
    float: right;
}
```

Wait, now we've screwed up our tab ordering! Our users spend all day in the application, adding and updating creations, and they rely on tabbing to quickly fill out the form. While we need the print details at the top of the form, we don't want them replacing more important, general-purpose fields in the tab order.

Thankfully there's a way to manually indicate how tabbing between form controls works: while by default tabs will cycle through any <a>, <area>,

<button>, <input>, <object>, <select>, or <textarea> element in the page, we can use tabindex to change this behavior.

First off, we need to think like a user. What are the first things our user would be likely to edit in our form? Probably the creation name and *not* the color space or bleed settings (nor the upsell link in the sidebar the guy in marketing added for clients to see). The tab ordering should directly relate to what's important for our users.

These should not be our navigation items. A good case in point from elsewhere in our application is the login form. tabindex="1" should probably be the user or email field, and the next item (2) should probably be the password field. And finally? You got it—the Submit button. We should take the same amount of care with all the forms in our application, especially a form as important as the creation form.

We can see this in our revised form in app/views/creations/_form.html.erb:

```erb
<%= form_for @creation, html: {multipart: true} do |f| %>
➤   <fieldset id='creation-print' class='inline'>
➤     <legend>Print Details</legend>
➤     <ol>
➤       <li>
➤         <%= f.label :color_space %>
➤         <%= f.select :color_space, %w(CMYK RGB Other),
➤                     tabindex: '4' %>
➤       </li>
➤       <li>
➤         <%= f.label :bleed, "Bleed size" %>
➤         <%= f.text_field :bleed, size: 5,
➤                                 placeholder: "Inches",
➤                                 tabindex: 5 %>
➤       </li>
➤     </ol>
➤   </fieldset>
    <fieldset>
      <ol>
        <li>
          <%= f.label :name %>
          <%= f.text_field :name, tabindex: '1' %>
        </li>
        <li>
          <%= f.label :description %>
          <%= f.text_area :description, cols: 80,
                                        rows: 4,
                                        tabindex: 2  %>
        </li>
        <li>
          <%= f.label :file %>
```

```
        <%= f.file_field :file, tabindex: 3  %>
      </li>
    </ol>
  </fieldset>
  <%= f.submit %>
<% end %>
```

Grouping Options

The <option> element is a child element of a form <select>. In our creation form, for instance, we'd like our designers to categorize the type and dimensions of a creation used in advertising across both print and Web.

We could mix these together, but as there's a pretty clear separation conceptually, why not group the options in our <select> as well? This will make it easier for users to find the option they're looking for when filling out the form. We can do this with <optgroup>.

The select() method on form builders doesn't support generating <optgroup> tags, so we'll need to create our <select> using a combination of the more general purpose select_tag() and grouped_options_for_select() helpers. Here's what we put in our form:

```
<%= ad_dimensions_tag(f) %>
```

In our CreationsHelper, we define ad_dimensions_tag():

artflow/forms/app/helpers/creations_helper.rb
```
def ad_dimensions_tag(builder)
  options = grouped_options_for_select(ad_dimensions_options,
                                       builder.object.ad_dimensions)
  select_tag('creation[ad_dimensions]', options)
end

def ad_dimensions_options
  [
   ['Print',
    ['legal', 'letter', 'half letter', 'half legal', 'other print']],
   ['Web',
    ['full banner', 'half banner', 'vertical banner', 'button']]
  ]
end
```

Our ad_dimensions_tag() helper calls ad_dimension_options() for the possible values of our tag. For the moment we're using a limited set of options—there are a lot of standard advertisement dimensions. Later we may want to pull these from another source or even create a model for them (with an association to Creation).

Automatically Focusing Form Elements

A nice touch to making web apps more usable is to automatically move the focus to the first form field in our form. It's just one less tab that users have to hit—potentially one of many, depending on their settings.

In HTML5, we can simply add `autofocus` to the input that we want to have this jump to, like so:

```
<%= f.text_field :name, autofocus: true %>
```

Since this only works in browsers that recognize HTML5 attributes on elements, we need to go ahead and provide a JavaScript fallback. We want to detect this so that it doesn't run on our newer browsers. We add a new CoffeeScript file at app/assets/javascripts/forms.js.coffee to handle this.

```
artflow/forms/app/assets/javascripts/forms.js.coffee
$(document).ready ->
  if not Modernizr.input.autofocus
    $('#creation_name').trigger 'focus'
```

Remember Modernizr? We added it to our layout in *Turning on HTML5 for Internet Explorer and Older Browsers*, on page 9. Here we use it to see if the browser supports autofocus. If it doesn't, we autofocus our creation name field manually with a bit of jQuery.

Let's make sure we add a `require` directive for our form's JavaScript to our application.js manifest:

```
artflow/forms/app/assets/javascripts/application.js
//= require modernizr-1.7.custom
//= require jquery
//= require jquery_ujs
//= require comments
➤ //= require forms
```

Now we'll add some more design metadata to our creations form.

To determine the current value of the field, ad_dimensions_tag() calls ad_dimensions() on builder.object, which is our creation instance.

The result speaks for itself (Figure 13, *Selection options for ad dimensions*, on page 131).

This provides a much clearer delineation and grouping of select options and allows for a user to find the ad dimensions faster; instead of hunting through a long list of mixed dimensions, a designer working on a legal-sized print ad can find it quicker under Print.

Now we'll see what we tell our users when they submit a form with bad or missing data.

Figure 13—Selection options for ad dimensions

Displaying Errors

Nothing's more frustrating to users than a form that they can't successfully submit for reasons they can't figure out. Providing users with useful feedback when they fail to provide a Rails action with the information it needs (to pass model validations, for instance) is something we need to take very seriously.

In our creation form, a number of the fields we've defined are required for validations. We've taken care to make this apparent by adding a required CSS class to the markup for those fields. For example, for name we use this:

```
<li class='required'>
  <%= f.label :name %>
  <%= f.text_field :name, autofocus: true %>
</li>
```

Our CSS for this is simple; we simply bold the <label>:

```
artflow/forms/app/assets/stylesheets/forms.css.scss
fieldset li.required label {
    font-weight: bold;
}
```

If a user submits our form and a validation for name fails, Rails will wrap both our <label> and <input> (generated by text_field()) in a <div> with a .field_with_errors CSS class when the form is re-rendered.

We can highlight our <input> tags and change the text color of our <label> easily enough to make the problem more obvious:

```
artflow/forms/app/assets/stylesheets/forms.css.scss
fieldset div.field_with_errors {
  label {
    color: #f00; /* red */
  }
  input {
    background: #ffc; /* light yellow */
  }
}
```

If we want to show the specific error messages, there are a number of options. We could use the error_messages() form builder method that's been extracted to a separate gem,[4] which would let us add the following to our form:

```
<%= f.error_messages %>
```

This is a pattern that was commonly used before Rails 3, and it provides a block of configurable errors that can be styled to look good, as Yahoo has done in its design pattern library.[5]

Another option is to check and display the errors beside the fields themselves. This is the preferred option, as it puts the cause of the problem directly next to the field where a user can fix it. Instead of adding this nice (but verbose) feature ourselves, we'll look at a prepackaged solution in *Formtastic*, on page 138.

We've put together a pretty solid beginning on our creation form, starting with a simple form_for() and adding <fieldset> tags, handling different form layouts, and tackling usability issues like grouped options, tabindex, and autofocus.

Next we'll look at how we can extend the form builders form_for() to do more of the heavy lifting, simplifying some of the semantic boilerplate we've been using.

5.2 Building Custom Form Builders

In Section 5.1, *Using Semantic Form Tags*, on page 119, we built a semantic form from the ground up using the form_for() helper and learned that it yields an object to the body of our form:

```
<%= form_for @creation, html: {multipart: true} do |f| %>
<% end %>
```

What is this mysterious object, this f that's yielded to the body of the form?

---

4.   https://github.com/joelmoss/dynamic_form
5.   http://developer.yahoo.com/ypatterns/ and http://developer.yahoo.com/ypatterns/about/stencils/.

Meet ActionView::Helpers::FormBuilder. It might just be the best friend you never knew you had.

The FormBuilder instance yielded to our block knows all about the object the form is handling (in our case, @creation) and has access to the template so that it can generate and insert tags. It can check for errors, create labels and inputs for attributes, and even change a portion of a form to handle a completely different object (using f.fields_for).

Since form builders know all about the object we're building the form to create or modify, it can really reduce the hoops we have to jump through to create our form fields: it can make decisions about fields so we don't have to. Take a simple text field, for example. If we were using the generic text_field_tag(), here's how we might add a <textarea> to allow designers to edit the body of a comment they made to a client (oops, they called him "Jim" instead of "James"!). We do this in app/views/comments/_form.html.erb:

```
<%= text_area_tag 'comment[body]', @comment.body %>
```

We need to provide the name of the field and the current value, since text_area_tag() doesn't have the first clue about our comment. When we're using a form_for @comment, things become significantly more succinct and magical:

artflow/forms/app/views/comments/_form.html.erb
```
<%= f.text_area :body %>
```

Here the form builder handles all the details. We don't need to tell it what to name the field; it knows what the standard convention is and applies it, freeing us from the vagaries of typos and accidental misnaming. It also deals with inserting the current value of the comment; since the record was supplied to form_for() and safely hidden away in the form builder (as its object>, as we'll see later), it can just ask the comment for its body. We don't need to get involved —it's a pretty boring conversation that we don't need to know about. Since we've got bigger fish to fry than mucking around with field names and value insertions that Rails can do easier, faster, and more reliably, we let it handle the details.

FormBuilder really shines, however, when we go beyond the stock helpers it provides and extend it to support the specific requirements of our applications. If our forms have been designed to follow a consistent pattern, why not codify that pattern in a little domain-specific language we can use easily? Why not convince our form builders to do a little more heavy lifting for us, building in the helpers for the look-and-feel of our forms instead of using them à la carte?

Defining a Form Builder

To create our own FormBuilder, we just create a new class that inherits from ActionView::Helpers::FormBuilder. For our application we'll create ApplicationFormBuilder in our lib/application_form_builder.rb:

```
class ApplicationFormBuilder < ActionView::Helpers::FormBuilder
end
```

Great, now we just need to make sure Rails can find it. Autoloading is a facility that Rails uses to automatically require() files when it encounters a constant that it doesn't recognize in an attempt to resolve the constant. It does this by a simple naming convention, looking under a whitelist of directories. New in Rails 3, lib/ has been removed from that list. Since we're going to conform to the naming conventions (putting modules in subdirectories, etc.), we'll tell Rails it's really okay to allow autoloading from lib/. We modify our config/application.rb and set the following:

artflow/forms/config/application.rb
```
config.autoload_paths += %W(#{config.root}/lib)
```

We can drop into the console quickly and see that our autoloading is working:

```
% rails console
>> ApplicationFormBuilder
 => ApplicationFormBuilder
```

Autoloading is working just fine, so our new form builder class is accessible and ready to be used. Now to make it do something useful!

Simplifying Markup

We've made a few important decisions about how the forms in ArtFlow should be structured. We'd like to make sure all of our forms follow this structure consistently, so we'll build some tools other developers on our team can use to make it as easy as possible.

In our forms all of our fields are surrounded by <li> tags and include a <label>. In the ArtFlow's creation form in app/views/creations/_form.html.erb, it would be nice to have a new method on our form builder, field_item(), that creates these tags for us:

```
<%= f.field_item :name do %>
  <%= f.text_field :name %>
<% end %>
```

Instant <li> and <label> tags! Now, how do we do it? We open up our form builder class in lib/application_form_builder.rb and add field_item():

```
def field_item(attribute, text = nil, &block)
  @template.content_tag :li do
    @template.concat @template.label(attribute, text)
    yield
  end
end
```

Our method starts out by calling a helper, content_tag(), to create our <li> tag. Since it's a normal helper (and not a method on the form builder itself, it needs to be called on @template, our form builder's reference to the template itself. We pass a block to content_tag(), which will be used to generate the tags inside the<li>.

The other method we call on @template is concat(). This method takes its argument (in this case, the generated <label> tag) and adds it to the template output at that point (just as if we used a <%= %> ERB tag.

Finally, our method calls yield, executing the block we passed to field_item() in the template, which inserts the text input for our name field (but could insert any form control we'd like).

The nice thing about this is that, once written, our team won't have to remember (or care about) the details of how fields are created, and in the future if we need to change the way fields are laid out, we only need to edit one place.

Before we can use our ApplicationFormBuilder in our application, we need to configure Rails to use it for forms.

Hooking It Up

The first à la carte method to tell Rails to use our form builder is the :builder option for form_for(). Let's modify app/views/creations/_form.html.erb:

```
<%= form_for @creation, builder: ApplicationFormBuilder,
                        html: {multipart: true} do |f| %>
<% end %>
```

This can get a bit tedious; it's unlikely we'd want to use multiple builders anyhow, so instead let's set our FormBuilder as the default for form_for(). To do this, we need to add an initializer in config/initializers:

artflow/forms/config/initializers/form_builder_initializer.rb
```
ActionView::Base.default_form_builder = ApplicationFormBuilder
```

Now all our forms will have access to the new form builder methods without using the :builder option.

Now we'll take a look at how we can make our form builder a bit smarter.

Getting Introspective

Often in a form builder we'll want to do more than just take the pain out of retyping commonly used tags; we may want to introspect and interact with the object the form references in new and interesting ways.

Getting a hold of the referenced object is easy in a form builder: it's assigned to the @object instance variable.

We'd love to add attribute-specific errors right next to the fields. We add an errors_on() method to our form builder:

artflow/forms/lib/application_form_builder.rb
```
def errors_on(attribute)
  if @object.errors[attribute].any?
    @template.content_tag(:span,
      @object.errors[attribute].to_sentence,
      class: 'error'
    )
  end
end
```

The idea here is simple—if there are any errors on the object for our attribute, we return a <span> tag flagged with an error CSS class. We can build this into our field_item() method:

artflow/forms/lib/application_form_builder.rb
```
def field_item(attribute, text = nil, &block)
  @template.content_tag :li do
    @template.concat @template.label(attribute, text)
    yield
    @template.concat errors_on(attribute)
  end
end
```

We can't forget that Rails already, by default, wraps all attribute-related fields in a <div> with a CSS class of field_with_errors. We don't really need that now, so we turn it off by changing out the field_error_proc it uses so that it just returns the generated field without adding a <div>; it changes the structure of our markup unnecessarily.

artflow/forms/config/initializers/form_builder_initializer.rb
```
ActionView::Base.field_error_proc = ->(field, instance) { field }
```

Great, now we have automatically generated <li> tags, labels, and error messages for each field. We can take it a level further, too; usually we're going to be building fields with text_field() anyway—and there aren't that many other types of form control. What if we created a method for each type, taking care of the whole thing? We can even throw in the new HTML5 input types, repurposing the helpers we added in Chapter 2, *Improving Readability*, on page 49.

artflow/forms/lib/application_form_builder.rb
```ruby
def email_field_item(attribute, *args)
  field = email_field_tag(attribute, @object.send(attribute), *args)
  field_item do
    @template.concat field
  end
end
def number_field_item(attribute, *args)
  field = number_field_tag(attribute, @object.send(attribute), *args)
  field_item do
    @template.concat field
  end
end
def range_field_item(attribute, *args)
  field = range_field_tag(attribute, @object.send(attribute), *args)
  field_item do
    @template.concat field
  end
end
```

It might be a little tempting to do something like this to try to guess the right form control for the attribute:

artflow/forms/lib/application_form_builder.rb
```ruby
def guess_field_item(attribute, *args)
  # Match on attribute name...
  if attribute =~ /_url$/
    url_field_item(attribute, *args)
    # Match on attribute column type
  elsif @object.class.columns_hash[attribute.to_s].type == :integer
    number_field_item(attribute, *args)
  else
    # More insanity...
  end
end
```

We don't do this! It's easy enough to explicitly state which form control we want for an attribute; often the tricks necessary to determine how attributes should be editable automatically become so overblown that the code becomes unmaintainable. Keep in mind the level of mental overhead we'd add to your applications with code like this; why perform code backflips to solve a problem that doesn't exist?

If we really want our forms shorter and more "magical," maybe we should look at some prepackaged form builders others have created. One popular choice that might be worth a look is Formtastic.

Formtastic

Formtastic is a plugin by Justin French (and contributors) that packs a punch when it comes to easily building forms with more semantic, modern markup.[6] It doesn't act as a drop-in replacement for form_for(), but rather it gives you an easy-to-recognize semantic_form_for() helper that offers a whole slew of handy methods to get the job done—without the manual boilerplate we hate to type ourselves (but which should be a part of our forms nonetheless).

Adding Formtatstic to our Rails application is easy. First, we add the following line to our Gemfile:

artflow/forms/Gemfile
```
gem 'formtastic'
```

Then we use Bundler to handle the install.[7]

```
% bundle install
```

Once the Formtastic plugin has been added, we need to add a require directive to our application.css to include its styling, making sure it's included before our own form styles:

artflow/forms/app/assets/stylesheets/application.css
```
/*
 *= require_self
 *= require normalize
 *= require layout
 *= require sidebar
 *= require navigation
 *= require notifications
 *= require blueprint/typography
➤ *= require formtastic
 *= require forms
 */
```

Let's convert our earlier form in app/views/creations/_form.html.erb to use Formtastic, shall we?

```
<%= semantic_form_for @creation do |f| %>
  <%= f.inputs %>
  <%= f.buttons %>
<% end %>
```

Wait, that can't be it, can it? Let's take a look at the top bit of the form from the browser:

---

6. http://github.com/justinfrench/formtastic
7. http://gembundler.com

Project	My Project ⬍
Name*	
Stage*	

If we look under the covers, we'll quickly notice a few things. First, the form correctly uses the <fieldset> tag and even uses <ol>/<li> tags, which makes sense, given that a form is an ordered list of fields. It even lets you select associations (in this case, the creation's project) and shows required attributes!

We submit the form without a name and see that Formtastic is even showing errors like the errors_on() method we added to our custom form builder:

Project	My Project ⬍
Name*	
	can't be blank
Stage*	
	can't be blank

All of our fields are jumbled together right now; we separate our fieldsets and put them where they're needed. Formtastic still gives us control over where we place fields, what to call them, and smaller details—including inline hints.

artflow/forms/app/views/creations/_form.html.erb
```
<%= semantic_form_for @creation, html: {multipart: true} do |f| %>
  <%= f.inputs 'Print Details', id: 'creation-print', class: 'inline' do %>
    <%= f.input :color_space, collection: %w(CMYK RGB Other) %>
    <%= f.input :bleed, size: 5, placeholder: 'Inches' %>
  <% end %>
  <%= f.inputs do %>
    <%= f.input :name %>
    <%= f.input :description, input_html: {cols: 80, rows: 4} %>
    <%= f.input :file %>
  <% end %>
  <%= f.buttons %>
<% end %>
```

That's quite a bit shorter than what we built ourselves!

The thing that's really compelling about Formtastic is that it is semantic HTML that's *out of your way*. Here we have the rare case where what is right and what is easy are the same thing.

Formtastic has a lot of bells and whistles we could look at later, including easy internationalization and ways to build on additional input types (without the work it takes to add them to a vanilla form builder on your own).

Sometimes a less opinionated library is warranted, especially when it comes to building complex forms. In that case we'd use SimpleForm, a very flexible alternative.[8]

We've certainly come a long way from our hand-built form and have learned a lot about how form builders (either ones we build from scratch or community-maintained projects we extend) can help us make our forms more powerful and still maintain the Rails simplicity we love so dearly.

5.3 Looking Toward the Future of HTML5 Form Elements

HTML5 has provided us with a large variety of new form elements that aim to take a lot of the JavaScript complexity out of forms and make these common-use cases into actual HTML tags and attributes. Doing this lets us improve the interaction with our users by changing keyboard layouts on mobile devices and by formatting text in fields.

As we move into the future, we'll be able to use these elements in our applications. Some of them we can use today, especially if we are developing for iOS or Opera environments. But for many of these elements, we'll have to wait a year or two before we start using them every day.

Let's take a look at what the future holds for our forms.

The Elements

There are some browsers that handle these new form fields today, and the most common of these are Mobile Safari and iOS. Anyone who has spent time with an iPhone, iPad, or iPod Touch has seen the keyboard change based on the input. If we look at Figure 14, *The various iOS keyboards*, on page 141, we can see what these keyboard types are.

There is a default keyboard, which is used in most typing instances. This is automatically changed by altering the type attribute of an <input>. If we change the attribute to type="email", we end up with a space bar broken into three buttons: the space bar, the @ symbol, and a period. Any email address includes each of those at least once, so this change cuts down on having to hit the number button to get to additional symbols. If we make it type="tel",

---

8. https://github.com/plataformatec/simple_form

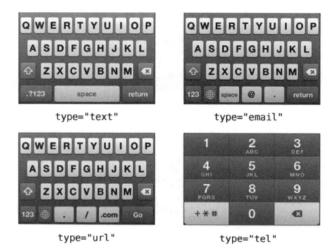

Figure 14—The various iOS keyboards

we get only a number pad with the ability to access some special characters. If we make it type="url", we are presented with something similar to email but without a space bar at all. Instead we see a period, a forward slash, and a ".com" button. The return key is replaced with a Go button as well.

The best part about using these new <input> types is that they will revert to a text input in browsers that don't understand the new functionality, so we can use them without fear of backward compatibility.

There are more than just these four types of inputs and other elements, but they aren't all currently supported in modern browsers. These include the following:

- color: An element to provide color picking.

- datetime: An input for putting in dates and times with various child elements of date, month, week, and time.

- keygen: An element to generate key pairs. Keeps the private key locally and sends the public key to the server.

- meter: A scalar measurement within a known range of numbers. Usable for scores, percentages, disk use, and more. Should not be used for progress of a download or other similar progress bar.

- output: An element for the result of a calculation between other inputs.

- progress: An element to show progress of a task, such as a file upload or server-side processing.

- range: An input for setting a range of options that a user can select within, such as "between 5 and 10."

- search: Widely supported in modern browsers and can be seen most dramatically in Safari, where Apple has changed the default look to have very rounded ends and a search icon inside of it.

In addition to these elements, there are a lot of new attributes to use in our form fields, such as required and placeholder. More information about these can be found on various sites on the Web, including the developers' specification.[9]

While the HTML5 elements promise that one day we'll be able to stop using JavaScript and have more semantic form tags for the core of interaction in our app, the reality is that they just aren't ready in most browsers (save Opera 11.50+).[10] For apps that only need brand-new browser support, experiment and see if they will work for you. The nature of working on the cutting edge is that you never know exactly when something will be supported. In some cases, some of these elements may have been removed from the working specification before you read this. Always check on the specification to see what is actually usable when it comes time to build out our forms.

5.4 Wrapping Up

During this chapter we've picked up a few techniques and tools that can help us clean up and make our forms more consistent by using semantic tags and form builders.

Unfortunately, many people never move beyond the most basic and shallow of helper methods, never embrace the idea of defining their own view-focused classes, and never reap the benefits we've discovered. In a way, it's a byproduct of the mixed nature of views; the templates make us forget that, just like the controller and model layers, the view layer has the full power of Ruby behind it.

As Rubyists, we should responsibly embrace the comprehensive and domain-specific use of our own Ruby classes in views. We'll be discussing some of these approaches in more depth in our next chapter, *Using Presenters*.

---

9. http://developers.whatwg.org/
10. http://wufoo.com/html5/

*I wouldn't give a nickel for the simplicity on this
side of complexity, but I would give my life for
the simplicity on the other side of complexity.*

➤ *Albert Einstein*

CHAPTER **6**

Using Presenters

There's a very limited amount of interaction between the view and controller layers in a Rails application. During rendering, instance variables are copied over, and the template has access to parameters and the session, but it's on its own to make sense of all the information that needs to come together to be displayed.

Sometimes the best way the view can do this is by using presenters, which are custom classes that simplify access to a model or other aggregation of information and know how to get at (or build) the information we need to display.

We've already run across this pattern when we worked with FormBuilder instances in Section 5.2, *Building Custom Form Builders*, on page 132, which knew how to build form fields for a record. It's time we learn how to build our own presenters from scratch. First we'll look at how we can use presenters in templates to help us more easily display information about model records, and then we will see how we can use presenters from controllers for data serialization.

In our ArtFlow application we need to display designer status information on the designer dashboard, the profile, and the administrative scheduling pages for our management team. The information shown for the designer status needs to be extracted from the objects associated with the designer: projects, creations, and clients that the designer is currently working with.

While we could do some of these lookups inline in our template and aggregate larger sets of data (like the project hours) in helpers or even in the model, it makes sense to live in our presenter instead because this data belongs together and is only used in this standardized view. Think of our presenter as a super-powered helper—a helper *object*.

6.1 Presenting a Record

Let's put together the presenter class to more easily expose the status data related to our Designer model. We call it DesignerStatus, since that's what it is, and to initialize it, we just pass in the Designer instance. We'll put it in lib/designer_status.rb:

```ruby
class DesignerStatus
  def initialize(designer)
    @designer = designer
  end
end
```

Our DesignerStatus inherits directly from Ruby's default Object class. While it's easy to become accustomed to using the classes that Rails provides, we're not limited to them. Just like Rails itself, we can build our own classes any time we like.

The data we need to pull together for the view is pulled from some associations on the designer. We add a few methods to our class:

```ruby
def active_projects_count
  active_projects.count
end

def pending_approvals_count
  active_creations.pending_approval.count
end

def approved_count
  active_creations.approved.count
end

def active_hours
  active_projects.total_hours
end

def hours_per_project
  active_projects.inject({}) do |memo, project|
    memo[project] = project.total_hours
    memo
  end
end

private

def active_projects
  @designer.projects.active
end
```

```
def active_creations
  @designer.creations.active
end
```

Our presenter only displays information on the active projects and creations for the designer, so we've created a couple of private methods, active_projects() and active_creations(), that handle getting that information for us. This way we won't need to have the same method chaining repeated in the methods we'll be calling from our template.

Now we need to instantiate our DesignerStatus presenter for use in our template. Sometimes it makes sense for the controller to set up the presenter, especially in cases where the presenter needs to be configured with session or request parameters. In this case, however, we prefer to instantiate our presenter in a helper because it's purely a view concern: it's only used from a template and it doesn't need any additional information about the request. The controller doesn't necessarily need to retrieve or instantiate every single object a template might need. Here it's the view's job. We'll use a helper method we'll put in app/helpers/designers_helper.rb to create the presenter instance.

```
module DesignersHelper
  def designer_status_for(designer = @designer)
    presenter = DesignerStatus.new(designer)
    if block_given?
      yield presenter
    else
      presenter
    end
  end
end
```

This helper takes an optional designer and defaults to the current @designer if it's not provided. When we're in an action template focused on a single designer (like the show() action of DesignersController), using this keeps our template brief and it doesn't lock us out of cases where we'd want to display status information for multiple designers on a single template, since we can just pass in the specific Designer record whenever we need it.

Once we instantiate our presenter, we yield it to the block if we can, which would let us invoke methods repeatedly on the presenter without having to assign it in the template (we *don't* do that, as we covered in Chapter 2, *Improving Readability*, on page 49).

Now that we have our presenter instance, let's put together the Designer Dashboard view that uses it, which is rendered by the DesignersController show() action from app/views/designers/show.html.erb:

```erb
<% designer_status_for do |status| %>
  <section class='designer-status'>
    <title>Status</title>
    <dl>
      <dt>Active Projects</dt>
      <dd><%= status.active_projects_count %></dd>
      <dt>Pending Approval</dt>
      <dd><%= status.pending_approvals_count %></dd>
      <dt>Approved</dt>
      <dd><%= status.approved_count %></dd>
    </dl>
    <h3>Active Project Hours</h3>
    <table>
      <tr>
        <th>Project</th>
        <th>Hours</th>
      </tr>
      <% status.hours_per_project.each do |project, hours| %>
        <tr>
          <td><%= link_to project.name, project %></td>
          <td><%= hours %></td>
        </tr>
      <% end %>
      <tr>
        <th>Total</th>
        <td><%= status.active_hours %></td>
      </tr>
    </table>
  </section>
<% end %>
```

This is great! We have all of these helpers bundled together into one unit without muddying our model or losing them in the crush of methods in our helper modules.

How can we support this more generically and make using the presenter elsewhere in the application as easy as possible? As we said before, we'd like to display this information in other places, too, but we'd like the information to be more condensed. Let's extract the designer status markup out of our show.html.erb into a partial, _status.html.erb, and add a condition to determine if we want the "expanded" view that includes our hourly breakdown by project. We'll also remove the designer_status_for() call since we won't need it; we'll be passing in our DesignerStatus instance when we render the partial, instead of creating it there.

artflow/presenters/app/views/designers/_status.html.erb
```erb
<section class='designer-status'>
  <title>Status</title>
  <dl>
```

> **Joe asks:**
> # When Should I Use a Presenter?
>
> Here are a few signs a part of your view could be better built or refactored as a presenter:
>
> - It displays specialized, complex data for a record or an aggregation of records, especially if it requires grouping, sorting, calculations, or transformation to new data structures for view-specific iteration.
>
> - It uses several interrelated helpers, especially if they call each other, pass around some type of shared state, are grouped together by a common prefix, or have been considered cohesive enough to be extracted into a separately named helper module.
>
> - It's displayed by an action whose authentication or other environmental constraints would make testing the view difficult or slow.

```erb
    <dt>Active Projects</dt>
    <dd class='active-projects'><%= status.active_projects_count %></dd>
    <dt>Pending Approval</dt>
    <dd class='pending-creations'><%= status.pending_approvals_count %></dd>
    <dt>Approved</dt>
    <dd class='approved-creations'><%= status.approved_count %></dd>
  </dl>
➤ <% if status.expanded? %>
    <h3>Active Project Hours</h3>
    <table>
      <tr>
        <th>Project</th>
        <th>Hours</th>
      </tr>
      <% status.hours_per_project.each do |project, hours| %>
      <tr>
        <td><%= link_to project.name, project %></td>
        <td><%= hours %></td>
      </tr>
      <% end %>
      <tr>
        <th>Total</th>
        <td><%= status.active_hours %></td>
      </tr>
    </table>
➤ <% end %>
  </section>
```

We need to add an expanded?() method to our DesignerStatus and support an options hash passed to our initializer:

```
artflow/presenters/lib/designer_status.v3.rb
def initialize(designer, options = {})
  @designer = designer
  @options = options
end
```

```
➤ def expanded?
➤   @options[:expanded]
➤ end
```

In expanded?() we just look for a non-nil or non–false :expanded option. Let's update our helper to accept additional options and pass them along. We'll make the default non-expanded, since usually we'll want the short status displayed:

```
➤ def designer_status_for(designer = @designer, options = {})
➤   presenter = DesignerStatus.new(designer, options)
    if block_given?
      yield presenter
    else
      presenter
    end
  end
```

Now we can change how our show.html.erb template renders the presenter now using the partial. We pass along the presenter instance using the :object option, which will make sure it's assigned to a variable with the same name as the partial (in this case, status):

```
artflow/presenters/app/views/designers/show.v2.html.erb
<%= render partial: 'status',
           object:  designer_status_for(@designer, expanded: true) %>
```

We can go even farther than this, tossing out the need for a render() in our template at all. We can make the DesignerStatus render *itself!* To do this, our class needs access to the template instance. This isn't a problem, since our helpers are executed in the context of the view; self is what we need to give our presenter. We edit our designer_status_for() helper and pass it along:

```
artflow/presenters/app/helpers/designers_helper.rb
  def designer_status_for(designer = @designer, options = {})
➤   presenter = DesignerStatus.new(designer, self, options)
    if block_given?
      yield presenter
    else
      presenter
    end
  end

end
```

Now the `DesignerStatus` `initialize()` method needs to be modified to accept the template argument:

artflow/presenters/lib/designer_status.rb
```ruby
def initialize(designer, template, options = {})
  @designer = designer
  @template = template
  @options = options
end
```

Now that our presenter has the template instance, what can we do with it? Well, let's look at how we *want* to add the markup for the designer status from our template:

artflow/presenters/app/views/designers/show.html.erb
```erb
<%= designer_status_for(@designer, expanded: true) %>
```

Wow, that's short! What's going on here?

When we insert content with ERB, it automatically calls to_s() (read: "to string") on the content first. Let's define that method on our `DesignerStatus` presenter so that inserting our presenter will work out of the box:

artflow/presenters/lib/designer_status.rb
```ruby
def to_s
  @template.render partial: 'designers/status', object: self
end
```

It's just as easy to generate the condensed version of our designer status elsewhere, as we do on the page for a project, showing the status for the designers styled as a badge:

artflow/presenters/app/views/projects/show.html.erb
```erb
<ul>
  <% @project.designers.each do |designer| %>
    <li><%= designer_status_for(designer) %></li>
  <% end %>
</ul>
```

Keep in mind we don't *need* to use the rendering shortcut or even need to use the partial at all. We can use designer_status_for() at any point, in any template, and extract any of the bits of data we need directly by calling methods on the `DesignerStatus` instance. We could support more options in our presenter, hide and show additional information, or even render an entirely different partial based on some criteria. Presenters can be amazingly flexible pieces of machinery.

Testing Template Presenters

There are a few aspects of these presenters that make sense to test. We should test the presenter instances themselves to make sure they're accurately extracting the data from the related records. We should also make sure users are seeing what we expect; that the helper creating the presenter instance behaves correctly, and that the template for the presenter displays the information as we'd like it to.

Let's focus on the DesignerStatus presenter, helper, and template that we put together in Section 6.1, *Presenting a Record*, on page 144, and look at how we might build our tests. We'll move from the core behavior of the presenter out to what the user sees.

Since presenters are just plain old Ruby objects, we can test them with a plain unit test. We'll use an ActiveSupport::TestCase, since it gives us some niceties (like String test names):

artflow/presenters/test/unit/designer_status_test.rb
```
require 'test_helper'
class DesignerTest < ActiveSupport::TestCase
  def setup
    setup_designer
    @status = DesignerStatus.new(@designer, nil)
  end

  test 'DesignerStatus instance calculates active projects' do
    assert_equal 3, @status.active_projects_count
  end

  test 'DesignerStatus instance calculates hours' do
    assert_equal [2, 2, 2], @status.hours_per_project.values
    assert_equal 6, @status.active_hours
  end
end
```

Here we instantiated our DesignerStatus just as our helper would, except we pass in nil instead of a template or a fancy mock. We're not testing the to_s() method: the template won't be tested.

In the test's setup() we create a Designer and related Project and Creation records by calling a method, setup_designer(), that we defined in our test helper:

artflow/presenters/test/test_helper.rb
```
require 'factories'
class ActiveSupport::TestCase

  # We don't use fixtures, so we comment this out:
  # fixtures :all
```

```
  def setup_designer
    @designer = Factory(:designer)
    3.times do
      creation = Factory(:creation, hours: 2, designer: @designer)
      @designer.projects << creation.project
    end
    @designer.save
  end

end
```

This setup_designer() utility method builds our objects using factory_girl, a test fixture library we prefer to Rails's built-in, static YAML-based fixtures.[1] Static fixtures are fine, but it's nice to be able to dynamically generate fixture data at will, trying out different combinations of data and using shortcuts like the Faker gem to give it a little variety.[2] Here are the definitions we're using and loading from factories.rb:

artflow/presenters/test/factories.rb
```
Factory.define :designer do |x|
  x.sequence(:email) { |n| "designer#{n}@artflowme.com" }
  x.password 'testtest'
end

Factory.define :project do |x|
  x.sequence(:name) { |n| "Project #{n}" }
  x.association :campaign
  x.active true
end

Factory.define :campaign do |x|
  x.sequence(:name) { |n| "Campaign #{n}" }
end

Factory.define :creation do |x|
  x.sequence(:name) { |n| "Creation #{n}" }
  x.association :project
  x.association :designer
  x.stage 'initial'
  x.revision 1
  x.description "This is a description"
end
```

With our prepopulated designer, we can test our active_projects_count(), hours_per_project(), and active_hours() methods to make sure they extract the data we expect from our record. We can build on this as the data we need to display

1. https://github.com/thoughtbot/factory_girl
2. http://rubygems.org/gems/faker

grows, and having these tests around will help prevent regression in the future; it seems likely time tracking and reporting will become more and more complex as our project grows.

Now let's make sure our helper behaves correctly. We'll do this with a Action-View::TestCase unit test:

artflow/presenters/test/unit/helpers/designers_helper_test.rb
```ruby
require 'test_helper'

class DesignersHelperTest < ActionView::TestCase

  def setup
    setup_designer
    @status = DesignerStatus.new(@designer, nil)
  end

  test 'designer_status_for helper returns a DesignerStatus instance' do
    assert_kind_of DesignerStatus, designer_status_for(@designer)
  end

  test 'designer_status_for helper yields a DesignerStatus instance' do
    yielded = nil
    designer_status_for(@designer) { |obj| yielded = obj }
    assert_kind_of DesignerStatus, yielded
  end

end
```

So far we're just concerned with making sure the helper returns or yields the DesignerStatus, but we can test the presenter to_s() method, too; since Action-View::TestCase sets up a template for us, we can use render()! We'll check that it's working as expected by checking a bit of the resulting content:

artflow/presenters/test/unit/helpers/designers_helper_test.rb
```ruby
test 'calling to_s returns status markup' do
  status = designer_status_for(@designer)
  assert status.to_s.include?('<title>Status</title>')
end

test 'non-expanded status markup does not include active hours' do
  status = designer_status_for(@designer)
  assert !status.to_s.include?('Active Project Hours')
end

test 'expanded status markup includes active hours' do
  status = designer_status_for(@designer, expanded: true)
  assert status.to_s.include?('Active Project Hours')
end
```

We're careful not to test too much of the markup. We want to avoid writing brittle tests that will break unnecessarily the next time someone tweaks the look and feel of the designer status widgets. Instead of ensuring that the structure of the returned markup meets today's expectations, we focus on verifying important pieces of information that are more likely to stand the test of time.

Let's add a quick test for our DesignersController show() action, where we display the "expanded" designer status. We'll limit our assertions to verifying that the presenter is rendered and just check the number of active projects displayed for our designer.

artflow/presenters/test/functional/designers_controller_test.rb
```
require 'test_helper'

class DesignersControllerTest < ActionController::TestCase

  def setup
    setup_designer
  end

  test "should render designer status presenter" do
    get :show, id: @designer.id
    assert_response :success
    assert_select 'section.designer-status .active-projects', text: '3'
  end

end
```

Once again we don't want to exhaustively test the structure of the markup, and since our unit tests will check the accuracy of the data our presenter extracts from the record, there's no need to double-check it here. Verifying the presenter is displayed for the designer is enough and is the best "bang for our buck."

Now that we've used a presenter to show information from one record, let's look at how we can use it to help us deal with aggregations of records.

6.2 Presenting Multiple Records

In ArtFlow we try to keep our clients up-to-date with our progress. Keeping the feedback loop short is key to making sure we deliver the best work we can in the shortest time possible. One of the ways we display status information to our clients is in a table, displaying specific pieces of information for the creations being worked on by our designers.

Over time, keeping the markup for the table nice and tidy has become more and more difficult. It's grown in size based on our clients' needs, and similar tables have popped up elsewhere in ArtFlow as well. We're going to try to clean things up using a presenter that will model the table's headers and columns for us. This will also make testing a lot easier, too!

We'll build the table presenter generically so we can reuse it elsewhere. We'll call it SimpleTable, and its initializer should just take a set of attribute names that it will display for a collection of records. We'll also pass along the current template so the presenter can render itself with to_s(). In lib/simple_table.rb:

```ruby
class SimpleTable

  def initialize(template, records, columns)
    @template = template
    @records  = records
    @columns  = columns
  end

  def to_s
    @template.render partial: 'presenters/simple_table', object: self
  end

end
```

We'll instantiate it from a helper we put in a new module, SimpleTableHelper. Just as with our DesignerStatus presenter, we pass in self, which is the current template instance.

artflow/presenters/app/helpers/simple_table_helper.rb
```ruby
module SimpleTableHelper

  def simple_table_for(records, columns = {}, options )
    presenter = SimpleTable.new(self, records, columns, options)
    if block_given?
      yield presenter
    else
      presenter
    end
  end

end
```

Now we create a partial that will render all the information from our presenter:

artflow/presenters/app/views/presenters/_simple_table.html.erb
```erb
<table>
  <thead>
    <tr>
      <% simple_table.columns.each_key do |title| %>
```

```
      <th><%= title %></th>
    <% end %>
  </tr>
</thead>
<tbody>
 <% simple_table.each do |record| %>
   <tr>
     <% simple_table.values(record).each do |title, value|
       <td><%= value %></td>
     <% end %>
   </tr>
  <% end %>
</tbody>
</table>
```

This builds our table headers from the column definitions and extracts the values from each record while building the rows. Let's add the methods we need to the SimpleTable class:

```
class SimpleTable

➤  attr_reader :columns
➤
➤  delegate :each, to: :@records

   def initialize(template, records, columns = {})
     @template = template
     @records  = records
     @columns  = columns
   end

➤  def values(record)
➤    @columns.each_with_object({}) do |(title, attribute), memo|
➤      memo[title] = record.send(attribute)
➤    end
➤  end

   def to_s
     @template.render partial: 'presenters/simple_table', object: self
   end

end
```

First we expose an attribute reader method so we can call columns(), then we delegate each() to our records so that we can easily iterate over them. Our values() method is a bit more complex: its job is to extract the values for the columns we've defined, building up a Hash using each_with_object() (a handy, easier-to-use method than the old standard for this sort of thing, inject()).

Let's use the simple_table_helper() we built earlier to display the list of creations awaiting approval by a client. We'll put it on the client dashboard:

artflow/presenters/app/views/clients/show.html.erb
```
<h3>Awaiting Approval</h3>
<%= awaiting_approval_table %>
```

We're calling a new helper in our template, awaiting_approval_table(). We'll define the helper to create our SimpleTable presenter instance for us, since putting the instantiation in the markup doesn't read as nicely as a descriptively named helper. Let's put awaiting_approval_table() in app/helpers/clients_helper.rb, since we're on a client page.

```ruby
module ClientsHelper
  def awaiting_approval_table
    simple_table_for(@client.creations.awaiting_approval,
                     'Name' => :name,
                     'Revision #' => :revision)
  end
end
```

This gives us a table with the name and revision of each creation, but the table implementation doesn't seem very flexible yet. We're limited to calling methods defined directly in our model class, Creation. We need to be able to show information from the Designer and from other records associated with the Creation as well.

There are three obvious options here, two of which we've already covered in Section 6.1, *Presenting a Record*, on page 144; we could either expose additional methods in our model, or we could pass our SimpleTable instance a collection of presenters exposing those methods for the model. The third option is to make our SimpleTable API more flexible, allowing us to define ad hoc strategies to extract the data we need. We'll support passing in Proc instances to extract the values for each column in addition to just calling specific methods on our records:

artflow/presenters/app/helpers/clients_helper.rb
```ruby
def awaiting_approval_table
  simple_table_for(@client.creations.awaiting_approval,
                   'Name'       => :name,
                   'Revision #' => :revision,
                   'Designer'   => ->(creation) {
                     link_to(creation.designer.name, creation.designer)
                   },
                   'File Size'  => ->(creation) {
                     number_to_human_size(creation.file.size)
                   })
end
```

We've provided some Proc objects to define how data will be pulled out. To get this to work inside our SimpleTable presenter, we'll use a little duck typing, checking to see if our extractor responds to the call() method.[3] We don't need to artificially limit ourselves to Proc, either; anything that responds to the call() method is good enough for us.

artflow/presenters/lib/simple_table.rb
```ruby
def values(record)
  @columns.values.each_with_object({}) do |(title, extractor), memo|
➤   memo[title] = extract_value(record, extractor)
  end
end

def to_s
  @template.render partial: 'presenters/simple_table', object: self
end

private

def extract_value(record, extractor)
➤ if extractor.respond_to?(:call)
➤   extractor.call(record)
  else
    record.send(extractor)
  end
end
```

We pulled our logic for extracting the value out of values() and into a private method, extract_value(). This keeps our code from becoming cluttered. After all, accumulating the data and extracting the data are two different operations.

We could expand our presenter considerably, extending support for column header and row element configuration and even polishing the API by crafting a column definition DSL. For now, however, we'll keep our SimpleTable, well, simple.

Presenters can be useful and elegant tools when we use them in our templates. They can let us access information we need from our models with cleaner, more readable semantics without muddying our models or turning our helper modules into junk drawers. There are existing libraries that simplify the creation of presenters, too. The Draper gem is a good example of a more comprehensive approach and is worth a look.[4]

3. http://c2.com/cgi/wiki?DuckTyping
4. https://github.com/jcasimir/draper

We can use presenters for more than just building markup, too. Building up a data structure for serialization to a JSON, XML, or other document format is another area where presenters can make our lives easier.

6.3 Using Presenters for Serialization

The term "presenter" doesn't just apply to domain objects used from a template. We can use presenters for formats other than HTML; this is a technique that works well for object serialization, where we might use a presenter to aggregate information for one or more records before returning it in serialized form.

Here in our CreationsController we offer a JSON version of the show() action that details important status and history information for the artwork our designers create.

```
artflow/presenters/app/controllers/creations_controller.rb
def show
  @creation = Creation.find(params[:id])
  @client = @creation.project.client
  respond_to do |format|
➤    format.json do
➤      render :json => CreationSummary.new(@creation, current_user).to_json
➤    end
    format.html
  end
end
```

The CreationSummary class here is the presenter responsible for extracting the information we'd like returned with the response for the current user. It lives in lib/creation_summary.rb:

```
class CreationSummary

  delegate :to_json, :to => :data

  def initialize(creation, user)
    @creation = creation
    @user = user
  end

  def data
    case @user
    when Admin
      data_with_estimate
    when Designer
      standard_data
    else
```

```
        sanitized_data
      end
    end
  end
```

We delegate to_json() to the result of the data() method, which determines the scope of the data to return based on the user type. The data contents are defined in data_with_estimate() to support tools for our management team, standard_data() for our designers and other staff, and sanitized_data() for clients.

```
artflow/presenters/lib/creation_summary.rb
def standard_data
  {
    campaign: @creation.campaign.name,
    client: @creation.client.name,
    designer: @creation.designer.name,
    hours: @creation.hours,
    name: @creation.name,
    project: @creation.project.name,
    revision: @creation.revision,
    stage: @creation.name
  }
end

def sanitized_data
  standard_data.reject do |k, v|
    [:hours, :client].include?(k)
  end
end

def data_with_estimate
  estimate_data = {
    hours: @creation.estimate.hours,
    rate: @creation.estimate.rate,
    total: @creation.estimate.total
  }
  standard_data.merge(estimate: estimate_data)
end
```

Putting this customized serialization logic in a separate presenter instead of our model keeps things clean; we only use this logic from this action anyhow; the separation lets us write more focused tests and documentation for the business logic.

Testing Serialization Presenters

One of the benefits we learned in *Testing Template Presenters*, on page 150, was how useful the extraction of logic from models and helpers can be for testing. When we have a decoupled, plain object to test, things get a lot easier.

This holds true with presenters used from the controller as well. Testing our CreationSummary is a lot more straightforward than testing a random collection of private methods in our controller or testing additional methods we've tacked onto our model. We also know where to put the tests and where to look for them later. There's a huge benefit just in being able to give this idea of a "creation summary" a real name!

Let's add some unit testing for our presenter. We'll get some data in place first:

artflow/presenters/test/unit/creation_summary_test.rb
```ruby
require 'test_helper'

class CreationSummaryTest < ActiveSupport::TestCase

  def setup
    @creation = Factory(:creation)
    @client = @creation.client
    @designer = @creation.designer
    @admin = Factory(:admin)
  end
end
```

Our setup() uses the factory_girl definitions we used earlier in *Testing Template Presenters*, on page 150, to create a Creation record. We assign the @designer and @client from the creation for convenience, then create an Admin and assign it to @admin. The factory for Admin, like Designer, was just a few lines:

artflow/presenters/test/factories.rb
```ruby
Factory.define :admin do |x|
  x.sequence(:email) { |n| "admin#{n}@artflowme.com" }
  x.password 'testtest'
end
```

First we'll test the CreationSummary for our @admin, an unadulterated dump of data for the Creation, including the initial estimate information:

artflow/presenters/test/unit/creation_summary_test.rb
```ruby
test "an admin sees data including the estimate" do
  summary = CreationSummary.new(@creation, @admin)
  fields = [:campaign, :client, :designer,
            :hours, :name, :project, :revision, :stage,
            :estimate]
  assert_serializes fields, summary
end
```

The assert_serializes() method we're using is one of our own design, added as a private method on our CreationSummaryTest. As the name indicates, it lets us verify that specific fields will be exposed in the serialized document.

```ruby
def assert_serializes(fields, summary)
  assert_equal(fields.sort, summary.data.keys.sort,
               "Serialization fields do not match")
end
```

Because assert_serializes() uses assert_equal() under the covers, it also verifies that the fields are the *only* fields serialized, which saves us from having to provide a negative assertion to verify our @designer doesn't get the estimate information:

```ruby
test "a designer sees the standard data" do
  summary = CreationSummary.new(@creation, @designer)
  fields = [:campaign, :client, :designer,
            :hours, :name, :project, :revision, :stage]
  assert_serializes fields, summary
end
```

Likewise, our client doesn't need to see the client name or the hours spent by the designer on this specific piece of artwork; that's information we prefer to provide on our invoices instead.

```ruby
test "a client only sees the sanitized data" do
  summary = CreationSummary.new(@creation, @client)
  fields = [:campaign, :designer,
            :name, :project, :revision, :stage]
  assert_serializes fields, summary
end
```

This is just the tip of the iceberg when it comes to testing this presenter. For now, we're focusing on ensuring that the policy we've defined for each requesting user is upheld, returning only the data the user needs to see. If we took this further, we'd want to dig into the individual bits of data themselves and verify that the values for each field are being returned correctly, though we wouldn't want to duplicate model unit tests that are already checking the logic.

For other, more complete approaches to serializing models, see the JBuilder (Builder-style DSL) and ActiveModel Serializers projects.[5] The latter is an especially elegant solution to the problem and sticks closer to presenter principles.

6.4 Wrapping Up

Now that we've tackled how to build presenters in our templates and controllers to make displaying information easier, let's turn to a design concern: how to present the data to the widest audience possible. In this day and age

---

5. https://github.com/rails/jbuilder and https://github.com/josevalim/active_model_serializers, respectively.

of mobile browsers and mixing of small screens with "traditional," larger desktop and (less mobile) laptop resolutions, how do we keep everyone happy with what they're seeing?

To be happy in this world, first you need a cell phone and then you need an airplane. Then you're truly wireless.

➤ *Ted Turner*

CHAPTER 7

Handling Mobile Views

These days, there are more and more users hitting our products and sites with mobile devices of all shapes and sizes, such as iPhones, Android devices, and iPads and other tablets. Mobile design and development gives us opportunities that don't exist in the desktop environment. With many mobile devices, we have access to multitouch input, user location from the GPS and compass, interaction with the accelerometer and gyroscope (which way the device is angled or positioned) and other items. These can improve and inform our users' interactions in ways previously unattainable outside the mobile space.

Mobile users often open a site in their mobile browser only to see text that is completely unreadable and content that requires constant zooming and panning for them to consume. This is what we get when we cram 800 to 1200 pixels into a screen that is 320 pixels or 480 pixels wide. This is just a bad experience and, with large downloads of images that get in the way of us getting to the content, can downright stop our users cold in their tracks.

Mobile usage continues to grow at an exciting pace and is poised to eclipse traditional desktop browsing by 2015, according to a 2011 study by Morgan Stanley.[1] To ignore this trend would be as foolish as ignoring the advent of the World Wide Web in the late 1990s. But we should not rush headlong into a mobile site without analyzing what we're doing and what our customers need.

The best way to approach mobile is to answer one simple question: What is the user trying to accomplish while mobile?

There are lots of ways to handle mobile users, and each method has benefits and detractions. We'll start by using a technique known as responsive design, where we use CSS media queries to transform our document for different

---

1.   http://www.morganstanley.com/institutional/techresearch/pdfs/MS_Economy_Internet_Trends_102009_FINAL.pdf

devices. Then we'll look into serving device-specific views using Rails's responders, and we'll wrap up by exploring how we can use jQuery Mobile to provide a version of our site that is optimized for touch devices.

Let's start with the foundation of a site that will work well on multiple screen sizes: the flexible layout.

7.1 Building a Flexible Layout

In the early days of the World Wide Web, designers complained that it didn't work like the printed page. They were accustomed to the "pixel-perfect layout" of the print world, where the page and every element on it are precisely sized and located. Web designers today complain about mobile not working like a full-screen browser. It's effectively the same short-sighted complaint and deserves the same kind of answer:

The medium of mobile is different and needs to be handled differently.

When we talk about a flexible layout, we're looking at creating a page that lays itself out in percentages of the whole. To do this we can use any nonabsolute value, such as %, em, and to a lesser extent the new rem type (or root ems in CSS3).

Let's take our app's two-column design. When we set it up in Chapter 1, *Creating an Application Layout*, on page 1, the page wrapper was 960 pixels wide, the left column was 800 pixels wide, and the sidebar was 150 pixels wide, which left us a gutter of 10 pixels between the two sides. Opening up app/assets/stylesheets/layout.css.scss, we see the following:

```
div#wrapper {
  width: 960px;
  margin: 0 auto;
}
section#content {
  float: left;
  width: 800px;
}
section#sidebar {
  float: right;
  width: 150px;
}
```

Translating that to percentages, roughly 83 percent is in the left column and 15 percent is in the right column. The actual math is achieved by dividing the child element's width by the parent element and moving the decimal over by two (also known as multiplying by 100). This results in values of

83.3333333333 percent and 15.625 percent for the left and right, respectively. Since the browser is translating this to pixels, having the extra decimals will help get us closer to the proper size.

```
div#wrapper {
  width: 960px;
  margin: 0 auto;
}

section#content {
  float: left;
➤ width: 83.333333333333%;
}
section#sidebar {
  float: right;
➤ width: 15.625%;
}
```

We would not notice much of a difference at this point, because the parent container is still determined in pixels. We'll need to change that to achieve the basics of a flexible layout.

```
div#wrapper {
➤ width: 95%;
  margin: 0 auto;
}

section#content {
  float: left;
  width: 83.333333333333%;
}
section#sidebar {
  float: right;
  width: 15.625%;
}
```

This will give us a slight margin on each side, which works out to 2.5 percent per side, or approximately 25 pixels when the screen is 1024px wide. We also need to plan for "browser chrome," or the space taken up by the edges of the application window and scroll bars. We don't want to actually max out at 100 percent, because in most cases the box model (which we discussed back in Section 1.3, *Building the Page Frame*, on page 14) will come back to haunt us and we will end up with more than 100 percent once we add padding into the equation.

We now have flexible columns set up for the page and can begin to bring our other elements into the framework as well. Looking quickly at our page layout from Chapter 1, *Creating an Application Layout*, on page 1, our header and footer elements were already set up to be flexible. In the header, our logo sits left and our background image floats right.

Building a Flexible Grid

We've got a pretty simple setup here, and as we move into multiple pages, it could be difficult to have an elegant, flexible solution by coding everything by hand. In this case, we're going to look at utilizing SCSS mixins to create a flexible—and semantic—grid.

Flexible layouts and grid layouts have both been around for a while, but combining the two is a more recent invention. Twitter was one of the first to codify it in their Bootstrap framework.[2] This set up both static and fluid layouts with predefined grid elements that would allow developers to reuse CSS across the Twitter front end without reinventing the wheel on every new page.

The problem with Bootstrap is similar to the problems that exist with other grid systems, such as 960.gs. They introduce excessive, nonsemantic class names into our HTML. This is where the power of Sass comes in. Semantic.gs uses mixins to move these presentation elements to the style sheet where they belong.[3] Semantic.gs is available on GitHub.[4]

First we'll get the contents of stylesheets/scss/grid.scss from the repository,[5] and we'll save it as vendor/assets/stylesheets/_semanticgs.scss in ArtFlow. We'll place it in vendor/assets to separate it from the stuff we've written in this application (placed in app/assets) and from the stuff we've written that is shared by other applications as well (placed in lib/assets). We may want to modify it to match our grid settings, and we'll want to @import it into files that need it.

Let's take a look at how semantic.gs works. At the top of the file, we have some default grid defined:

```
artflow/responsive/app/assets/stylesheets/_semanticgs.scss
// Defaults that you can freely override
$column-width: 60px;
$gutter-width: 20px;
$columns: 12;
```

The system defaults to a grid 960 pixels wide. If we have twelve columns with 20-pixel gutters between them, that would be 60 pixels for each column. The next line does most of the work in our file:

---

2. http://twitter.github.com/bootstrap/
3. http://semantic.gs/
4. https://github.com/twigkit/semantic.gs
5. https://github.com/twigkit/semantic.gs/blob/master/stylesheets/scss/grid.scss

```
artflow/responsive/app/assets/stylesheets/_semanticgs.scss
// Set $total-width to 100% for a fluid layout
$total-width: ($column-width*$columns) + ($gutter-width*$columns);
```

This utility variable does the calculation to figure out how large the page actually is. Basically, it adds the columns and gutters together to get a total width. We're going to change that to be 100 percent:

```
artflow/responsive/app/assets/stylesheets/_semanticgs.scss
$total-width: 100%;
```

By setting $total-width to 100 percent, we override the static layout and make the layout flexible. It will work in the proportions defined at the 960-pixel fixed size. We have to go to 100 percent to engage the flexible layout aspects of the tool. We'll make margins to pull the content back from the edges.

Now all we need to do is change the values in our layout.css.scss to use the semantic grid measurements, then use the column Sass mixin that semantic.gs provides to place our <section> elements correctly on the page:

```
➤ @import "semanticgs";

  div#wrapper {
➤   width: $total-width;
    margin: 0 auto;
  }

  section#content {
➤   @include column(10);
  }
  section#sidebar {
➤   @include column(2);
  }
```

This gives us a lot of power and clarity in our source code and lets us work with a grid system that is both flexible and powerful. We can use these declarations on any of our elements as we move forward.

Flexible layouts and flexible grids provide us a lot of power and embrace the nature of the Web with multiple sizes of screens, but at some point, the screen is too small or too large for content originally designed for a different size. Next we're going to take a look at @media queries and utilize their conditional nature to improve our view for the small and the large screen.

7.2 The Next Level with Responsive Design (@media queries)

The Web is a dynamic medium. Designers have fought with this for years and we, as the implementers of those designs, have had to deal with striving for pixel perfection. This chapter is about letting go. The power of the Web is that the content can be experienced in a variety of ways on a variety of devices. We should build applications and websites that let the content be easily accessible on those devices.

Responsive design means that we as developers try to build our apps and sites in a way that lets any device access them. We are providing a response based on various conditions, including the user's role, the task the user is trying to accomplish, and the tool with which the user intends to accomplish the task. It's specifically being used as a term right now to refer to using @media queries to change the way a page is rendered depending on the device that is rendering it. While we can zoom in and out on an iPhone, it would be better if the page realized it was on an iPhone and changed its layout accordingly.

The term was first introduced by Ethan Marcotte on *A List Apart* in May 2010.[6] He used @media queries with flexible layouts to create a site that would render differently depending on the width of the screen.

Flexible layouts have been around for a while and work relatively well when you're looking at a specific type of browser (e.g., desktop only). Once someone accesses that site or app with a mobile device, things get messy because you can only go so small with floated elements, such as a right-side column.

We pulled up our app on our mobile device (an iPhone in this case) and it's unusable. Let's not mince words. Working with this all day would be on par with reading in 6 point lawyer font. Zooming in and zooming out, mixed with a limited visual area, creates a bad experience.

We will look at serving mobile specific templates in Section 7.3, *Using Mobile-Specific Templates*, on page 174, but our VP of marketing isn't happy waiting for us to deliver that. He wants to drink from the fire hose and he wants it today. If he can do it on his desktop, he wants the same on his iPad and iPhone too.

@media queries and flexible layouts to the rescue!

---

6. http://www.alistapart.com/articles/responsive-web-design/

We can tackle this using flexible layouts and something new in CSS3 called @media queries. These techniques will allow us to build something that will work for future devices of all shapes and sizes and keep us from needing to write a custom page for each and every device type that comes into use in our organization.

There are two steps we're concerned about as we build this solution. The first is when a user's window is under 800 pixels wide. This covers the iPad and most tablet or netbook kinds of devices. The next is when it goes below 640 pixels in width. This is for when we access the site from most mobile phones, including iPhones with the Retina display. We then have a rule block for the smallest and lowest resolution of devices that we want to support.

A Simple View

We'll add a new file to hold our media queries, media.css.scss. First let's edit our application.css to make sure it pulls them in at the end. We want them to apply after any other rules have been rendered; otherwise, they may be overruled by other CSS declarations:

`artflow/responsive/app/assets/stylesheets/application.css`

```
/*
 *= require_self
 *= require normalize
 *= require layout
 *= require sidebar
 *= require navigation
 *= require notifications
 *= require blueprint/typography
 *= require formtastic
 *= require forms
➤ *= require media
 */
```

Here are the basic definitions we'll stick in a new file, app/assets/stylesheets/media.css.scss:

```
@media screen and (max-width: 800px) {
}

@media screen and (max-width: 640px) {
}

@media only screen and (min-device-width: 320px) and (max-device-width: 480px) {
}
```

We've got an @media query for the screen only and we've got maximum width settings. These could be any value. We could even do variations for people with *really* large screens by saying (min-width: 1600px). We could target people with HDTV 1080p equivalent monitors (1920 x 1080) or almost any device we can think of by having our CSS affect devices within certain parameters.

We are going to start by turning off the columns by disabling floats and making the former columns the full width of the screen.

```
@media screen and (max-width: 800px) {
➤   /* Kills columns */
➤   section#content,
➤   section#sidebar {float: none; width: $total-width; margin-bottom: 5px;}
➤   section#page {min-width: 310px;}
}

@media screen and (max-width: 640px) {
}

@media only screen and (min-device-width: 320px) and (max-device-width: 480px) {
}
```

This looks great, but the sidebar info really isn't valuable here for our users, so let's hide that entirely.

```
@media screen and (max-width: 800px) {
  /* Kills columns */
  section#content { float: none; width: $total-width; margin-bottom: 5px; }
  section#page { min-width: 310px; }
➤   section#sidebar {display: none;}
}

@media screen and (max-width: 640px) {
}

@media only screen and (min-device-width: 320px) and (max-device-width: 480px) {
}
```

Because media queries run after the content is loaded in the browser, the content is loaded and then acted on by the CSS. We can only show or hide or reposition content and elements within the page. This can be problematic if there's a lot of content hidden because download times can seem really long for a small amount of visible content.

We also need to address smaller screens, as most of our truly mobile users will be checking this on a small screen no more than four inches wide. We're going to drop the body font size to 70 percent of what it is and resize elements to be smaller.

```
@media screen and (max-width: 800px) {
  /* Kills columns */
  section#content { float: none; width: $total-width; margin-bottom: 5px; }
  section#page { min-width: 310px; }
  section#sidebar {display: none;}
}

@media screen and (max-width: 640px) {
  /* Kicks the size down on smaller windows,
   * e.g., iPhone, to fit the nav
   */
  body { font-size: 70%; }
  header#page_header {
    background-image: url('../images/brandtag_sm.png');
    height: 30px;
  }
  header #appbar img#logo {width: 127px;}
  header img#logo {
    top: 10px;
    width: 140px;
  }
  section#page {margin: 5px; }
  a, a:link {font-weight: bold;}
}

@media only screen and (min-device-width: 320px) and (max-device-width: 480px) {
}
```

We've shrunk everything down and effectively redesigned the screen specifically for this type of interface (one that is smaller than 640px wide). Remember, we're not limited here to only certain numbers or a certain device. We can create as many of these rules as we want in order to target specific devices for that guy in accounting who just won't stop whining. Remember that the more rules we have, the more things we'll need to test to make sure they work. Great power means great responsibility and whatnot.

Getting Horizontal

Until now we've been working only in portrait mode with these devices. What happens when the user turns the device? Do we ignore that the device has changed orientation and simply zoom? Or do we want to recast the screen to use the real estate in a different way?

We're going to try the latter. To start, let's write an @media query that specifies this type of device (tablets in the horizontal position).

```
@media only screen and (device-width: 768px) and (orientation: landscape) {
}
```

We've sketched a quick mockup of what we want to do, and we're going to build to this. In this case we will need to add some HTML to the design specifically for this horizontal view. We can hide it in our web version of the app.

So, first things first, let's add the HTML placeholder we need into our application.html.erb file.

artflow/responsive/app/views/layouts/application.html.erb
```erb
<% if content_for?(:ipad_sidebar) %>
  <div id="ipad_sidebar">
    <%= yield :ipad_sidebar %>
  </div>
<% end %>
```

By default we don't want this showing up, so let's modify our application.css, adding display: none;.

artflow/responsive/app/assets/stylesheets/layout.css.scss
```scss
div#ipad_sidebar {
  display: none; /* Needed to hide for regular app users */
  background-color: #999;
  border: 2px solid #444;
  border-left: none;
  -moz-border-radius-topright: 10px;
  -moz-border-radius-bottomright: 10px;
  -webkit-border-top-right-radius: 10px;
  -webkit-border-bottom-right-radius: 10px;
  border-top-right-radius: 10px;
  border-bottom-right-radius: 10px;
  -moz-box-shadow: 0px 0px 10px #333 inset;
  -webkit-box-shadow: 0px 0px 10px #333 inset;
  box-shadow: 0px 0px 10px #333 inset;
  color: #fff;
  float: left;
  padding: 10px;
  @include column(3); /* approx 200px */
}
```

We will now turn this on for our users of horizontal devices with a width of 768 pixels, aka iPads.

```scss
@media screen and (max-width: 800px) {
  /* Kills columns */
  section#content { float: none; width: $total-width; margin-bottom: 5px; }
  section#page { min-width: 310px; }
  section#sidebar {display: none;}
}

@media screen and (max-width: 640px) {
```

```
/* Kicks the size down on smaller windows,
 * e.g .iPhone, to fit the nav
 */
body { font-size: 70%; }
header#page_header {
  background-image: url('../images/brandtag_sm.png');
  height: 30px;
}
header #appbar img#logo {width: 127px;}
header img#logo {
  top: 10px;
  width: 140px;
}
section#page {margin: 5px; }
a, a:link {font-weight: bold;}
}

@media only screen and (device-width: 768px) and (orientation: landscape) {
  div#ipad_sidebar {
    display: visible;
  }
}

@media only screen and (device-width: 768px) and (orientation: landscape) {
}

@media only screen and (min-device-width: 320px) and (max-device-width: 480px) {
}
```

Now wherever we want to surface page-specific content or general functionality, we can provide a content_for :ipad_sidebar block, and the app will display it within the gray, rounded sidebar.

How Does It Look?

There are a few ways we can test our @media queries site. The easiest is simply to resize our browser window down to each size we'd like to test, either by using a plugin or extension to give us a specific size or by just grabbing and dragging.

We can also look at using some development tools, such as the Opera Mobile Emulator,[7] the Opera Mini Simulator,[8] iOS simulator,[9] and the Android emulator,[10] to view our application from the desktop.

---

7. http://www.opera.com/developer/tools/mobile/

8. http://www.opera.com/mobile/demo/

9. http://developer.apple.com/library/ios/#documentation/Xcode/Conceptual/ios_development_workflow/25-Using_iOS_Simulator/ios_simulator_application.html#//apple_ref/doc/uid/TP40007959-CH9-SW1

10. http://developer.android.com/guide/developing/tools/emulator.html

For a quicker overview, we can use a tool by Matt Kersley that shows us the site in a variety of predefined widths.[11]

Conclusion

Media queries are a flexible way to quickly provide some CSS-only changes to our app and get it working better on a slew of devices with browsers. To see what can be done with this approach, check out the http://mediaqueri.es/ site.

One of the problems that we have with this approach is download size. Even though we've hidden images with CSS and resized many of them to be smaller, mobile users are still downloading the full size and all these images. They're also downloading all of the JavaScript and stylesheet assets, even ones they probably will not use.

Interaction is different on mobile. There's no hover state, but there's a tactility of "pushing" a button with your finger that needs to register more so than for a typical browser. How do we overcome these issues? In some cases, they aren't relevant and we'd stop here. But since we need to provide our end users with the fastest experience possible (sales people can be needy that way), we're going to examine some other options.

7.3   Using Mobile-Specific Templates

How do we handle cases where we want to give mobile users special features? What happens when the content we want to show our mobile users is so different from our standard templates—exposing special mobile functionality —that CSS media queries don't go far enough?

We could provide a mobile-specific site, but this creates a sandboxed experience that can sometimes be forgotten and seem overly dumbed down for people with higher-end smartphones. We also don't want people sharing a URL that is specifically for mobile browsers and having people on a desktop or tablet open up a mobile page instead of the expected experience. Finally, can we really prove that a tablet is in fact a mobile device? More and more, these are being used in place of home computers.

Instead, we will let Rails do some heavy lifting! We make use of its extensible templating system, which allows us to register new MIME-type aliases for formats and, when requests come from mobile user agents, render the matching templates we've prepared especially for our mobile users.[12]

---

11. http://mattkersley.com/responsive/
12. http://en.wikipedia.org/wiki/Internet_media_type

Let's make a mobile-specific version of the creation index in ArtFlow that shows a grid of creation previews—a different, quicker navigation interface than the normal version—where the workflow is a lot more about editing metadata and managing the list, not browsing.

Identifying Mobile Requests

Let's identify our incoming requests as coming from a mobile user agent. Unlike normal nonmobile requests, where format is pulled directly from the "file" extension of the request path (and defaults to html), we're going to instruct ArtFlow to be a bit sneakier. We'll be looking out for specific user agents.

Rails makes this easy: the information is available on the request object and readily available to the controller. Let's add a private method that we can use on our ApplicationController to figure it out for us. For now we'll just look for iOS devices, checking the user agent against a regular expression. In our app/controllers/application_controller.rb we add the following:

```
def mobile_request?
  request.user_agent =~ /iP(?:hone|ad|od)/
end
helper_method :mobile_request?
```

We'll use this to change the request's format if it looks like a mobile request. Because we've made mobile_request?() a helper_method, we can also use it from the view to include mobile-specific markup. Now let's figure out how to register a new MIME-type alias for the text/html content type. There are plenty of examples commented out in config/initializers/mime_types.rb, so we just add the following at the bottom of the file:

artflow/responsive/config/initializers/mime_types.rb
```
Mime::Type.register_alias "text/html", :mobile
```

So we have a new MIME-type alias, and we have a way to check if a request is mobile (at least for iOS). Now we need to put these two together and let Rails know that the requests from mobile devices are implicitly asking for mobile templates. We do this with a before_filter setting the format of the request. Rails will use this later when determining which template to render for the request. Let's edit our app/controllers/application_controller.rb:

```
before_filter :prepare_mobile_request!

def prepare_mobile_request!
  if mobile_request?
    request.format = :mobile
  end
end
```

We've added our MIME-type alias and identified when to display a mobile page to our users—now we get down to the business of creating our views.

Creating Mobile Templates

First up, we tackle the layout. Because we've added a mobile, the filename should be application.mobile.erb instead of application.html.erb. Since we're catering to a crowd with smaller screens, we keep the layout minimal:

```
<!DOCTYPE html>
<html lang="en">
  <head>
    <title>ArtFlow: Mobile Edition!</title>
  </head>
  <body>
    <%= yield %>
    <%= render partial: 'layouts/footer' %>
  </body>
</html>
```

Let's focus the creation listing that we want inserted at the yield in our layout. We'll build this as a list that we'll use CSS to style into a flexible grid and put it in app/views/creations/index.mobile.erb:

```
<ul>
  <%= render @creations %>
</ul>
```

We can render each Creation record differently than we do on the main site by creating a _creation.mobile.erb partial. Here we link to a square thumbnail image of the creation:

artflow/responsive/app/views/creations/_creation.mobile.erb
```
<li>
  <%= link_to(image_tag(creation.url(:square_thumb), alt: creation.name) %>
</li>
```

There we go—a view of our creations specifically for our mobile users. Right now it's the only listing they can see, and they're not allowed to view the standard interface. Is that too strict?

Letting Users Decide

Let's be honest. It's not nice to force users into a mobile layout. Sometimes they may be trying to find something they saw earlier on a nonmobile device, and the changes we've made to make the mobile experience "better" for them just end up getting in their way. While our mobile layout should be the default for mobile users, we don't want to lock them to it unnecessarily. Mobile users should be able to see the normal, unadulterated version of our application when they want, but how?

If we break it down, we see a couple of things need to be done. We need to add a way for a mobile user to let us know which type of view is preferred, and we need to store that preference for the duration of the session. We can do this by looking for a query parameter and toggling a session variable. We handle these issues in the ApplicationController.

```ruby
before_filter :set_preferred_view!
before_filter :prepare_mobile_request!
def set_preferred_view!
  if mobile_request?
    case params[:prefer_view]
    when 'standard'
      session[:preferred_view] = :standard
    when 'mobile'
      session[:preferred_view] = :mobile
    end
  end
end
```

Notice we made sure this new before_filter runs *before* the prepare_mobile_request!() logic we worked on earlier. We need to use the user's preference there. We'll also allow Ajax requests (request.xhr?) to pass through without being modified, since we don't want to stop JavaScript responses from being returned:

```ruby
def prepare_mobile_request!
  if !request.xhr?
    if mobile_request? && preferred_view == :mobile
      request.format = :mobile
    end
  end
end
def preferred_view
  if mobile_request?
    session[:preferred_view] || :mobile
  else
    :standard
  end
end
helper_method :preferred_view
```

We've added a convenience method, preferred_view(), to make checking the preference easier. We'll use this in a helper method we'll add to make links in our footer—these links will let the user change the preference by sending mobile or standard as the value of the prefers_view parameter to the current URL, which will be caught by set_preferred_view!().

```
artflow/responsive/app/helpers/application_helper.rb
def link_to_prefer_view(name)
  link_to_unless(preferred_view == name,
                 "#{name.capitalize} View", prefer_view: name)
end
```

The helper we've defined here uses link_to_unless() so it will only create a link for the *other* view preference. Now all we need to do is use this helper twice in our footer—once for mobile and once for the standard preference.

Because the footer partial is an html.erb instead of a mobile.erb template, we need to be specific about the file extension. If we wanted to get rid of this requirement, we could rename the file to footer.erb to make it apply to any format, but for now we'll just be specific. We might want to create a mobile-specific footer.mobile.html later that's a bit more compact and shows links to items of special interest to our mobile users (like the new iOS app we've just released):

```
artflow/responsive/app/views/layouts/_footer.html.erb
<% if mobile_request? %>
  <%= link_to_prefer_view :mobile %>
  |
  <%= link_to_prefer_view :standard %>
<% end %>
```

The choice will only be shown to mobile users, and it should make it easy to switch.

Shortcut: mobile-fu

Remember how we only supported iOS mobile devices? Felt like a bit of a cop-out, didn't it? We did this because the list of mobile devices we could support is *long*, and, sadly, they don't all include a simple mobile identifier in their user agent strings to take it easy on us.

Thankfully, someone's taken the pain out of the process and built a library for us to use, mobile-fu, which we add to our Gemfile:[13]

```
artflow/responsive/Gemfile
gem 'mobile-fu'
```

Then we install the library with Bundler:

```
% bundle install
```

The mobile-fu library identifies a wide range of mobile devices and automatically sets :format for us with a single line in our ApplicationController:

---

13. http://github.com/brendanlim/mobile-fu

```
artflow/responsive/app/controllers/application_controller.rb
class ApplicationController < ActionController::Base
  has_mobile_fu
end
```

The library includes per-device CSS overrides and an ability to turn off the mobile views with a bit of extra work and a session variable, similar to what we did in set_preferred_view!.

The decision to use mobile templates instead of just media queries, client-side JavaScript modifications, or a completely separate application isn't one to make lightly. We could even combine mobile templates together with the power of @media queries to provide a better experience to our users. There are definite trade-offs involved when you're supporting multiple types of devices, but sometimes the ability to sit our views on top of controller and model code we're already using means it's worth it.

7.4 Using jQuery Mobile

As we saw in Section 7.2, *The Next Level with Responsive Design (@media queries)*, on page 168, and Section 7.3, *Using Mobile-Specific Templates*, on page 174, building our Rails applications to recognize mobile users and modify the layout accordingly (and even decide which templates to render) isn't difficult. What *is* tricky is keeping up-to-date with all the mobile devices out there and designing interfaces that work well with them. New touch-enabled devices are crowding the market—and our applications. How do we make the user experience and interaction work for these mobile users as quickly as possible?

jQuery Mobile, a library that addresses a lot of the issues we run into while developing and designing for mobile devices on the Web,[14] is built on top of the semantic HTML we know and love and offers niceties like page transitions (a mainstay of mobile applications), themes, and ready-to-go mobile icons.

A lot of our clients are constantly on the go, and getting them to approve creations can be a bit of a struggle. It sure would be helpful to tighten up the feedback loop with a mobile version of our creation-commenting workflow in ArtFlow to speed things along. Clients could slip in some feedback on the taxi ride to the airport, which would give us the chance to deliver a new iteration by the time they land!

---

14. http://jquerymobile.com/

Creating a Page

After we download jQuery Mobile,[15] we get the CSS and JS linked into our layout, making sure that the images are accessible. We download the zipfile and unzip it in vendor/assets/javascripts. Mobile's a moving target, and by keeping things together now (and not modifying the file contents), we make upgrades easier later.

```
% unzip jquery.mobile-1.0.zip
Archive:  jquery.mobile-1.0.zip
   creating: jquery.mobile-1.0/
   creating: jquery.mobile-1.0/images/
  inflating: jquery.mobile-1.0/images/ajax-loader.png
  inflating: jquery.mobile-1.0/images/icon-search-black.png
  inflating: jquery.mobile-1.0/images/icons-18-black.png
  inflating: jquery.mobile-1.0/images/icons-18-white.png
 extracting: jquery.mobile-1.0/images/icons-36-black.png
  inflating: jquery.mobile-1.0/images/icons-36-white.png
  inflating: jquery.mobile-1.0/jquery.mobile-1.0.css
  inflating: jquery.mobile-1.0/jquery.mobile-1.0.js
  inflating: jquery.mobile-1.0/jquery.mobile-1.0.min.css
  inflating: jquery.mobile-1.0/jquery.mobile-1.0.min.js
```

We can then remove the minified files.

Now we'll create a new file, vendor/assets/javascripts/jquery.mobile.js, to pull in the versioned JavaScript file with a Sprockets require directive:

artflow/responsive/app/assets/javascripts/jquery.mobile.js
```
//= require 'jquery.mobile-1.0/jquery.mobile-1.0'
```

Since jQuery Mobile includes a style sheet and images, we need to tell Rails to serve them as well. We do that with a couple of provide directives in the same file:

```
//= provide 'jquery.mobile-1.0/jquery.mobile-1.0.css'
//= provide 'jquery.mobile-1.0/images'
```

While we could have edited the library's JavaScript directly (jquery.mobile-1.0.js) and just added our provide directives at the top, we use this little configuration stub so we can leave files in vendor untouched. We view files in vendor as someone else's (the vendor's!) and easily replaceable when a new version comes out. Then there's no need to worry about losing our modifications.

Starting the server, we test by hitting our stub at /assets/jquery.mobile.js (pulling in the library's JavaScript), the style sheet at /assets/jquery.mobile-1.0/jquery.mobile-1.0.css, and an image at /assets/jquery.mobile-1.0/images/ajax-loader.png. It works!

---

15. http://jquerymobile.com/download/

Now we link jQuery and our assets in a .mobile.erb layout (just like we set up in Section 7.3, *Using Mobile-Specific Templates*, on page 174):

artflow/responsive/app/views/layouts/application.mobile.erb
```
<%= javascript_include_tag 'jquery', 'jquery.mobile' %>
<%= stylesheet_link_tag 'jquery.mobile-1.0b3/jquery.mobile-1.0b3' %>
```

Our list of project creations will live at /projects/:project_id/creations and will be one of the most important pages for our clients. We'll show a thumbnail of the creation and allow quick access to a larger view of the creation, complete with comments and metadata. Pay special attention to the data-role attributes we use in the markup:

artflow/responsive/app/views/creations/index.mobile.erb
```
➤ <article data-role='page'>
➤   <header data-role='header'>
      <h1><%= @project.name %></h1>
    </header>
➤   <section data-role='content'>
➤     <ul data-role='listview'>
        <% @creations.each do |creation| %>
          <li>
            <%= image_tag creation.file.url(:thumb) %>
            <%= link_to creation.name, [@project, creation] %>
          </li>
        <% end %>
      </ul>
    </section>
  </article>
```

The data-role attributes are used to provide jQuery Mobile with the information it needs to map components to areas of the view.[16] In this template we've identified four components: the page-level container, the header, the content portion of the page, and a listview containing our creations. jQuery Mobile supports a wide range of roles, but these are the only ones we need for this template.

We can see the results of this in Figure 15, *Creation list*, on page 182.

Since we put the image thumbnails in at the beginning of each list item, JavaScript has automatically handled its placement for us, and the default right arrow icons work perfectly. Those are pretty good defaults!

We have our list. Now we'll put together the pages for the individual items.

---

16. http://jquerymobile.com/demos/1.0/docs/api/data-attributes.html

Figure 15—Creation list

Going Deeper

When we click or touch a creation, jQuery Mobile will load the show() action of the CreationsController asynchronously and, after a page transition, display it. The template we build for that page is similar, with a few additions:

```erb
artflow/responsive/app/views/creations/show.mobile.erb
<article data-role='page' data-theme='c'>
  <header data-role='header'>
    <h1><%= @creation.name %></h1>
  </header>
  <div data-role='content'>
    <p><%= image_tag @creation.file.url %></p>
  </div>
  <footer data-role='footer'>
    <div data-role='navbar'>
      <ul>
        <li><%= link_to_preview(true) %></li>
        <li><%= link_to_comments %></li>
        <li><%= link_to_modify %></li>
      </ul>
    </div>
  </footer>
</article>
```

Here we added a few components, namely footer and navbar, which we use for lateral navigation between the creation image preview, comments, and metadata pages. We also specified a theme swatch with data-theme,[17] since our designers wanted the pages for the individual creations to have a distinct feel that was different from the project pages. Our navigation bar icons were added with data-icon attributes,[18] and we used some helpers to create the links:

```
artflow/responsive/app/helpers/creations_helper.rb
def link_to_preview(active = false)
  navbar_link_to('Preview', [@project, @creation], 'grid', active)
end

def link_to_comments(active = false)
  navbar_link_to('Comments', [@project, @creation, :comments], 'info', active)
end

def link_to_modify(active = false)
  navbar_link_to('Modify', [:edit, @project, @creation], 'gear', active)
end

def navbar_link_to(text, url, icon, active = false)
  link_to text, url, 'class' => navbar_link_class(active),
                     'data-icon' => icon
end

def navbar_link_class(active = false)
  active ? 'ui-btn-active' : nil
end
```

We now see the page (in Figure 16, *Creation preview*, on page 184), with the navbar showing the active page (set with the ui-btn-active CSS class):

Clients can browse their creations but can't add feedback yet. Let's fix that by building the commenting page next.

Adding a Form

The comments page sits at /comments, displays the full list of comments on the creation, and allows our users to quickly add another. Adding a form to a page is as easy as anywhere else in Rails; in fact, because jQuery Mobile handles laying out the labels and inputs automatically, it's arguably easier. We create comments/index.mobile.erb and add this code:

---

17. http://jquerymobile.com/demos#docs/api/themes.html
18. http://jquerymobile.com/demos#docs/buttons/buttons-icons.html

Figure 16—Creation preview

artflow/responsive/app/views/comments/index.mobile.erb

```erb
<article data-role='page' data-theme='c'>

  <header data-role='header'>
    <h1><%= @creation.name %></h1>
  </header>
  <div data-role='content'>
    <% if @comments.any? %>
      <ul>
        <%= render @comments %>
      </ul>
    <% end %>
    <%= form_for [@project, @creation, Comment.new],
          :html => {'data-transition' => 'pop'} do |f| %>
      <%= f.label :body, 'Comment' %>
      <%= f.text_area :body, :cols => nil %>
      <%= f.submit 'Add' %>
    <% end %>
  </div>
  <footer data-role='footer'>
    <div data-role='navbar'>
```

Multiple Pages per Template

In this tip we focus on building out a min–mobile application, with each page served up by a different request. This isn't a constraint that jQuery Mobile forces on us—in fact, we can include as many data-role="page" elements in a template as we'd like and the library will manage their visibility for us. Instead of linking to full URLs to change pages, we just refer to the page we'd like to display with a named anchor; for instance, in this example we link from one page to another:

```
responsive/jquerymobile/_page_link_example.mobile.erb
<article data-role='page' id='first-page'>
  <header data-role='header'>
    <h1>First Page</h1>
  </header>
  <section data-role='content'>
➤    <p><%= link_to 'Show second page', '#second-page' %></p>
  </section>
</article>

➤ <article data-role='page' id='second-page'>
  <header data-role='header'>
    <h1>Second Page</h1>
  </header>
  <section data-role='content'>
    <p>Welcome to Page #2!</p>
  </section>
</article>
```

We might use this in situations when it made sense to render all the data for a resource all at once but only display it in pieces on a mobile device.

```
      <ul>
        <li><%= link_to_preview %></li>
➤       <li><%= link_to_comments(true) %></li>
        <li><%= link_to_modify %></li>
      </ul>
    </div>
  </footer>
</article>
```

This form is pretty vanilla, except we're setting a custom page transition with the data-transition set to pop; we'll show this same page after the comment is added, so this effect seems like a better choice than the default page slide, which gives the impression of forward movement.

The form looks as we'd expect in Figure 17, *The Comment form*, on page 186.

New comments are displayed using the simple comment template we added, which just shows the comment body and author (as seen in Figure 18, *Displaying comments*, on page 187).

Figure 17—The Comment form

That was relatively painless. Forms just worked out of the box and jQuery Mobile handled the bulk of our UI concerns. Now we'll tweak the header of our creation pages a little.

Customizing the Header

jQuery Mobile automatically adds a Back button to the header, but we'll remove it. Because this should feel like an application and not like a web page, retaining browsing history as people change from page to page in the navbar isn't a requirement. Instead, we'll add a Home button to get back to the creation list. Since this will make our header a little more complex, we'll extract it to its own partial and render() inside our templates.

```
artflow/responsive/app/views/layouts/_header.mobile.erb
<header data-role='header' data-backbtn='false'>
  <h1><%= @creation.name %></h1>
  <%= link_to_home %>
</header>
```

Turning off the Back button was just a matter of setting data-backbtn to false. Adding the Home button is a bit more complex, so we use a helper:

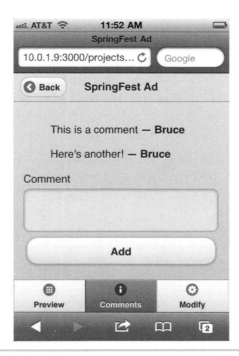

Figure 18—Displaying comments

---

artflow/responsive/app/helpers/creations_helper.rb
```ruby
def link_to_home
  link_to('Home', [@project, :creations],
          'class' => 'ui-btn-right',
          'data-icon' => 'home',
          'data-iconpos' => 'notext',
          'data-direction' => 'reverse')
end
```

Here we tell jQuery Mobile to put the button on the right (with class), to use the little home icon (with data-icon), to hide the button text (with data-iconpos), and to show a reverse page transition without touching the page history (with data-direction). While this might seem complex, keep in mind that each of these provides a specific visual or behavioral flavor that makes the effect more closely match what users would expect to see in a native application.

jQuery Mobile is a serious painkiller. Sure, it's a lot to learn—as any large, magical library is (Rails, anyone?)—but the time savings and stress relief we get by using it, even in the most shallow, incomplete way, makes it well worth the effort. After all, with your company bent on world domination, don't you have more important things to focus on than the intricacies of (and differences in) mobile interaction on the Web?

7.5 Wrapping Up

We've looked at a few different means of handling mobile users. For most content sites, responsive design solutions with @media queries will get us to the finish line. For web applications, we need to determine if our users are going to be served better by minimum web pages returned with responders or by a full-blown experience in jQuery Mobile.

We now have a pretty robust system running, but we're missing out on how we interact with our users most often, and that is email. From notifications to marketing, we'll take a look at how we should best handle email delivery in the next chapter.

CHAPTER 8

Working with Email

Since the early days of the Internet, email has provided one of the main methods of interaction with website users. Users receive updates, transaction notices, activity alerts, and more in their inboxes on a daily basis. Since this is one of the main starting points for users interacting with our application, we need to pay it some serious attention while we work on other aspects of the Rails view.

In ArtFlow, we want to send a notification to our users when someone adds a creation to a campaign. An iOS push notification, which is a way we can send a quick message to a user on a mobile platform, might look like Figure 19, *A sample push notification*, on page 190. We can see from this notification that Bruce just posted a creation in a specific campaign, but we can't provide more information than that. This is the perfect opportunity for us to send an email notification with more specific information. We'll create a notification that includes the creation's synopsis, date and time added, and some information about its project.

Let's dive in! Before we create the template, let's configure ArtFlow to send out emails.

8.1 Building a Mailer

For our email testing, we're going to configure our application to use our company's SMTP account but deliver the test emails locally. There are many other options for delivery, and you can read about those in the API or in *Agile Web Development with Rails* [RTH11]. For this setup we're going to need to edit development.rb in the directory config/environments in our application.

Figure 19—A sample push notification

```
artflow/email/config/environments/development.rb
config.action_mailer.delivery_method = :smtp
config.action_mailer.smtp_settings = {
  :address         => "smtp.gmail.com",
  :port            => 587,
  :domain          => "artflowme.com",
  :authentication  => "plain",
  :user_name       => "artflow",
  :password        => "secret",
  :enable_starttls_auto => true
}
```

We need to restart our application if we have it running locally. After we've restarted, let's generate an ActionMailer.[1] We'll just call it Notifier to keep it simple:

```
% rails generate mailer Notifier creation_added
   create  app/mailers/notifier.rb
   invoke  erb
   create    app/views/notifier
   create    app/views/notifier/creation_added.text.erb
   invoke  test/unit
   create    test/functional/notifier_test.rb
```

Our Notifier is similar to a controller in that there are templates associated with its methods, but instead of rendering for the Web, it sends an email.

```
artflow/email/app/mailers/notifier.rb
class Notifier < ActionMailer::Base
  default :from => 'Art Flow <artflow@artflowme.com>'
  def creation_added(creation)
    @creation = creation
    @campaign = creation.project.campaign
    mail to: "test@artflowme.com",
       subject: "Creation Added"
  end
end
```

---

1.   http://api.rubyonrails.org/classes/ActionMailer/Base.html

> ## Always Ask: What Is the Action?
>
> With emails we need to provide a call to action to users. What do we want them to do with this email? Is it simply for their notification, or do we require their approval or review? If this was an e-commerce project and we were sending out sales emails, what would we want them to do? In many cases, this call to action encourages our users to "click through" to the website.
>
> There's also nothing as frustrating as seeing something that we need to visit with no clear way to get there. As users, we don't want to go to a site and dig around for the place the email spoke about.
>
> We shouldn't send an email without a call to action.

We are going to change out our development code for our production code once we've finished developing these emails. We've put it in and commented it out for right now. We have a mailer ready to go, but we need to get a template for it to send to our users. That's where we'll head next.

8.2 Handling Email Templates

We know that the majority of our internal users are using either Mac OS X Mail or our internal Google Mail for Domains setup, and therefore we can assume certain capabilities about our users. This is good, because internal messages can rely on a cleaner markup and can use CSS for styling.

However, our external clients use a myriad of systems, including Microsoft Outlook. How can we ensure that our company's main interaction with them (email) is not an abysmal failure? The answer is to have contingencies in the way we build our emails. Every graphical email will have a plain text alternative. Since plain text is far easier to implement, we'll start with that and get sending!

Creating Plain Text Emails

While HTML emails are nice, starting with straightforward text-based emails gets us communicating a lot faster and supporting every email client in the world from the get-go, including Blackberry and other older mobile platforms (such as Symbian).

Plain text isn't just dumping the content of the email into a paragraph and handing it off to Postfix to deliver, lest we end up with the nightmare that appears in Figure 20, *A plain-text dump with no treatment*, on page 192. A

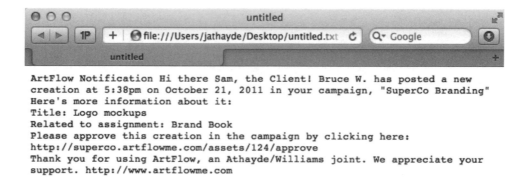

ArtFlow Notification Hi there Sam, the Client! Bruce W. has posted a new
creation at 5:38pm on October 21, 2011 in your campaign, "SuperCo Branding"
Here's more information about it:
Title: Logo mockups
Related to assignment: Brand Book
Please approve this creation in the campaign by clicking here:
http://superco.artflowme.com/assets/124/approve
Thank you for using ArtFlow, an Athayde/Williams joint. We appreciate your
support. http://www.artflowme.com

Figure 20—A plain-text dump with no treatment

plain-text email can be as difficult to design as a regular email. A lot of our own best practices from writing readable code apply here as well.

We want to keep our column count under eighty characters wide, regardless of if we're using fixed or variable-width fonts. We want to make paragraphs logical and provide clarity of content. Since we won't have font size, bold, italics, and other typographic standards to play with, we need to use ASCII punctuation and lines to aid with breaking up the page and providing hierarchy. Rows of equal symbols and hyphens can help create some visual breaks. Underscores and other punctuation marks can also be used. We could even use something as a brand element (such as a row of forward slashes) if we use it graphically in our brand. If we are presenting financial or columnar data, we want to use a monospace font.

This email notification is going to be sent to members of a project or a campaign when another user adds a new creation. We'll want context as well as some details about the file. To this end, we'll include the following information in this email:

- Creation title
- Creation created_at
- Campaign name
- Project name
- The user who added it
- A clear call to action (or CTA) to the recipient

artflow/email/app/views/notifier/creation_added.text.erb

```
=============================================================================
| ArtFlow Notification                                                      |
=============================================================================


Hi there <%= @creation.client.name %>!

<%= @creation.designer.name %> has posted a new creation at
<%=l @creation.created_at %> in your campaign, <%= @campaign.name %>.

Here's more information about it:

Name: <%= @creation.name %>
Project: <%= @creation.project.name %>

<% if @creation.approvable? %>
This creation is <%= link_to "awaiting approval",
                            edit_creation_url(@creation) %>.
<% end %>


=============================================================================
| Thank you for using ArtFlow, http://www.artflowme.com                     |
=============================================================================
```

By using some hard returns and some ASCII characters, we were able to break up the awful dump of plain text with nothing in it and provide clarity to our end user for when the email is opened. The only thing left to do is to actually have it send on an event, namely when a new creation is added. We'll do this with an after_create() Creation model:

artflow/email/app/models/creation.rb

```
after_create :notify_created

def approvable?
  status == 'awaiting_approval'
end

private

def notify_created
  Notifier.creation_added(self).deliver
end
```

We've built a plain-text email that will be readable on a wide variety of low-end devices and email clients, but it doesn't reinforce our brand. Let's take this a step further and build an HTML email template that lets us use our brand and design elements to present a more engaging experience, including showing a preview of the asset.

Using Graphics-Based Emails

Supporting a broad variety of email clients means that we have to code to the lowest common denominator. Email clients, unlike web browsers, still have very poor support for HTML and CSS standards. It's as if we are still living in 1998 with some of them, and that means we need to code like it's 1998.

We have to resort to old-style table-based markup to lay out the email. (This is probably the only case for using table-based markup outside of tabular data.) While we could design an email that has excessive graphics, the best course of action is to not look like a spam email and to use the design elements to support the content.

First we need to create a new template in our app/views/notifier folder named creation_added.html.erb. This will be our HTML version of the email. According to *Agile Web Development with Rails* [RTH11]:

> If you create multiple templates with the same name but with different content types embedded in their filenames, Rails will send all of them in one email, arranging the content so that the email client will be able to distinguish each.

Voilà—instant multipart awesomeness! So now all we need to do is to write up the HTML email template and give it a whirl.

`artflow/email/app/views/notifier/creation_added.html.erb`
```erb
<h2>ArtFlow Notification</h2>

<p>Hi there, <%= @creation.client.name %>!</p>

<p>
  <%= @creation.designer.name %> has posted a new creation at
  <%=l @creation.created_at %>
  in your campaign, <i><%= @campaign.name %></i>.
</p>

<h3>Here's more information about it</h3>

<dl>
  <dt>Name</dt>
  <dd><%= @creation.name %></dd>
  <dt>Project</dt>
  <dd><%= @creation.project.name %></dd>
</dl>

<% if @creation.approvable? %>
<p>
  This creation is
  <%= link_to "awaiting approval",
        edit_creation_url(@creation) %>.
```

```
</p>
<% end %>

<p class="footnote">
  Thank you for using <%= link_to 'ArtFlow', root_url %>.
</p>
```

We can now add our styles either in a <style> block at the top of the email or inline. Some email clients just play nicer with them inline. And since we're going to support the lowest common denominator, we're going to use inline styles.

While HTML emails are great, don't forget that not all clients will support them and that some connections, especially mobile ones, can be very slow to download a lot of images. Let's write another rule up on the whiteboard:

> With an HTML email, always provide a plain-text alternative and a link to view the email on a website.

We can send this URL to a controller that shows email contents from a database or simply to a controller handling static pages to show these off. Since the email is a standalone HTML entity, we'd show it without a layout or within an iFrame on a page.

We've finished generating our emails, but we are by no means ready for production yet. We first need to test these and refine them. While we can constantly send them to our test email account, this becomes burdensome and slows down our development. In the next section we're going to build a Rake task to help us with this issue and then look at some testing services for checking different email clients.

8.3   Testing Locally

Testing our emails is a bit more difficult, as we don't generally have access to every email client with our email accounts. Sending and checking each one by hand would also be tedious. The process we are going to follow is more iterative.

Normally, when our email service does its job, it creates a message, connects to an SMTP server, and sends that to an account somewhere in the ether (or to a "series of very large tubes"). This can be time-consuming and completely clog up our email inbox in order to do testing, so we need a shortcut.

The best way to do this is to take the sending issue out of the equation. We can do rapid development in the web browser itself. While many email clients are not as sophisticated as browsers, the prevalence of web-based email clients lets us choose this as the primary environment. We'll get to debugging across multiple clients in Section 8.4, *Testing Across Clients*, on page 196.

The Letter Opener gem by Ryan Bates is a nifty tool that lets us skip the configuration to send our emails and lets us just open them in a web browser.[2] This really speeds up our development cycle!

artflow/email/Gemfile
```
group :development do
  gem 'letter_opener'
end
```

We put the gem in our :development group in order to keep this out of our production environment. After running bundle install, we have to change our ActionMailer delivery method in our config/environment/development.rb:

artflow/email/config/environments/development.rb
```
config.action_mailer.delivery_method = :letter_opener
```

This tells Rails to pass emails over to Letter Opener for email delivery. Now in order to test our email, we're going to trigger an email out of our system from the console using our Notifier:

```
>> Notifier.creation_added(Creation.first).deliver
```

This creates an email that is saved in the tmp/letter_opener directory and then opens it for us in a browser. Now we can see how our email should be rendered. This helps us proof our HTML email, but it would be nice to see if our email design works in all our situations for the email clients we need to support.

8.4 Testing Across Clients

Once we have our email looking good locally, we need to venture into the world of the various email clients that our users might be using. With most of ArtFlow, it's easier to control what people are using, since it's an internal application. But our external clients could be using anything from Outlook to OS X Mail to Gmail to AOL. Some might even be so brave as to only use PINE.

Regardless of their client choice, we want to make sure that they are getting the information in a manner that looks good and reflects well on our company. To this end, we need to test our emails in these clients.

---

2. https://github.com/ryanb/letter_opener

Do we set up lots of accounts on every possible service and check these by hand? Well, that certainly is one solution, but it's a bit of a waste of our time. In this instance, we find it far more valuable to use a system like Litmus to test our emails and send us screen shots.[3] Litmus has a seven-day free trial account to see if you like it.

Enter the Marketing Email

So far we've been working with transactional emails that are notification and interaction based. They're pretty simple. We've just been handed our new marketing email design for the next quarter and we need to make sure it looks great in as many email clients as possible.

This will be easy to crank out. We break it into HTML and call our CSS files and...wait a minute—not so fast. In some cases, email clients will ignore style sheets referenced in <link> tags, and some remove the <head> tag contents entirely. Most won't load an external style sheet either, so we need to use inline styles for our email.

email/marketing_email.html
```
<!DOCTYPE html>
<html>
  <head>
    <style>
      #page {
        min-width: 600px;
      }
      #header {
        background-color: #bc471d;
        height: 94px;
        overflow: hidden;
        padding: 0 10px;
      }
      img#logo {float: left;}
      img#cloud {float: right;}
      img#subhead {margin-top:7px;}
      img#creatives {float: right;}
      p {
        color: #666666;
        font-family: verdana, arial, sans-serif;
        font-size: 14px;
        line-height: 20px;
        margin-bottom: 12px;
        margin-top:15px;
        width: 315px;
      }
```

---

3.   http://www.litmus.com

```
      #footer p {
        color: #999999;
        font-size: 10px;
        margin-bottom: 12px;
      }
    </style>
    <meta http-equiv="content-type"
         content="text/html; charset=ISO-8859-1">
    <title>25% off ArtFlow for a limited time</title>
  </head>
<body>
    <p style="font-family: verdana, arial, sans-serif;
             font-size: 9px;">
      Can't view this email? <a href="">View it on the Web</a>.
    </p>
    <div id="header">
      <img src="http://artflowme.com/images/email/logo.gif"
          alt="ArtFlow" id="logo">
      <img src="http://artflowme.com/images/email/cloud.gif"
          alt="cloud icon" id="cloud">
    </div>
    <div id="page">
      <img src="http://artflowme.com/images/email/creatives.jpg"
          alt="image of creative elements"
          id="creatives">
      <img src="http://artflowme.com/images/email/subhead.gif"
          alt="Creative File Management Made Easy"
          id="subhead">
      <p>
        We here at AwesomeCo know how the end of the year can just be too much
        for keeping your files in order. Lots of &quot;get it out the door
        before the holiday&quot; projects end up in file server soup when you
        get back after New Year's.
      </p>
      <p>
        That's why, for a limited time only, we're offering all new customers:
      </p>
      <a href="http://www.artflowme.com/holiday/">
        <img src="http://artflowme.com/images/email/pitch.gif"
            alt="Sign up today and get 25% off artflow">
      </a>
      <p>
        Make your New Year's resolution to not have any more &quot;to
        sort&quot; folders. Get your team and your clients communicating
        better with our industry-changing software.
      </p>
      <p>
        Because no designs should be alone this holiday season.
      </p>
      <a href="http://www.artflowme.com/holiday/">
```

```
        <img src="http://artflowme.com/images/email/button1.gif"
            alt="Sign up today and get 25% off artflow"
            border="0">
    </a>
    <br><br>

    </div>
    <div id="footer">
        <img src="http://artflowme.com/images/email/footer.gif"
            alt="&copy;2011 John Athayde, Bruce Williams. All Rights
                Reserved, All Wrongs Reversed.">
        <p>
        We hate spam too, so if you received this in error, or simply no
        longer wish to receive our marketing emails,
        <a href="http://www.artflowme.com/marketing/unsub">simply click here</a>
        to unsubscribe.
        </p>
    </div>
  </body>
</html>
```

You'll notice that we actually spell out our CSS declarations entirely instead of using the shorthand methods we've used throughout our application. This is due to the fact that some clients don't yet support the shorthand declarations. To find a list of supported features for various email clients, visit CampaignMonitor, which has a handy chart. We're going to try to support as many clients as possible,[4] so we will approach this as a lowest-common-denominator solution. But first, we need to see how bad off we are with our existing email template.

Before we do that we need to change our image paths to absolute paths (or to paths that start with http://) and make sure that those images exist on our server. FTP, Capistrano, or some other method will suffice to get our assets where they need to be on the server.

Once our image paths are fixed, we can set up our application to send to Litmus so we can see how this email renders. We're going to create a new test and select our clients, as seen in Figure 21, *Starting a new test in Litmus: Choose your clients*, on page 200. When we click Start Test at the bottom, the system will give us the option to send the email to a certain address or upload the HTML. Since we already have letter_opener generating local HTML files, we'll just upload the HTML.

If we look at Figure 22, *Litmus: HTML/CSS email results*, on page 201, we see that Apple Mail, AOL, and many of the Outlooks and newer Lotus Notes, as

---

4.   http://www.campaignmontior.com/css/

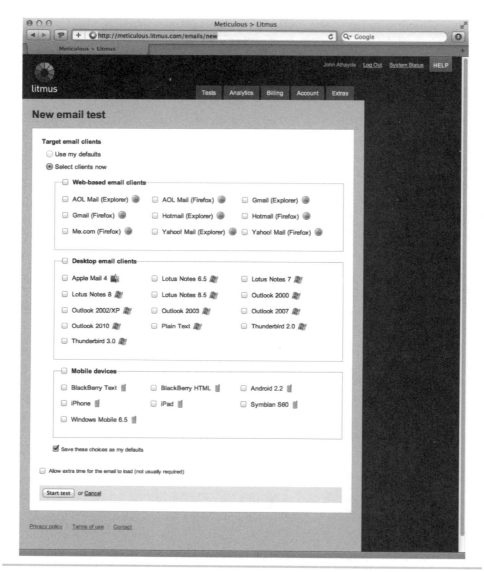

Figure 21—Starting a new test in Litmus: Choose your clients

well as iOS clients, look pretty good. The newer Outlooks don't get the float right. We also see some other clients that don't play so nicely, such as Gmail and Hotmail.

The reason is that a lot of these email clients don't support proper HTML and CSS layout. Many of them strip out the entire <head> section or remove head styles. In order to get this working globally, we have to take a trip back to 1998 and think in table-based layout for these emails.

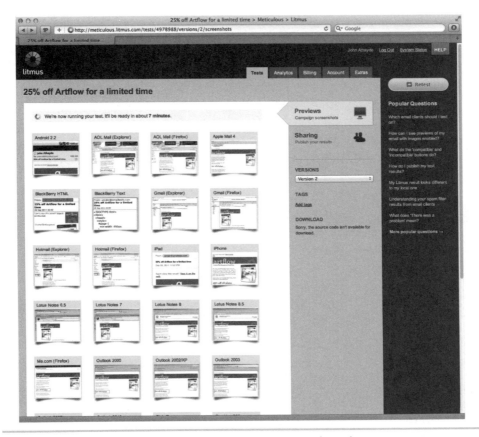

Figure 22—Litmus: HTML/CSS email results

Table-Based Layout

Tables? Yes, tables. Table-based markup was so vilified in the early 2000s that it created a backlash and caused DIVitis, which occurs when you see markup that only uses <div> and <span> for everything. For those of you who never learned about table-based markup before <div>s and CSS ruled the Web, the only way to achieve layout control was to design your site as a fixed-width table and break out various images into a grid of cells. This was the dominant method of layout from about 1997 until the early 2000s, and it is going to get us as close as we can to a unified look across our email clients.

If you haven't learned or need a refresher on table-based layout, you can find some excellent resources online at Campaign Monitor and Sitepoint.[5]

---

5. http://www.campaignmonitor.com/blog/post/2491/tables-in-html-emails-nesting/ and http://www.sitepoint.com/code-html-email-newsletters/, respectively.

This leads us to another of our rules for the wall:

> *When building complex emails, use table-based markup to ensure similar presentation across a variety of email clients.*

Let's take the marketing email that we see in *Enter the Marketing Email*, on page 197, and change it to a table-based layout. We'll think of things as rows (<tr>s) and then add additional cells (<td>s) as needed. This is designed as 600 pixels wide, which is about as wide as we want to go in email design. Many desktop email client's chrome covers anything over this, and the actual message window is quite small. Also, our mobile email clients will be limited to smaller sizes as well.

email/marketing_email_tables.html

```html
<!DOCTYPE html PUBLIC "-//W3C/DTD HTML 4.01//EN"
        "http://www.w3.org/TR/html4/strict.dtd">
<html>
  <head>
    <style>
      table, tr, th, td {margin: 0; padding: 0;}
      a img { border: 0; }
    </style>
    <meta http-equiv="content-type"
        content="text/html; charset=ISO-8859-1">
    <title>25% off ArtFlow for a limited time</title>
  </head>
  <body>
    <center>
      <p style="font-family: verdana, arial, sans-serif;
                font-size: 9px;">
        Can't view this email? <a href="">View it on the Web</a>.
      </p>
      <table border="0" cellpadding="0" cellspacing="0" width="100%">
        <tr>
          <th bgcolor="#bc471d">
            <img src="http://artflowme.com/images/email/spacer.gif"
                width="10" height="1">
          </th>
          <th bgcolor="#bc471d" align="left" valign="top">
            <img src="http://artflowme.com/images/email/logo.gif"
                alt="ArtFlow">
          </th>
          <th bgcolor="#bc471d" align="right" valign="top">
            <img src="http://artflowme.com/images/email/cloud.gif"
                alt="cloud icon">
          </th>
          <th bgcolor="#bc471d">
            <img src="http://artflowme.com/images/email/spacer.gif"
                width="10" height="1">
          </th>
```

```
      </tr>
      <tr>
        <td>
          <img src="http://artflowme.com/images/email/spacer.gif"
              width="10" height="1">
        </td>
        <td align="left" valign="top">
          <img src="http://artflowme.com/images/email/subhead.gif"
              alt="Creative File Management Made Easy"
              style="margin-top:7px;">
          <p style="color: #666666;
                    font-family: verdana, arial, sans-serif;
                    font-size: 14px;
                    line-height: 20px;
                    margin-bottom: 12px;
                    margin-top:15px;">
          We here at AwesomeCo know how the end of the year can
          just be too much for keeping your files in order. Lots
          of &quot;get it out the door before the holiday&quot;
          projects end up in file server soup when you get back
          after New Year's.
          </p>
          <p style="color: #666666;
                    font-family: verdana, arial, sans-serif;
                    font-size: 14px;
                    line-height: 20px;
                    margin-bottom: 12px;">
          That's why, for a limited time only, we're offering all
          new customers:
          </p>
          <a href="http://www.artflowme.com/holiday/">
            <img src="http://artflowme.com/images/email/pitch.gif"
                alt="Sign up today and get 25% off ArtFlow">
          </a>
          <p style="color: #666666;
                    font-family: verdana, arial, sans-serif;
                    font-size: 14px;
                    line-height: 20px;
                    margin-bottom: 12px;">
          Make your New Year's resolution to not have any more
          &quot;to sort&quot; folders. Get your team and your
          clients communicating better with our industry-changing
          software.
          </p>
          <p style="color: #666666;
                    font-family: verdana, arial, sans-serif;
                    font-size: 14px;
                    line-height: 20px;
                    margin-bottom: 12px;">
          Because no designs should be alone this holiday season.
```

```
        </p>
        <a href="http://www.artflowme.com/holiday/">
          <img src="http://artflowme.com/images/email/button1.gif"
              alt="Sign up today and get 25% off ArtFlow"
              border="0">
        </a>
        <br><br>
      </td>
      <td align="right" valign="top">
        <img src="http://artflowme.com/images/email/creatives.jpg"
            alt="image of creative elements">
      </td>
      <td>
        <img src="http://artflowme.com/images/email/spacer.gif"
            width="10" height="1">
      </td>
    </tr>
    <tr>
      <td>
        <img src="http://artflowme.com/images/email/spacer.gif"
            width="10" height="1">
      </td>
      <td colspan="2">
        <img src="http://artflowme.com/images/email/footer.gif"
            alt="&copy;2011 John Athayde, Bruce Williams.
                All Rights Reserved, All Wrongs Reversed.">
        <p style="color: #999999;
                font-family: verdana, arial, sans-serif;
                font-size: 10px;
                margin-bottom: 12px;">
          We hate spam too, so if you received this in error, or
          simply no longer wish to receive our marketing emails,
          <a href="http://www.artflowme.com/marketing/unsub">
            simply click here</a> to unsubscribe.
        </p>
      </td>
      <td>
        <img src="http://artflowme.com/images/email/spacer.gif"
            width="10" height="1">
      </td>
    </tr>
  </table>
  </center>
  </body>
</html>
```

That sure takes us back. We used images where we needed to and used plain
text for the body font. This way, if people have images disabled, they can still
see some of the content. We also provided alt attributes for every image because
many users have their clients configured to block images on emails. We've
defined the styles inline for the paragraph tags as well. We also used a spacer.gif,

which is a 1-pixel-by-1-pixel transparent GIF, to create our left and right margins, since just defining width and height doesn't always work.

Let's send this to Litmus now and see what we get. As it's working, it will have placeholders for the email clients we selected. They will become thumbnails as soon as they are processed, as we see in Figure 23, *The results of our first test*, on page 206.

The first thing that jumps out is the blue box around our images that are links. We have to go in and add a border="0" attribute to each <img> element that falls inside a link/anchor to take those out.

```
email/marketing_email_tables.html
<a href="http://www.artflowme.com/holiday/">
  <img src="http://artflowme.com/images/email/button1.gif"
      alt="Sign up today and get 25% off ArtFlow"
      border="0">
</a>
```

For good measure, we'll also add a style to our header:

```
email/marketing_email_tables.html
a img { border: 0; }
```

We'll also add an inline style attribute to those same tags and say style="border:0;". That will take care of Gmail stripping out the <style> in the header. We'll use both because certain clients look in different places for styles.

We'll go back to Litmus now and click Retest in the upper right corner. By using Retest instead of sending a new test to the system, it will keep the tests together and give us a new version number so we can compare our tests as we fix problems.

Our email looks much better now, but our users who prefer text-only email clients remind us that we have not put in a plain-text alternative. Litmus doesn't support uploading HTML and text-only emails together, so we'd need to make sure we take care of this in whatever email sending solution we choose. Most third-party systems will simply have a field to fill in with the alternative. Remember that this needs some design love too!

Email is one of the more complex pieces of the view, but it can be essential to marketing and interaction with customers. It has more possible clients than the Web side of our application, and special considerations need to be taken into account so that we can deliver the content in a manner that suits our users.

Figure 23—The results of our first test

8.5 Wrapping Up

Now that we've figured out how to send both transactional and marketing emails, as well as how to design them within the complex constraints of the mail readers available, let's tackle some post-launch concerns for our ArtFlow application and ask ourselves some difficult questions about how our application is performing and how we can make it better.

Without continual growth and progress, such
words as improvement, achievement, and
success have no meaning.

> ➤ *Benjamin Franklin*

CHAPTER 9

Optimizing Performance

There are two basic types of performance characteristics we can look at as our application grows and gains users: how efficiently it's performing technically (in terms of concurrent requests and other code metrics) and how effectively it's serving our business interests. As we build our ArtFlow application, we need to ask ourselves a few important questions.

Is the way we've built our views making things run slower, possibly necessitating higher hosting costs? Is the marketing copy or the design stale and uninviting, hindering user acquisition? Is the user interface confusing and unintuitive, preventing users from fully connecting with the product?

Let's tackle these questions head on, getting the answers we need with some tools we can use to objectively measure how fast our application is running and how effectively it's catering to our customers. Once we have our answers, we'll use some optimization techniques to make things better.

The first tool we'll look at is "A/B" testing, which we'll use to see how ArtFlow users interact with the system.

9.1 A/B Testing with Vanity

We live in exciting times. We've built such a good asset manager that we're now selling it as a SaaS (software-as-a-service) to other firms, and the subscriptions are rolling in. Never complacent, though, what we're doing this bright and sunny morning is asking the question "How do we sell more subscriptions?"

We're focused on optimizing conversion, the number of users that go from casually perusing the site to signing up to becoming paying members. To increase our conversion rate, we need to rapidly determine which elements of the application increase (or decrease) it, then tweak it, and then rinse and repeat until we win.

To help us measure how each part of the application is helping (or hurting) our conversion, we are going to integrate a system to do A/B testing (also called multivariate testing[1]). These methods compare two or more options of the same item, be it a Submit button, a logo, a color, or anything else we (or our friends in marketing) can come up with to test and give us statistics we can use to make decisions.

It's important for any organization to improve its online presence and offerings to its users. We, as the front-end developers, are responsible for providing tools to let the company's presence move from nice-in-theory to awesome-in-practice. So we'll test everything from varying headlines on stories to price points to colors on buttons and everything in between.

We'll use a Ruby library called Vanity to help us automate this testing.[2] That way we can skip the whole "let's write an A/B testing engine from scratch" problem and get right down to providing business value.

Setting Up Vanity

To store Vanity's metrics, we'll use Redis, which is fast and easy to install.[3] On OS X, the easiest way to get Redis is with Homebrew,[4] and it's as simple as:

```
$ brew install redis
```

If we weren't using OS X or Homebrew, we'd need to see the Redis site for the appropriate installation details.[5]

Next, let's get the gem into our application by adding it to our Gemfile:

artflow/performance/Gemfile
```
gem 'vanity'
```

Run Bundler and we're in business. Next, we need to create some folders to place our ongoing files in for the tests and metrics.

```
$ mkdir -p experiments/metrics
```

---

1. http://en.wikipedia.org/wiki/Multivariate_statistics
2. http://vanity.labnotes.org/
3. http://redis.io/
4. http://mxcl.github.com/homebrew/
5. http://redis.io/download

We edit our ApplicationController to tell Vanity to track the account that is currently signed in.

artflow/performance/app/controllers/application_controller.rb
```
use_vanity :current_user
```

We need to add a Vanity configuration file, config/vanity.yml, that points the library at our local Redis server:

artflow/performance/config/vanity.yml
```
development:
  collecting: false
  adapter: redis
  host: localhost
  port: 6379

production:
  collecting: true
  adapter: redis
  database: vanity

test:
  collecting: false
```

Vanity comes with a built-in dashboard tool, so we won't have to write a front end to view our results and switch between tests. We do, however, need to tell our application where to make the interface available, so we add a quick route:

artflow/performance/config/routes.rb
```
match '/vanity(/:action/:id)', :controller => :vanity, :as => :vanity
```

Now we make a basic controller, VanityController, to run the dashboard:

artflow/performance/app/controllers/vanity_controller.rb
```
class VanityController < ApplicationController
  include Vanity::Rails::Dashboard

  layout false
end
```

When we browse to http://localhost:3000/vanity, we'll see our dashboard. This has all our tests that are active in the experiments directory as well as the ongoing metrics that are being tracked. We'll set up those metrics now.

Setting Up a Test

We don't want to just change items on the page on a whim. What are we planning for? We should approach these as science experiments. We want a control and a variable and a hypothesis about what will happen. The test proves or disproves that hypothesis.

We need to establish a funnel, or a path we want users to take. This generally ends up in a conversion (be it a signup or a purchase). From there we want to install analytics, such as Google Analytics,[6] and figure out what people are doing. Do they bounce from (immediately leave) our landing page once they get there? Do they browse around but not sign up? Do they sign up for more info? Do they sign up for a free plan but not a paid one? We should find out those pain points and then base our tests on those. Testing without a target and adequate measurement tools is worthless.

We need to talk about what we want to measure here. In Vanity, these are called *metrics*. A metric could be anything from opening a page to adding items to a cart to checking out. We can also track any element of the data model—for example, the quantity of items in the cart.

Metrics run even when tests are not running, and we'll see them in the dashboard. This is important because we want to know what the "normal" baseline is before we can adequately judge if our test is helping or hurting.

We define metrics in our /experiments/metrics directory. A metric for someone clicking to buy would look like this:

artflow/performance/experiments/metrics/subscriptions.rb
```ruby
metric "Subscriptions" do
  description "Measures how many visitors subscribe to ArtFlow"
end
```

It's that simple. We give it a name and a description. It'll track the number of times this happens. Nothing too crazy, as we're just capturing event counts, but this data is critical for analysis.

To get this recording data, we need to tell the system to track it. We can do this two ways: from the controller or from the model. Since the subscriptions metric is tied to the number of Subscription records we have, we'll have the Subscription model increment the metric every time one is created by using the track!() method in our after_create callback in app/models/subscription.rb:

```ruby
after_create :increment_subscriptions!

def increment_subscription!
  track! :subscriptions
end
```

---

6.   http://www.google.com/analytics/

Now when a new Subscription is created, Vanity will know when subscriptions happen and increment our subscriptions metric. It turns out that this is such a common case that, instead of putting this in the model, we can just bake it directly into the metric itself. Let's edit our experiments/metrics/subscriptions.rb again:

artflow/performance/experiments/metrics/subscriptions.rb
```
metric "Subscriptions" do
  description "Measures how many visitors subscribe to ArtFlow"
➤ model Subscription
end
```

Now the Vanity metric definition can handle the business of tracking its value instead. Since metrics on record counts are so common, this handy decoupling keeps the number of times we manually have to call track!() in our controllers and models to a minimum.

Now we're getting data on those metrics, so we can see how our changes affect them. We'll capture these in an experiment and then watch how much the metric changes (either improves or declines). Depending on our customer base, this could be a big or a small change. If we are dealing with hundreds of thousands of users every day, then a small percentage change is a very large number. We should always know what our metric goals are before we start, such as "Improve conversion by 1 percent."

We want to have our metrics collecting regardless of whether a test is running or not so we can see the change and also avoid any other statistical anomalies or other issues that arise, which is why we enabled collection in the production environment portion of our config/vanity.yml:

artflow/performance/config/vanity.yml
```
production:
  collecting: true
  adapter: redis
  database: vanity
```

We spoke with our product team and they're convinced we have what is called a *paradox of choice.*[7] A paradox of choice is a hypothesis that too many choices can create anxiety with customers when they are looking to purchase something and actually hurt conversion. With three choices, there's less self-filtering required, less information on the page, and a better chance, we believe, that users will convert on that page. It's a great hypothesis and something we can easily check with A/B testing. We'll write this up as an experiment file, 3_vs_5_plans.rb, and put it in our experiments folder.

---

7. http://en.wikipedia.org/wiki/The_Paradox_of_Choice:_Why_More_Is_Less

artflow/performance/experiments/3_vs_5_plans.rb
```ruby
ab_test "3 vs 5 plans" do
  description "Testing to see if 3 plans converts better than 5."
  metrics :subscriptions
end
```

We display the plans to our users in a partial, so to build our A/B test we'll split this into two different partials, one that shows three plans and one that shows five. We'll put a conditional statement on the partial call. If the test is active, it will render the variable option of three plans.

artflow/performance/app/views/subscriptions/_form.html.erb
```erb
<% if ab_test(:3_vs_5_plans) %>
  <%= render '3plans' %>
<% else %>
  <%= render '5plans' %>
<% end %>
```

These two options provide a distinct difference for our users. We are mainly interested in testing the paradox of choice. We don't want to completely change the design because we want to have as few variables as possible to see which option outperforms the other so we can move forward with other tests.

Now we just sit back and wait for the results to roll in!

Reading the Results

The metric we are tracking is conversion. We want to increase the number of people buying a plan subscription. When there is no change in other factors, if that number goes down, we have done something wrong. When we set up the test, we set it to turn off at a thousand visitors. Based on our site stats, we know this will take about a week to run. We could set it higher, but we want to actually move forward on A/B tests, not just be stuck in one.

We go and load up the Vanity dashboard that comes with the plugin and take a look at our metric graphs. It looks like our test was a success. During the period that we had it enabled, conversion went up. But let's dig a little deeper. What exactly happened? Is it statistically significant? What does that even mean?

Statistical significance is when a result in a test is unlikely to have occurred by chance or randomness.[8] If our result just looks great but had a low number of users or some other event occurred, it may not be as significant as we think. The significance is referred to as the *p-value* and we want our p-values in Vanity's dashboard to be over 95 percent.

---

8. http://en.wikipedia.org/wiki/Statistical_significance

Looking at our results we see that the three-price options variable converts 7.2 percent better than the control. We ran this over a week with twenty thousand views, so, for our business, we'll go ahead and switch to only showing the three main options for price. And now we can look at the next test that our marketing guys want to run.

We could, in the future, get more detailed and set other metrics in place, such as saving which plan the user signed up for (compared to our current mode of "they signed up or not"). There are all sorts of things we can track as we move forward. Remember that it's not just about the quantity of throughput but the quality as well. Getting a lot of clicks that don't convert is not worth as much fewer clicks that convert at a higher rate.

Moving Beyond A/B: Multivariate

Vanity supports more than two variables in a test, but it takes a little more configuration to handle the potential mix of variables.

Say we've been doing some research and found that the color of the button can affect if people click on it or not. We're going to test the color and text of our main call-to-action button. Right now it's a green button that says "Find Out More." We are going to test the following options: "Try Now" vs. "Find Out More" for the wording, and blue vs. green for the button color.

The control in this experiment is the Find Out More button in green. We have three other variables that we are also going to test: "Find Out More" in blue, "Try Now" in green, and "Try Now" in blue.

With multivariate tests we need to have a much larger sample size, and the sample size can grow exponentially with the number of variables in the test. We're able to roughly calculate the potential number of variations by using a factorial.[9]

It's not too difficult to set these up. Instead of our basic true/false, we're going to be looking at various states. We have two widgets. We want to show both, show one or the other, and finally show neither to see what works better with conversion.[10]

This test would run in the same way and show us four options in the end. When our site has enough throughput, multivariate can get a solution much faster than many single control/variable experiments. When to use which type of test depends on our traffic and who we are targeting.

---

9. http://en.wikipedia.org/wiki/Factorial
10. http://vanity.labnotes.org/ab_testing.html#multiple

Testing is an excellent way for us to incrementally improve certain metrics, or, in simpler terms, to help improve our business. At the end of the day, we can test everything in the world, but keeping our focus on the customer will always win the field.

9.2 Performance Testing and Maintenance

Inevitably in our application's life cycle, we'll experience some slow page loads. These are caused by a variety of issues that can range from server configuration to how our models interact with ActiveRecord and the database layer to inefficiencies in our view code. These problems take a long time to manifest themselves, and we should remain vigilant about preventing them before the symptoms appear. Many of these are beyond the scope of this book, so we are going to focus on the things that we can affect as view layer developers.

We are going to look at some tools for keeping our view code running like a well-oiled machine. These include tools to find unused CSS classes, manage our load times, and implement quick caching, as well as a brief overview of what we can ask our Ops guys to do on their end to help speed up our site and improve our customer's experience.

Auditing and Cleaning CSS Declarations

Over time, our application changes. We add new screens, remove screens, implement redesigns, and more. With these changes comes the potential for lots of cruft in our CSS files, stuff that is no longer needed or called. These files, while only transferred once and cached, can add up on large traffic sites. Since one of our highest costs is going to be transfer costs, optimizing these files can save us costs. These dead code areas can get really out of control in larger apps when our team is big. Lucky for us, there are some great tools we can use to attack this issue.

Auditing from the Browser

The first and easiest way to start auditing pages for unused CSS is to install the Firefox extension called Dust Me Selectors, which is available from Sitepoint.[11] This hasn't been updated in a while, and there's a replacement for newer browsers (up to Firefox version 8) called CSS Roundup.[12] In it's simplest form, this will compare all the IDs, classes, and DOM elements on the page

---

11. http://www.sitepoint.com/dustmeselectors/
12. http://blog.brothersmorrison.com/?p=198

with our style sheets and tells us what is not used on the page. Google's PageSpeed tool, which we'll use in a little bit, also does this for us.

Let's take a look at our login page at http://localhost:3000/designers/sign_in and see where we can clean it up. Once the page loads, we can click the small broom in the lower right of the status bar. It will prompt us with what it is going to do (review selectors) and then we'll see it start counting. When it's done, it will display results similar to Figure 24, *Results from Dust Me Selectors*, on page 216.

That returned a whole bunch of stuff! Is our CSS actually that bad? No. Because our style sheet covers our whole application, and Dust Me Selectors is only looking at one page, it's going to say that we have a whole lot of unused CSS. While we could script it to spider the application, we'd then have to share that script by hand and make sure people have the newest version.

There's a Ruby gem that will let us create a Rake task to do this for us and walk through the application looking for errant CSS that is hiding out.

Using the Deadweight Gem

Once an application gets a few years on it, we end up with large chunks that get rewritten or altered. Designs change, and with them, CSS. If we don't remove old CSS when we make those edits, we'll end up with a bloated stylesheets directory, with all sorts of declarations that are never used.

To find these unused declarations, which are called "deadweight,"[13] we can add something to our application and our test suite to search through and find the cruft. The Deadweight gem takes a given set of style sheets and URLs and determines which CSS selectors are being used and which ones aren't. Its report will let us know what we can delete and, in doing so, will reduce the size of the style sheet that we serve.

We'll install Deadweight by adding it to our Gemfile, but we'll do so in our test group, like so:

artflow/performance/Gemfile
```
group :test do
  gem 'capybara'
  gem 'cucumber-rails'
  gem 'database_cleaner'
  gem 'turn', :require => false
  gem 'factory_girl'
➤ gem 'deadweight', require: 'deadweight/hijack/rails'
end
```

---

13. https://github.com/aanand/deadweight

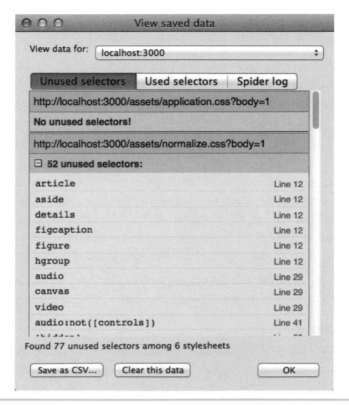

Figure 24—Results from Dust Me Selectors

After doing that, we need to run bundle install and make sure it is in our system. We're going to create a new Rake task in lib/tasks/deadweight.rake:

artflow/performance/lib/tasks/deadweight.rake

```
require 'deadweight'

Deadweight::RakeTask.new do |dw|
  dw.stylesheets = ["/assets/application.css",
                    "/assets/normalize.css",
                    "/assets/layout.css",
                    "/assets/sidebar.css",
                    "/assets/navigation.css",
                    "/assets/notifications.css",
                    "/assets/creations.css"]
  dw.pages = ["/creations/index",
              "/creations/1"]
end
```

This will load all our relevant style sheets and then check them to see what is used and what is not. To run this task, we need to start our application running on localhost:3000 with the rails server command. Once that's up we can run rake deadweight from our terminal session.

Deadweight can also be used with the Mechanize library to improve its analysis of applications by actually interacting with pages.[14] More information can be found in Deadweight's documentation.[15]

Now that we've cleaned things up a bit by getting rid of unnecessary style declarations, let's look at measuring and optimizing our page load times.

Speeding Up Page Load Time

There are many ways to speed up the load time of our pages, and while none alone is the end all be all, performing these audits and cleaning up will help create a more efficient site and a better user experience. One of the biggest wins since Rails 3.1 has been the built-in asset pipeline, which bundles and minifies our JavaScript and CSS through YUI and UglifierJS, respectively.

This helps us reduce the number of http requests and speeds up our pages. But there are many other things we can tackle.

Finding Problems with ySlow and PageSpeed

The developer team at Yahoo has spent a lot of time figuring out things that affect web page performance and has codified them into a testing tool for our usage called ySlow.[16] This is available as an extension for Firefox, Chrome, and Opera and as a bookmarklet.

The tool comes with three predefined rulesets, or we can create our own. When we run it against a ruleset, it will provide suggestions for improving our page's performance, such as reducing http requests, reducing DNS lookups, minifying JavaScript and CSS, and other best practices.

Google PageSpeed is a similar extension that fills a similar role. One of the main differences (and why we prefer it over Yahoo's ySlow) is that PageSpeed does not dock us points for not using a CDN, or content delivery network. There is also a PageSpeed online tool that saves us the extension download (for those who don't want to use Chrome or Firefox) available at http://page-speed.googlelabs.com/pagespeed/.

---

14. http://mechanize.rubyforge.org/
15. https://github.com/aanand/deadweight
16. http://developer.yahoo.com/yslow/

> ## Generating a Sitemap.xml
>
> There are a few different sitemap utilities available for Rails apps, but two of the best (and most complex) are https://github.com/christianhellsten/sitemap-generator and https://github.com/alexrabarts/big_sitemap. The latter is great for exceptionally large sites. For something simpler or to roll your own, take a look at the sitemap fork of the Enki blog system for inspiration.[a]
>
> ---
>
> a.   https://github.com/fernandogomes/enki/blob/sitemap/app/controllers/sitemap_controller.rb

Both of these tools work through the Firebug extension for Firefox and live on a tab in the interface.[17] To use PageSpeed, we hit the PageSpeed tab and run the analysis. After running the test, we get a 39/100, and the tool gives us some suggestions for speeding up our site: we should gzip certain resources (we will look at this later), we should minify JavaScript, and we may have some unused CSS selectors.

In order to precompile and minify our assets, we can use the `bundle exec rake assets:precompile` command locally, or we can use Capistrano (in 2.8.0 and above), loading a recipe:

```
load 'deploy/assets'
```

There are lots of configuration options in the asset pipeline that can be set for this, depending on the need and the level we are trying to get things running at, with details available in the Asset Pipeline guide.[18]

Once we're sure our assets are being precompiled as they're deployed, we should use some analysis tools to look for other holes in our interface.

Ongoing Auditing with Google Webmaster Tools

Google has an online suite of analysis tools that help us figure out where links are coming from, where we have crawl errors, what search queries are coming in, if our sitemap.xml has problems, and a variety of other items.[19]

This will integrate with the PageSpeed browser extension for some of the newer Google Labs functionality Google has as well. These tools help us to control the site links served in Google results, identify web crawl errors, and manage other things to keep us running smoothly.

---

17.   http://getfirebug.com/
18.   http://guides.rubyonrails.org/asset_pipeline.html
19.   https://www.google.com/webmasters/tools/

There are a number of local tools we can use as well, some of which are even built into our browsers!

Analyzing with Web Inspector, ApacheBench, and More

Some of the most overlooked tools when trying to get our site moving faster are right under our noses. In Safari, we have the built-in Web Inspector, which has a tab for viewing the speed of downloads for the elements that make up each page. With this we can quickly see what items the page is hanging on and fix those problems.

Is our jQuery loading slow from a third-party server? Maybe we want to bring that in-house. Lots of images taking a while? Maybe we should use image sprites (which we covered in Section 3.3, *Adding Sprites*, on page 88). The results in Figure 25, *The Safari/WebKit Web Inspector*, on page 219, are from our development environment, so we don't have any of the benefits of asset minification and precompiling occurring, and we have a twenty-second page load time from start to finish.

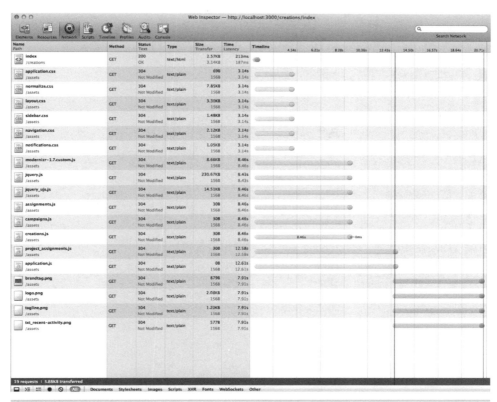

Figure 25—The Safari/WebKit Web Inspector

We know that's not going to cut it in production, so we can make sure our asset pipeline is configured correctly, bundle our static assets, and work from that baseline.

```
$ bundle exec rake assets:precompile
```

This dropped our development environment request time from 20.71 seconds to 8.91 seconds. That's under half the time!

That's great for one request, but what happens to our servers when they get hammered? We can use a tool that comes built into Mac OS X (and available on most Unix systems) called ApacheBench.[20] If we run this, we can see what is going on with our site and where problems may occur. Running this on therailsview.com, for example, yields:

```
$ ab -n 100 -c 5 therailsview.com/
This is ApacheBench, Version 2.3 <$Revision: 655654 $>
Copyright 1996 Adam Twiss, Zeus Technology Ltd,
http://www.zeustech.net/
Licensed to The Apache Software Foundation, http://www.apache.org/

Benchmarking therailsview.com (be patient).....done


Server Software:        Apache
Server Hostname:        therailsview.com
Server Port:            80

Document Path:          /
Document Length:        1605 bytes

Concurrency Level:      5
Time taken for tests:   3.631 seconds
Complete requests:      100
Failed requests:        0
Write errors:           0
Total transferred:      188000 bytes
HTML transferred:       160500 bytes
Requests per second:    27.54 [#/sec] (mean)
Time per request:       181.572 [ms] (mean)
Time per request:       36.315 [ms] (mean, across all concurrent requests)
Transfer rate:          50.56 [Kbytes/sec] received

Connection Times (ms)
              min  mean[+/-sd] median   max
Connect:       55  174 103.8    150    763
Processing:     0    5  11.3      2     61
Waiting:        0    4  11.3      1     59
```

---

20. http://httpd.apache.org/docs/2.0/programs/ab.html

```
Total:          99  179 102.0    152      763

Percentage of the requests served within a certain time (ms)
   50%     152
   66%     175
   75%     190
   80%     197
   90%     225
   95%     256
   98%     629
   99%     763
  100%     763 (longest request)
```

We see that our requests range from 99 ms to 763 ms. With this baseline, we can start optimizing both the server settings (with the help of our DevOps guys) and other page elements to lower these times.

We can start by using our Web Inspector and see if certain requests are getting tied up and then target those. After that, we can look at merging our CSS and JavaScript files and creating image sprites. This is all about reducing requests to the server. A page served in five requests is much faster than one served in thirty.

After we've spent some time dialing in the request side of the equation, we want to start looking at the transfer side. How can we get the data transferred to our customer's browser with a smaller amount of information?

Image Optimization

One of the easiest wins in loading our pages is to optimize our images. On the (Mac) desktop, one of the best solutions for this is a program called ImageOptim.[21] This wraps up seven different optimization tools into a single interface (and an optional eighth tool with some extra work). It also has a sister application called ImageAlpha, where we can convert 24-bit PNGs down to PNG8+alpha, saving a lot of size with little visual change.

The quickest thing we can do is to run our public/images directory through this tool. It will reduce the images by taking 24-bit PNGs and changing them to PNG8+alpha, as well as removing gamma information and other content that is not needed in most cases.

Real quick, let's just drop our images directory into ImageOptim and see what happens. It looks like we save, on average, 65 percent in file size. (See Figure 26, *ImageOptim compressing our site graphic elements*, on page 222.) That's a big win for static assets, especially as we scale to handle more customers.

---

21. http://imageoptim.pornel.net/

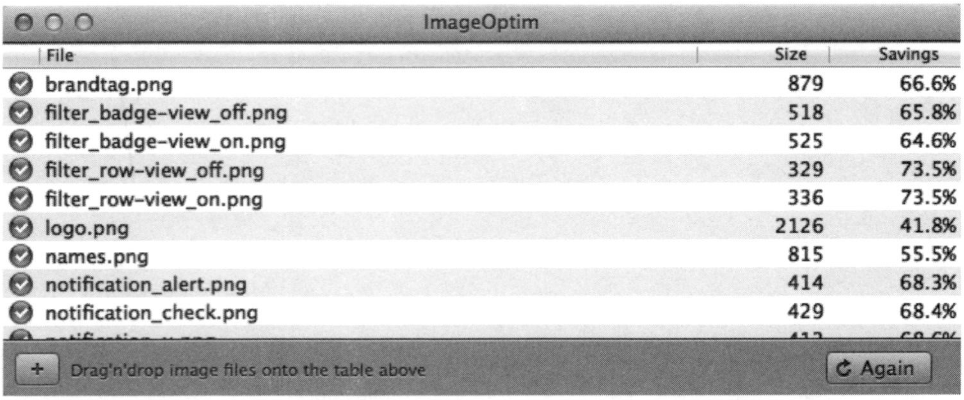

Figure 26—ImageOptim compressing our site graphic elements

ImageOptim saved us so much space by converting any image with under 256 colors to a PNG8+alpha format. Photoshop doesn't support this format, so therefore "Save for Web" only gives us 24-bit when we want true alpha transparency. We can replicate some of this in Adobe Fireworks, but since our team doesn't use that tool, we don't see those benefits.

For Windows and Unix systems, we can download and run these tools on our own or make them part of our application's image processing tools, such as OptiPNG and the Ruby Gem interface to it, also called optipng.[22]

Outside of this, we can also look at SVG and SVGZ images. SVGs are "scalable vector graphics" and the SVGZ is a gzipped equivalent.[23] Many modern browsers support this (including IE9+) and as a vector file, we can scale them quite large with no file size increase. We can also include raster elements within an SVG.

Many browsers don't deal with this right, and there are a handful of tools available online, such as "SVG to HTML" and more.[24] This has a very limited use for dealing with really large images of a specific type.

Speeding Up the Web Server

On the server itself, we want to ensure that our site keeps humming along and serving files quickly and without too much hand-holding from us. There are a few ways we can help it accomplish that.

---

22. http://optipng.sourceforge.net/ and https://github.com/martinkozak/optipng, respectively.
23. http://www.adobe.com/svg/illustrator/compressedsvg.html
24. http://www.irunmywebsite.com/raphael/SVGTOHTML_LIVE.php

First, we want to send any file types that we can down as gzip compressed. In Apache-based web servers, there's a module called mod_deflate that will do this.[25] This lets us compress things on a browser-by-browser basis as well as on a file-type basis. This is really a DevOps kind of fix, but it's one of the first things we should do when we're getting set up for production.

Another tool is Google's mod_pagespeed.[26] It optimizes both our web pages and the resources on them to implement web performance best practices. This will also bat cleanup for us on our finished code. While we can control the code that renders the pages, it's difficult to control the code that comes out of text fields, especially in content management systems and places where we allow HTML-formatted comments. If we have a missing end tag or things of that nature, mod_pagespeed can help us clean those up before we send them to the client machine.

We have a wide variety of tools for auditing and catching problems on the server and as we develop, and our site is already running faster. Now let's look at some Rails stack solutions for speeding up request times and improving performance.

Implementing Caching

Many of our application's pages don't change all that often. They change due to actions our users engage in, such as adding assets, creating new projects, and posting comments. One of the fastest ways we can speed up our site is to add page caching to serve static HTML files whenever there is no new information on the page. Not only will this help with page load on the customer side, but it will reduce the load on our application and database servers as well.

Caching is already enabled in our production environment, as we can see by opening up config/environments/production.rb:

artflow/performance/config/environments/production.rb
```
config.action_controller.perform_caching = true
```

There are a few types of caching we can do to help speed up our server. For pages that don't require authentication or have restricted access, we can use *page caching*. If we need to have filters run before a page is served, we need to use *action caching*. We can also cache pieces of a page using *fragment caching*.

---

25. http://httpd.apache.org/docs/2.0/mod/mod_deflate.html
26. http://code.google.com/speed/page-speed/docs/module.html

Page Caching

Our creations index is a view that gets a lot of mileage in our application. What happens in a request is that Rails processes the commands in the controller and turns it into a web page that is served. It's destroyed as soon as it's done, and it has to start all over the next time.

We don't add creations as often as people view the index, so we can save some time by caching the results of our controller action and serving them a static HTML file (let's call it creations.html) instead.

To turn on page caching, we simply open up our controller and add one line above our method definitions.

```
class CreationsController < ApplicationController

➤   cached_page :index

    # The rest of the controller...

end
```

This static file will be placed in the default public_path and will be called instead of the action if it is present. The default public_path is typically the public/ directory, but it can be changed by altering config.action_controller.page_cache_directory in our environment file.

So we are now serving a static file, which is much faster than running through the actual database calls. But what happens when we add a file? Since the static creations.html is present, it will serve that first. We need to tell Rails that the cached page is no longer valid, and we do that in app/controllers/creations_controller.rb again, but this time for the create action (and probably the update action as well):

```
def create
  @creation = Creation.new(params[:creation])
  if @creation.save
➤    expire_page action: :index
    flash[:notice] = "Creation added!"
    redirect_to @creation
  else
    flash.now[:alert] = "Could not save creation!"
    render action: 'new'
  end
end
```

That's the simplest form of caching. It generally works only for pages that don't need a login. So how do we handle that state? We use action caching.

Action Caching

Most of our application is one that restricts access. Users must log in to see creative files associated with their accounts. Page caching won't work for this situation, so we need to look at using action caching instead. It acts similarly to page caching except that it runs through the Action Pack part of the Rails stack before the cache is served. This lets before_filter directives, such as authentication, actually work first.

So for our authenticated CreationsController.rb, our code would look something like this:

artflow/performance/app/controllers/creations_controller.rb
```
class CreationsController < ApplicationController

  before_filter :authenticate_user!
➤ caches_action :index

  def index
    @creations = current_user.creations
  end

  def create
    @creation = current_project.creations.new(params[:creation])
    if @creation.save
➤     expire_action action: :index
      flash[:notice] = "Creation added!"
      redirect_to @creation
    else
      flash.now[:alert] = "Could not save creation!"
      render action: 'new'
    end
  end
end
```

We simply change the caches_page directive to caches_action and do the same for our expiration function. This kind of caching is an after filter, so we'll only get caches of successful requests.

Fragment Caching

What do we do when we only want to cache part of a page? The solution here is to use fragment caching. It's completely done in our view layer as well, so we can cache as we go without having to delve too deep into the internals.

Let's look at our CreationsController index action again. We have an area for "Recent Activity" in our sidebar. This will probably change at a different rate than the creations themselves, so we're going to set up two separate fragment caches.

Fragment caches work in a similar way to action caches and store their data in the same place.

```
artflow/performance/app/views/creations/index.html.erb
<% cache action: 'index', action_suffix: 'all_creations' do %>
  <ul id='creations'>
    <%= render @creations %>
  </ul>
<% end %>
```

We also add caching to our sidebar partial, app/views/creations/_sidebar.html.erb:

```
<% content_for :sidebar do %>
  <% cache action: 'index', action_suffix: 'recent_activity' do %>
    <section id="recent_activity">
      <header>
        <h1 class="ir" id="recent">Recent Activity</h1>
      </header>
      <%= render 'activity_items/recent' %>
    </section>
  <% end %>
<% end %>
```

The expiration of this is as easy as using the expire_fragment method, like so:

```
expire_fragment(controller: 'creations',
                action: 'index',
                action_suffix: 'recent_activity')
```

But say we want to use the same recent activity cache on other controllers. We can use a globally keyed fragment by adding a key in the cache() call.

```
artflow/performance/app/views/creations/_sidebar.html.erb
<% content_for :sidebar do %>
➤  <% cache action: 'recent_app_activity' do %>
    <section id="recent_activity">
      <header>
        <h1 class="ir" id="recent">Recent Activity</h1>
      </header>
      <%= render 'activity_items/recent' %>
    </section>
  <% end %>
<% end %>
```

And then to expire it, simply expire that key:

```
expire_fragment('recent_app_activity')
```

There's more complexity we can investigate, such as sweepers for cleaning up caches and other tricks; details can be found in the "Caching with Rails" guide or through other online articles.[27]

Caching will make our production application feel much snappier and help reduce load on our server resources as well. Whenever we find things are slowing down, we should look at what we can cache.

DevOps Fixes

To some extent, we can only do so much in our code to make the site more efficient. A certain number of requests will overload any hardware setup in the world. Here are some things that we should discuss with our DevOps team to see if we can implement them.

Load Balancing

Once our application moves beyond one server or instance, we want to start splitting up our web, application, and database servers. Once we get more than one of each, we need to have a way to share the love and the load among the servers. A load balancer, which is typically another machine or instance that routes requests, will be an essential part of scaling our systems.

We'll also need to make sure our database servers replicate each other, and we'll need to update our Capistrano tasks to push to all the right places.

Fixing Query Times

For all the power that ActiveRecord gives us, it can also lead to massive joins in queries that take a long time to process. If this is the case, we'll need to either add indexes to our database tables or look at utilizing find_by_sql() and drop down to calling our data by hand. We can also investigate utilizing something like Memcached to help with caching queries and speeding up response times.

Static Asset Servers and CDNs

If we're dealing with a lot of images or video creations as we grow, we might consider using a static asset server or even a CDN (content delivery network) to handle our static files. This will help our servers focus on what they need to do, which is run the application, and allow us to offload the high bandwidth static files to dedicated, stripped-down servers.

---

27. http://guides.rubyonrails.org/caching_with_rails.html

CDNs are a unique class in this group. While having static asset servers with your other servers lets us dial in our web server software (Apache, Nginx, etc.), we're still limited by the connection from our customer's ISP to the server and back again. Any hiccups along that path or a lot of concurrent users can really hurt the experience on the customer side.

Enter the CDN.

This service has mirrored copies of our static assets all over the world, and load balancing servers will send from the fastest available machine at any given point. This keeps videos streaming, large images downloading, and software updating in a smooth fashion.

Two of the largest CDNs are Akamai and Amazon's CloudFront.[28] They have various pricing plans based on bandwidth or files served. When the app gets to a point that our own static asset servers don't cut it anymore, it's time to look into these tools.

Varnish and RAM Caching (Reverse Proxies)

For extreme performance on caching, we can look at Varnish Cache,[29] a caching tool that speeds up our pages by caching them in RAM instead of on disk. It can eat up a lot of resources and basically intercepts all requests on port 80. We'd then have it talk to our application on, say, port 8080. Varnish Cache uses the expiration in the Apache config for time-based expiration and has an API, so we can talk to it and tell it when to expire pages. If Rails caching and memcached aren't enough, this is where we'd need to go next.

Remember that in speeding up our server and providing better content flows, we are going to reduce the amount of time people spend on our site and the number of pages they visit. In an age of TL;DR ("too long; didn't read"), efficiency is the name of the game.

9.3 Wrapping Up

Ongoing performance testing and refactoring our code to run smoother and faster makes for a better experience for our customers. It also makes our code easier to maintain and lets us keep up with current best practices. A little extra time out of our iterations will help us from having whole iterations of "fixing problems" and make for a smoother work flow for all.

---

28. http://www.akamai.com and http://aws.amazon.com/cloudfront/, respectively.
29. https://www.varnish-cache.org/

9.4   Where Do We Go from Here?

We've got ArtFlow up and running and in production, and we're now optimizing performance and adding new features for our users. Our View layer has come a long way from the start of this adventure. Here, at the end, we have a toolkit full of new libraries, gems, and techniques to keep our future development on the right track.

But we can't rest on our laurels. The view is constantly changing. Today's cutting-edge techniques are tomorrow's old news. It's important that we stay caught up on developments with the myriad of technologies that make up the view and continue to adjust our approach.

Good luck! It's a [code] jungle out there!

Part I

Appendices

The Rails View Rules

Throughout the book we've been establishing rules of thumb for use in our daily development tasks. Here they are, all collected in one place. We've also provided a handy PDF download to print out at http://therailsview.com/rules.pdf.

1. Our markup should have meaning. We write templates using semantic HTML.

2. Our style sheets should handle presentation. We don't use markup to style or use images when CSS will do.

3. Our templates should be free of client-side code. We unobtrusively attach behavior from our JavaScript files.

4. Our templates should be easy to read. We consistently indent correctly using spaces instead of tabs, type lines no longer than eighty characters, and extract complex logic to helpers and presenters.

5. Our templates should be easy to find. We use standard naming conventions and place them in the directory for the related resource (or the layout).

6. Our markup should be easy for the entire team to modify. We prefer rendering partials over generating markup from Ruby code.

7. Our technology choices should help, not hinder, the team. We use the templating language and tools that work best for all of us.

8. Our designs for the Web should work on a variety of devices and browsers. We build for the simplest interactions first and support progressive enhancement.

9. Our designs for email must work for a wide range of providers. We use HTML tables and images as necessary and always provide a plain-text alternative.

10. Our application should perform as well as it needs to, when it needs to. We implement the most elegant approach first, then we optimize when necessary.

Bibliography

[BK10]   Bear Bibeault and Yehuda Katz. *jQuery in Action*. Manning Publications Co., Greenwich, CT, Second Edition, 2010.

[CC11]   Hampton Catlin and Michael Lintorn Catlin. *Pragmatic Guide to Sass*. The Pragmatic Bookshelf, Raleigh, NC and Dallas, TX, 2011.

[Dee08]   Ian Dees. *Scripted GUI Testing with Ruby*. The Pragmatic Bookshelf, Raleigh, NC and Dallas, TX, 2008.

[HT00]   Andrew Hunt and David Thomas. *The Pragmatic Programmer: From Journeyman to Master*. Addison-Wesley, Reading, MA, 2000.

[HWWJ12]   Brian P. Hogan, Chris Warren, Mike Weber, Chris Johnson, and Aaron Godin. *Web Development Recipes*. The Pragmatic Bookshelf, Raleigh, NC and Dallas, TX, 2012.

[Hog10]   Brian P. Hogan. *HTML5 and CSS3: Develop with Tomorrow's Standards Today*. The Pragmatic Bookshelf, Raleigh, NC and Dallas, TX, 2010.

[Mar08]   Robert C. Martin. *Clean Code: A Handbook of Agile Software Craftsmanship*. Prentice Hall, Englewood Cliffs, NJ, 2008.

[Pil10]   Mark Pilgrim. *HTML5: Up and Running*. O'Reilly & Associates, Inc., Sebastopol, CA, 2010.

[RTH11]   Sam Ruby, Dave Thomas, and David Heinemeier Hansson. *Agile Web Development with Rails, 4th Edition*. The Pragmatic Bookshelf, Raleigh, NC and Dallas, TX, 2011.

Index

What you Need to Know

Each new version of the Web brings its own gold rush. Here are your tools.

HTML5 and CSS3 are the future of web development, but you don't have to wait to start using them. Even though the specification is still in development, many modern browsers and mobile devices already support HTML5 and CSS3. This book gets you up to speed on the new HTML5 elements and CSS3 features you can use right now, and backwards compatible solutions ensure that you don't leave users of older browsers behind.

Brian P. Hogan
(280 pages) ISBN: 9781934356685. $33
http://pragprog.com/titles/bhh5

Modern web development takes more than just HTML and CSS with a little JavaScript mixed in. Clients want more responsive sites with faster interfaces that work on multiple devices, and you need the latest tools and techniques to make that happen. This book gives you more than 40 concise, tried-and-true solutions to today's web development problems, and introduces new workflows that will expand your skillset.

Brian P. Hogan, Chris Warren, Mike Weber, Chris Johnson, Aaron Godin
(344 pages) ISBN: 9781934356838. $35
http://pragprog.com/titles/wbdev

Welcome to the Better Web

You need a better JavaScript and more expressive CSS and HTML today. Start here.

CoffeeScript is JavaScript done right. It provides all of JavaScript's functionality wrapped in a cleaner, more succinct syntax. In the first book on this exciting new language, CoffeeScript guru Trevor Burnham shows you how to hold onto all the power and flexibility of JavaScript while writing clearer, cleaner, and safer code.

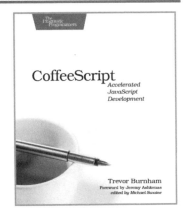

Trevor Burnham
(160 pages) ISBN: 9781934356784. $29
http://pragprog.com/titles/tbcoffee

CSS is fundamental to the web, but it's a basic language and lacks many features. Sass is just like CSS, but with a whole lot of extra power so you can get more done, more quickly. Build better web pages today with *Pragmatic Guide to Sass*. These concise, easy-to-digest tips and techniques are the shortcuts experienced CSS developers need to start developing in Sass today.

Hampton Catlin and Michael Lintorn Catlin
(128 pages) ISBN: 9781934356845. $25
http://pragprog.com/titles/pg_sass

Go Beyond with Rails and NoSQL

There's so much new to learn with Rails 3 and the latest crop of NoSQL databases. These titles will get you up to speed on the latest.

Thousands of developers have used the first edition of *Rails Recipes* to solve the hard problems. Now, five years later, it's time for the Rails 3.1 edition of this trusted collection of solutions, completely revised by Rails master Chad Fowler.

Chad Fowler
(350 pages) ISBN: 9781934356777. $35
http://pragprog.com/titles/rr2

Data is getting bigger and more complex by the day, and so are your choices in handling it. From traditional RDBMS to newer NoSQL approaches, *Seven Databases in Seven Weeks* takes you on a tour of some of the hottest open source databases today. In the tradition of Bruce A. Tate's *Seven Languages in Seven Weeks*, this book goes beyond a basic tutorial to explore the essential concepts at the core of each technology.

Eric Redmond and Jim Wilson
(330 pages) ISBN: 9781934356920. $35
http://pragprog.com/titles/rwdata

Testing is only the beginning

Start with Test Driven Development, Domain Driven Design, and Acceptance Test Driven Planning in Ruby. Then add Shoulda, Cucumber, Factory Girl, and Rcov for the ultimate in Ruby and Rails development.

Behaviour-Driven Development (BDD) gives you the best of Test Driven Development, Domain Driven Design, and Acceptance Test Driven Planning techniques, so you can create better software with self-documenting, executable tests that bring users and developers together with a common language.

Get the most out of BDD in Ruby with *The RSpec Book*, written by the lead developer of RSpec, David Chelimsky.

David Chelimsky, Dave Astels, Zach Dennis, Aslak Hellesøy, Bryan Helmkamp, Dan North
(448 pages) ISBN: 9781934356371. $38.95
http://pragprog.com/titles/achbd

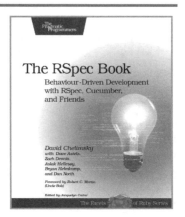

Rails Test Prescriptions is a comprehensive guide to testing Rails applications, covering Test-Driven Development from both a theoretical perspective (why to test) and from a practical perspective (how to test effectively). It covers the core Rails testing tools and procedures for Rails 2 and Rails 3, and introduces popular add-ons, including RSpec, Shoulda, Cucumber, Factory Girl, and Rcov.

Noel Rappin
(368 pages) ISBN: 9781934356647. $34.95
http://pragprog.com/titles/nrtest

The Pragmatic Bookshelf

The Pragmatic Bookshelf features books written by developers for developers. The titles continue the well-known Pragmatic Programmer style and continue to garner awards and rave reviews. As development gets more and more difficult, the Pragmatic Programmers will be there with more titles and products to help you stay on top of your game.

Visit Us Online

This Book's Home Page
http://pragprog.com/titles/warv
Source code from this book, errata, and other resources. Come give us feedback, too!

Register for Updates
http://pragprog.com/updates
Be notified when updates and new books become available.

Join the Community
http://pragprog.com/community
Read our weblogs, join our online discussions, participate in our mailing list, interact with our wiki, and benefit from the experience of other Pragmatic Programmers.

New and Noteworthy
http://pragprog.com/news
Check out the latest pragmatic developments, new titles and other offerings.

Save on the eBook

Save on the eBook versions of this title. Owning the paper version of this book entitles you to purchase the electronic versions at a terrific discount.

PDFs are great for carrying around on your laptop—they are hyperlinked, have color, and are fully searchable. Most titles are also available for the iPhone and iPod touch, Amazon Kindle, and other popular e-book readers.

Buy now at *http://pragprog.com/coupon*

Contact Us

Online Orders:	*http://pragprog.com/catalog*
Customer Service:	*support@pragprog.com*
International Rights:	*translations@pragprog.com*
Academic Use:	*academic@pragprog.com*
Write for Us:	*http://pragprog.com/write-for-us*
Or Call:	+1 800-699-7764